ICEMAN

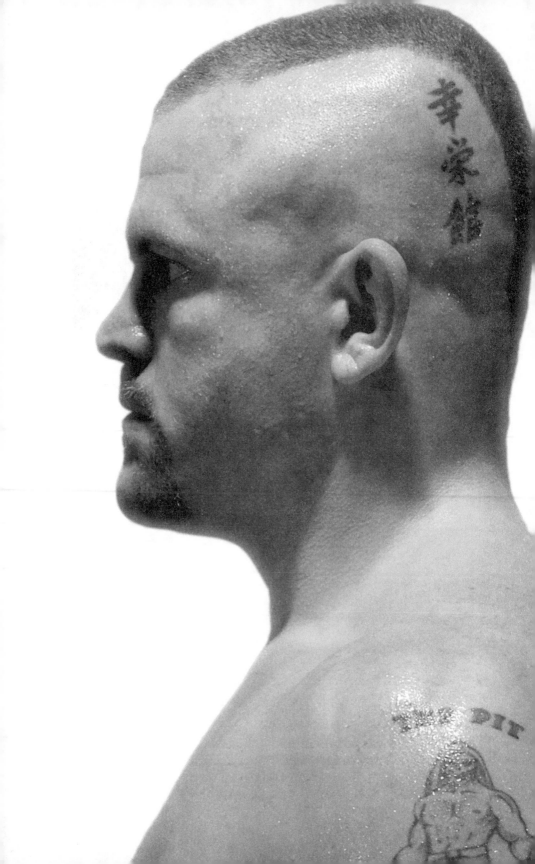

MY FIGHTING LIFE

CHUCK LIDDELL

WITH CHAD MILLMAN

NEW AMERICAN LIBRARY

New American Library
Published by New American Library, a division of
Penguin Group (USA) Inc., 375 Hudson Street,
New York, New York 10014, USA
Penguin Group (Canada), 90 Eglinton Avenue East, Suite 700, Toronto,
Ontario M4P 2Y3, Canada (a division of Pearson Penguin Canada Inc.)
Penguin Books Ltd., 80 Strand, London WC2R 0RL, England
Penguin Ireland, 25 St. Stephen's Green, Dublin 2,
Ireland (a division of Penguin Books Ltd.)
Penguin Group (Australia), 250 Camberwell Road, Camberwell, Victoria 3124,
Australia (a division of Pearson Australia Group Pty. Ltd.)
Penguin Books India Pvt. Ltd., 11 Community Centre, Panchsheel Park,
New Delhi - 110 017, India
Penguin Group (NZ), 67 Apollo Drive, Rosedale, North Shore 0632,
New Zealand (a division of Pearson New Zealand Ltd.)
Penguin Books (South Africa) (Pty.) Ltd., 24 Sturdee Avenue,
Rosebank, Johannesburg 2196, South Africa

Penguin Books Ltd., Registered Offices:
80 Strand, London WC2R 0RL, England

Published by New American Library, a division of Penguin Group (USA) Inc. Previously published in a
Dutton edition.

First New American Library Printing, January 2009
10 9 8 7 6 5 4 3 2

For author copyrights and permissions, see page 319.

 REGISTERED TRADEMARK—MARCA REGISTRADA

NAL Caliber Trade Paperback ISBN: 978-0-451-22540-5

The Library of Congress has cataloged the hardcover edition of this title as follows:

Liddell, Chuck.
Iceman: my fighting life / by Chuck Liddell with Chad Millman.
   p.   cm.
ISBN 978-0-525-95056-1 (hardcover) 1. Liddell, Chuck. 2. Kickboxing. 3. Kickboxing—United States—
Biography I. Millman, Chad. II. Title.
GV1114.65.L53 2008
796.815—dc22   2007043746
[B]

Set in Dante MT with DIN Schrift
Designed by Daniel Lagin

Printed in the United States of America

For Pops, who taught me how to fight and always thought I was the best fighter in the world. And for Trista and Cade, who make me want to be the best dad in the world.

CONTENTS

PROLOGUE   1

CHAPTER 1
GET THE F**K UP   5

CHAPTER 2
LISTEN TO YOUR MOTHER   9

CHAPTER 3
KNOW YOUR STUFF   15

CHAPTER 4
BE WILLING TO LEARN   21

CHAPTER 5
WHY? 'CAUSE SCREW THEM.   27

CHAPTER 6
DON'T ALWAYS FOLLOW MOM'S ADVICE   35

CHAPTER 7
NO COWERING, NO SCOWLING, JUST STARING   41

CONTENTS

CHAPTER 8
PRACTICE WHAT YOU LOVE   45

CHAPTER 9
NEVER UNDERESTIMATE ANYONE   49

CHAPTER 10
BEING MENTALLY TOUGH IS NOT A SOMETIMES THING   55

CHAPTER 11
SIZE DOESN'T MATTER   59

CHAPTER 12
TAKE IT TO THE NEXT LEVEL   65

CHAPTER 13
YOU'RE NEVER TOO TOUGH TO SHOW THE LADIES
YOUR SENSITIVE SIDE   71

CHAPTER 14
THE MORE YOU MOVE, THE MORE SOMEONE HAS TO
TRY TO KEEP YOU STILL   79

CHAPTER 15
APPRECIATE RISK   83

CHAPTER 16
NEVER LET A LITTLE THING GET IN THE WAY OF
MAKING A BIG THING HAPPEN   89

CHAPTER 17
A FIGHT'S A FIGHT, NO MATTER WHERE IT IS   97

CHAPTER 18
BE ABOUT BEING THE BEST   103

CHAPTER 19
TURNS OUT MOJO DON'T PAY THE BILLS   109

CHAPTER 20
IF YOU DON'T FIGHT, YOU DON'T TRULY KNOW IF
YOU CAN WIN   117

CHAPTER 21
ALTITUDE TRAINING IS BULL   125

CHAPTER 22
REGULATION IS GOOD   129

CHAPTER 23
WITHOUT ANY SUBSTANCE, YOU CAN NEVER HAVE
ANY STYLE   135

CHAPTER 24
TO LEAVE NO DOUBT, YOU'VE GOT TO KNOCK A GUY OUT   143

CHAPTER 25
LOYALTY IS EVERYTHING   151

CHAPTER 26
FORGET PLANS AND EXPECTATIONS   161

CHAPTER 27
LOSING AS A MAN IS BETTER THAN WINNING
AS A COWARD   167

CHAPTER 28
YOU CAN WORRY ABOUT LOSING, OR YOU CAN DO
SOMETHING ABOUT IT   175

CHAPTER 29
IT NEVER PAYS TO MOUTH OFF   179

CONTENTS

CHAPTER 30

NEVER LET 'EM BREATHE   183

CHAPTER 31

IT'S NOT ABOUT STRENGTH; IT'S ABOUT STRENGTH
OVER A LONG TIME   191

CHAPTER 32

WHEN YOU GET AN OPPORTUNITY TO HAVE A GOOD
TIME, YOU'VE GOT TO TAKE IT   203

CHAPTER 33

WHEN YOU'VE GOT A GUY DAZED, KNOCK HIM OUT   209

CHAPTER 34

PATIENCE DOES PAY OFF   217

CHAPTER 35

HAVING A GOOD CHIN COMES NATURALLY   219

CHAPTER 36

YOU NEED TO BEAT SOMEONE OVER THE HEAD
TO GET WHAT YOU WANT   223

CHAPTER 37

WE'RE FIGHTERS. A LOT OF US HAVE ISSUES.   231

CHAPTER 38

SOMEONE UP THERE HAS A GREAT SENSE OF HUMOR   235

CHAPTER 39

IF A GUY SAYS HE'S READY, HE'S READY. WHO AM I
TO SHOW MERCY?   241

CHAPTER 40

A MOHAWK ENHANCES YOUR COMMERCIAL APPEAL   249

CHAPTER 41
REVENGE IS PRETTY DARN SWEET   255

CHAPTER 42
YOU CAN'T WAIT TO FINISH A GUY   259

CHAPTER 43
SCREW IT. RETAKE IT.   265

CHAPTER 44
IT'S A PRETTY GREAT LIFE WHEN YOU MAKE IT DOING WHAT YOU LOVE   271

CHAPTER 45
NEVER CHOKE ANYONE OUT UNLESS YOU'RE GETTING PAID FOR IT   279

CHAPTER 46
YOU HAVE TO STAY CHILL WHEN THE LIGHTS ARE BRIGHTEST   285

CHAPTER 47
GET THE F**K BACK UP   291

EPILOGUE
WHEN YOU'RE GRATEFUL YOU CAN'T BE ANGRY   295

APPENDIX
307

ACKNOWLEDGMENTS
315

ICEMAN

PROLOGUE

WHAT'S IT LIKE TO WALK DOWN THE STREET AND have no fear? What's it like to turn the corner and know I can handle anything that comes my way? What's it like to be the guy people are afraid to meet in a dark alley? People ask me those questions more than any others. That's what happens when you're six-two, 205 pounds, sport a low-and-tight Mohawk, and have a tattoo etched onto the side of your skull. That's what happens when you've got a rep as the hardest puncher in what is arguably the toughest sport since the 300 were doing battle. People want to know what it's like to be fearless more than they want to know how much money I make (enough), or how much it hurts to be an ultimate fighter (not much), or would I let my nine-year-old son step into the Octagon when he's older (sure, if he trained).

Well, here's the answer: I have no idea, because I've got nothing to compare it to. I've never been afraid of a fight. In fact, I like fighting, always have. Not that I'm looking for a brawl every time I hit the bars. I stopped doing reckless stuff like that when I was a teenager. Back then I'd walk into a room trying to figure which guys I was going to end up throwing down with at the end of the night. I didn't care if I was taking on five other people. I figured, no matter what happened to

This is my "don't mess with me" stance.

me, by the time it ended I'd have taken care of at least three or four of them. Ever since my grandpa taught me how to throw a punch, I've known how to handle myself in those situations. And having that kind of confidence frees me up to think about something other than "Wow, I can pretty much kick anyone's ass." It just doesn't cross my mind. At least not when I'm walking down the street.

But heading toward the cage, that's a different story. Then, I never doubt. When I walk out of the tunnel, I can see the lights, hear the music, feel the crowd, but it all begins to close off as I near the cage. By that point I'm thinking, I've been training hard; it's time to focus. I play to the crowd because that is part of the show, but I can't hear what anyone is saying. Good or bad. All the best MMA (mixed martial artist) fighters feel exactly the same way, because most of us were competitive athletes long before joining the UFC (Ultimate Fighting Championship). I played football and wrestled at Cal Poly San Luis Obispo. Randy Couture was an all-American wrestler at Oklahoma State and was an alternate on three Olympic wrestling teams. The UFC welterweight champ Matt Serra won a Brazilian jujitsu gold medal at the Pan American Games. What we're doing is sports in its most basic form. We don't have teammates. It's a one-on-one battle, with no place to hide. Every man is born with a fight-or-flight instinct, and mine is to fight. It always has been.

I've been in twenty-four professional MMA fights since turning pro in 1998. I've won twenty, seven of those by knockout, and lost four, three of those by knockout. That's a total of less than three matches a year, which usually equals fewer than forty minutes total of actual fight time. Yet for each of those fights I work out twice a day, five times a week, for three straight months (give or take a day here and there to blow off some steam). My trainer at The Pit in San Luis Obispo, John Hackleman, has me throw a 125-pound medicine ball against a wall. I run with a wheelbarrow full of rocks up hills. I do fight drills, fitness drills, and bag work. I spar. I wrestle. I take kicks to the head and knees to the stomach. And that is just for practice. After that kind of effort, if I walk into the cage and don't think I can whip anyone I'm facing, I'm in the wrong sport.

I'm pretty sure I made the right choice. And while you're reading this book, I think you'll agree. I wrote this because I wanted people to know the guy beneath the Mohawk, to understand why I love stepping into the cage and beating up on people. And while I begin the story with my days growing up in Santa Barbara and end it living the good life as a UFC star in San Luis Obispo, I'm hoping this serves as more than just a year-by-year record of my life story, because that's not all it is to me. I didn't just wake up one day and decide I could be a UFC champion. I worked toward it every day of my life, even before there was such a thing as the UFC. All I ever wanted to do was make a living fighting. It didn't have to be professionally. Before becoming a UFC fighter I was working in a dojo and as a bartender. I could have done those two things forever. And if I had written a book about that kind of life, except for the fights themselves, most of it wouldn't be all that different. Every chapter in this book features a lesson that helped me become who I am in and out of the cage, from the time I learned to box when I was three years old to the days both of my kids were born to the night that Rampage knocked me on my butt. You may finish this book and not remember one detail of my life—although I'm sure you'll be telling your friends some stories. But at the least, if you rip out the table of contents and carry it with you (after you buy the book), you'll have the road map that helped me become the light heavyweight titleholder. And the lessons apply whether you're studying for the SATs, sitting in a cubicle hating your boss, or training to be a UFC fighter.

Hackleman likes to say that I was nothing but a 220-pound slab of clay who couldn't fight when he met me. He also tells reporters that before big fights I get really nervous, head to his house, sit on his couch, put my head on his shoulder, and ask him to rub the tattoo on the side of my head until I fall asleep. Only one of those things is true.

Read this book and you'll find out.

CHAPTER 1

GET THE F**K UP

I WAS BORN CRIPPLED. AT LEAST THAT'S HOW MY MOM, Charlene, likes to put it. You couldn't tell at first. I did all the things a baby was supposed to do: roll over, sit up, and crawl. By nine months I was walking—actually running—as fast as I could. I wanted to chase down my older sister, Laura. I fell, I bruised, I cried; then I got back up. But when I was around eighteen months old, my mom noticed that I was falling more than usual, and for no reason at all. Not just when I was running, but when I was standing in the kitchen drinking milk or pulling myself up onto a chair in the living room. My body would just crumple. I looked like a mannequin as my legs folded underneath me and I collapsed to the floor.

My mom wasn't the kind to coddle her kids. This was a woman who, as the shortest girl in her class, played right

Don't be deceived by the Mickey Mouse ears. I may have looked harmless, but I wasn't afraid to take a kid out if I had to.

guard on the boys' football team when she was in sixth grade. When she got to high school, her mom made her stop playing sports so she could be more feminine. She grew to be five-eleven, got a job working in the social services office in our hometown of Santa Barbara, and was raising her kids on her own. She still has a sweet voice and a good heart. And she had the perfect attitude for bringing up four kids. No amount of crying seemed to unsettle her. She had her own ideas about parenting, especially single parenting. Most of all, she wanted her children to be independent, because she believed that was the only way they'd be happy. If I whined about being tired and wanting to be carried, she'd tell me how great my legs worked and how strong I was, and bottom line, she wasn't about to let me waste them by carrying me home. When we were hurt, unless the gash was big enough to see bone or someone took a hammer to one of our heads (which Laura pulled on me twice one afternoon), her response was to wipe it off with a towel and tell us to get up and get back outside. She was—and still is—strong and fierce and determined. And she wanted her kids to be more than that.

But my frequent spills surprised—and even concerned—her. One afternoon she took me to the doctor, who was concerned enough that he sent me to a specialist. He could tell right away what the problem was: My joints kept slipping out of my sockets. And every time it happened, I flopped to the ground. The doctor told my mom I wasn't going to grow out of it and suggested I get braces on both legs, which would then be connected at the knee by a steel rod, so the bottom half of my body was stable and the problem would be corrected. It meant I wouldn't be able to walk for a while and that I'd have to stop doing all the things a rambunctious eighteen-month-old kid likes to do. But when I got the braces off, I'd be fine. My mom hated that idea. She had grown up in the sixties, and while she hadn't ever lived on a commune, she did think of herself as a modified hippie. The image of my legs being locked up with braces stuck in her head, and she immediately worried about—her words not mine—my "psychological develop-ment." If I couldn't walk for a long time, it wouldn't be long before my six-month-old brother, Sean, passed me by. She knew that wouldn't sit well.

So she asked the doctor what else we could do to fix the problem. He laid out a schedule of physical therapy that makes my twice-a-day-five-days-a-week-for-three-straight-months-before-a-fight workout ses-sions seem like a restless nap. It was even harder for my mom. I was eighteen months old; where did I have to be? But my mom, after nights spent trying to keep infant Sean happy, woke up with me extra early in the morning. Before getting Laura ready for school she contorted and twisted my legs into pretzels. I screamed in agony, and it broke her heart. Then she'd come home from work and do it all again. Basically, she was telling me to get the fuck up. For a year and a half we went through this routine nearly every day. But, by the time I was three, I was falling less and felt sturdier on my feet. I was putting plenty of distance between Sean and me and had no problem keeping up with Laura when we played on the school playground across from our town house.

However, my mom's grand plan not to stunt my development didn't work out exactly as she had planned. Years later I was trying out for the football team at San Marcos High School. I wanted to be a run-ning back, and the coach put us through different drills to get a sense of how fast we were. I wasn't that fast. I couldn't get into a smooth stride because I had a hitch when I ran. It was an aftereffect of how my legs had developed. I still have it when I walk.

During those drills, the mile, especially, killed me. One day I came home and mentioned how frustrated I was that I couldn't make any progress. My mom reminded me of the joint problems I had had and the therapy I'd gone through. At one point she mentioned that if I had done the braces, I probably wouldn't have had the hitch. I kind of lost it.

"Mom," I whined, "you should have put me in the braces."

Always be prepared . . .
for a fight.

"Sweetie," she told me, "I didn't want you to feel different than the other kids and stop walking. I was worried about your psychological development."

"You should have known I could handle it."

"Hey, you were new to me. How was I supposed to know you were going to be such a determined young child?"

She was right. How could she know? I was an average kid, never that tall, kind of thin, not particularly outgoing. Some kids can't wait to jump into the sandbox and take other kids' toys. That wasn't me. I liked things to be in order, preferring to stand on the side, assessing the situation and taking my time. When I was really young, I used to line my trucks up in the same order every day. Before I ever took a karate class, I was in the chess club because I liked to study what my opponents were going to do for as long as possible before attacking. I'd go to skate parks and watch for thirty minutes before getting on my board, then perfectly mimic the moves I was watching. My youngest brother, Dan, who is five years younger than me (as well as three inches taller and seventy pounds heavier), likes to joke that I'm like a general: I like to figure everything out before I make a move.

LISTEN TO YOUR MOTHER

'M NAMED AFTER MY GRANDFATHER CHARLES LIDDELL (most of my family still calls me Charlie). Pops was a first-generation American whose parents came over from Ireland during the great migration in the early 1900s and settled in the Red Hook section of Brooklyn. In those days gangs were everywhere, and Lucky Luciano was running the harbor that bordered Red Hook. My grandpa liked to say that only three types of people came out of Red Hook: cops, hoods, and priests. At the time, he didn't see himself becoming a priest and he didn't like the cops. But the life of a hood, that was something he could get used to. When he was just a kid, during Prohibition, he helped roll barrels of liquor for Lucky's guys.

His family lived near the harbor, and most of the people they knew worked on the docks, loading and unloading the ships. When the market crashed and the Depression hit in 1929, my grandpa was fourteen years old. He was never the kind who sat in the front of the class, so he didn't need an excuse like the Depression to get him out of school and onto the docks earning a living.

Then, when he was in his early twenties, a couple of his buddies were arrested. Another was killed. He understood he was an Irish guy working for an Italian gang. He'd never become a made man, and the life he was leading became less appealing, less glamorous. He realized he would have little chance to see old age if he didn't find a way out of Red Hook. So, at the end of the 1930s, when it looked as if there was no way to avoid a war with Hitler, he joined the military and was sent to California for training.

Pops was in one of the first units shipped to the Pacific after Pearl Harbor. When he came home, he wasn't interested in going back to his life in Red Hook. Instead he settled near where he'd trained, in Santa Barbara, and decided he wanted to be, of all things, a cop. But it wasn't that easy. He was so broke while waiting for the sheriff's department to accept him that he had to drive a beer truck to support his family. The only place he could afford to put them up was in an army barracks. They were poor and had plenty of meals consisting of nothing but a plate of beans.

My grandpa was also proud. He made $25 a month driving the beer truck, which was $3 less a month than he would have made from the government after getting out of the war. But he didn't want the handout. And when he finally joined the sheriff's department, he assumed everyone else—especially the prisoners—had the same sense of pride. Whenever he was working with criminals, he would think back to his days in Red Hook and say, "There but for the grace of God." He decided early on that everyone deserved to be treated with respect and common decency, until they proved they didn't deserve it anymore. Of course, he was a tough guy—around six-one, two hundred pounds, with a high-and-tight buzz cut that he'd picked up in the army—so people didn't often challenge him.

He used to drive around town picking the drunks up off the street. He'd put them in a hotel for the night and give them some meal money. One guy he met was in his early twenties and already had most of his front teeth knocked out. Every few weeks he'd see the guy in prison. He finally asked him, "How come you're in here so often?" The guy told him that he was always getting in fights because people were making fun of his teeth. So my grandpa gave him some money to get his teeth fixed. He didn't see the guy again for about three years. And then one day he showed up with a wife, a kid, and a job working for the county. He just wanted to tell Pops thanks for helping him turn his life around.

It was easy for Pops to show his soft side, maybe because he had spent so much time causing trouble when he was younger. Plus, it's always easier to be nice if you know how mean you can be. My family is Irish, which means we've all got tempers. And my grandpa learned early on that if you're going to fight, the only way to win is to know what you're doing. That meant understanding how to throw punches that actually hurt someone. It also meant recognizing that being out of control—of your body and of your emotions—did you more harm than good. My grandpa always used to say that if you get mad, then you lose your edge and you can't think clearly. You need to think to be a winner when you're fighting.

He gave his two daughters—my mom and my aunt—boxing lessons when they were young. He didn't care that they were girls. He knew they were Liddells and, on some days, their tempers were going to get the best of them. But it was about more than that, too. Once he was older, my grandpa wasn't the type to start fights. My mom isn't the type to start fights. And I'm not the type to start fights either. But you'd better believe that knowing how to fight, knowing if it comes down to it we can handle ourselves, makes us a lot more likely to stand up for our-

One morning I was at the IHOP in San Luis Obispo with my kids, Trista and Cade. Trista decided she had a story to contribute and grabbed the microphone so she could be heard. This is what she had to say:

"My dad cheats. One time he and I were boxing on the Wii and every time I tried to punch him, he pushed me over. He was cheating and I ended up losing because I couldn't hit him. Another time we were playing cards at my grandparents' house and I saw him swipe two cards from the deck. I didn't know what they were, and he didn't know that I saw him, but when we put our hands down, he had two aces. Clearly he cheats."

selves, and anyone else we see in trouble, for that matter. I'm not just talking about going toe-to-toe with some guy in an alley. My mom was able to raise four kids on her own, without any financial support from my dad, because she wasn't afraid to stand up for herself. Everyone has a fight-or-flight instinct. The Liddells' instinct is to fight. And my grandfather tried to nurture that.

Me, my brothers, and my sister got boxing lessons when we were young, too. They started when we'd all fight over each other's toys. My mom knew right away we had all inherited the Liddell temper, and she was going to have to find a way to get us to control it. Or at least

Pops was my biggest supporter. He taught me everything I know about loyalty and honor.

harness it. So we learned that we should not wrap our fingers around our thumb when we threw a punch, because our thumb would break if we actually connected. We learned how to duck out of the way of punches. My mom and my grandpa would get on their knees, hold out their hands like stop signs, and let us whale away on their palms for practice. We learned how to turn our bodies and lean into a punch, getting power from our legs and waist so we didn't just swing limply with our arms. We learned how to throw straight, tight punches that had more of a chance of connecting, rather than the wild swings most kids make that never hit anything. (Ironic, since I'm known for throwing roundhouses now.) When we'd get too rambunctious, my grandpa would build a ring in the backyard and let us go at it until we all calmed down. We weren't a family of thugs. But my grandpa grew up in Brooklyn working for Lucky Luciano, went to war, and became a cop. My mom had been through a nasty divorce. They knew firsthand that life was full of confrontations, that not everyone you met always played nice. When you're faced with those kinds of challenges, you can either run away and start over somewhere else, or you can stay and fight. So if fighting was going to be a part of life, we might as well be really good at it.

Of course, my mom the modified hippie didn't want us to be bullies. And to be honest, my grandfather didn't love the idea of a Liddell gang roaming the streets of Santa Barbara, picking fights. They knew what they were teaching us could be dangerous, and they both preached that before ever throwing a punch, we should apply the talk-and-walk method: Talk your way out of it. Walk away from it. Only when those two things didn't work did they want us defending ourselves. It was a lot for us, as young kids, to wrap our heads around.

But we tried. At least I did. And until I was five years old, what I took away from the lessons was that I shouldn't be getting into fights—at all. Then, after a tough week at day care, I learned what it truly means to listen to your mother.

Where I lived and went to day care, being a small, shy white kid

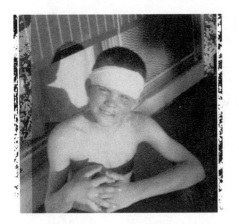
I was never afraid to get a little roughed up.

put me in the minority, and that made me a target. Not because the kids I went to school with were prejudiced, but kids pick on kids who look different. And for a while, I was getting my butt handed to me. The teachers were always coming to my rescue—I wouldn't fight back—and after a week, they finally asked me, "Why don't you try to defend yourself?" I answered, "Because my mom told me she doesn't want me to fight."

That day my mom was called into day care, and the teachers told her what was happening. They explained that when they came to break things up, they'd see that I was standing there with my fists clenched at my sides, but I would never throw a punch. Then they mentioned that I wasn't defending myself because my mom told me not to fight.

That night at home we had a chat. She said she was proud of me for not hurting anyone and for not starting something with anyone. But she didn't want me to stand around and get beat up without standing up for myself. That wasn't what she and my grandpa had been trying to teach me. Basically she let me loose. And the next time I was picked on at day care, I didn't need the teachers to come and break it up. I ended it myself.

CHAPTER 3

KNOW YOUR STUFF

SANTA BARBARA IS NOT EXACTLY FILLED WITH ghettos, but if there was a poor part of town, we were living in it. At the time the five of us—my mom and her four kids—were living in a three-bedroom town house that cost $400 a month. But my mom made so little money that she qualified for the government's assisted-living program, so she got help paying the rent. Even then, after all the expenses were paid, we usually had less than $100 a

Sean, me, and Laura. The three of us were always getting into trouble.

month to feed a family of five. My mom could make it stretch, though. She shopped at the day-old-bread store, where she would get two loaves for fifteen cents. And we got lucky, too. One time, when we were out of cash and my mom's payday was still four days away, she won a raffle during parents' day at my school. The prize: two bags of groceries.

When I turned eight, the cost of living in Santa Barbara had become too high for my mom, even with the help from the government. The five of us had to move in with my grandparents, who lived a few blocks away. It hurt my mom's pride, but all us kids were thrilled. My grandparents lived closer to the beach than we did, had a bigger yard, and were across the street from a school, where Laura and I played one-on-one tackle football. It was an all-or-nothing game—you either scored or you got slammed. By now Dan, who was three but big for his age, followed me, Laura, and Sean everywhere we went. Half the time he'd end up running back inside and crying to Mom because he'd been hurt. She'd tell him what she had told the rest of us growing up: He had two choices, play inside by himself or play outside with the kids. Either way, she didn't want to hear him whining.

The house was crowded. It was three bedrooms, with a small guesthouse in the backyard. My great-grandma lived back there for a while—which meant seven of us were splitting those three bedrooms. When she passed away, my grandparents moved into the guesthouse, basically giving us five the run of their house. They were just incredibly generous. We never wanted for cleats or equipment or support at our games because they were always helping out. People who don't know me, who try to tell my story, like to think that I fight because of some deeply hidden anger because my father wasn't around. Sorry to disappoint, but that's not the case, although he gave me—and my family—plenty of reasons to be mad. One time when I was two and he was still living with us, my mom came home to find me in a room by myself eating an onion that my sister had given me. I was starving and my father didn't want to get off the couch to feed me. Another time,

It was crowded in our house, but I always loved having Grandma and Pops around.

when I was eight, Pops, a guy everyone called Smiley because he never got mad at anyone or swore around us, came running into the house muttering, "I saw him, I swear to God I saw that fucker and I'm going to kill him." It didn't take us long to realize he was talking about my dad—the guy I would eventually just refer to as the sperm donor. Pops ran out of the house with his handgun and his billy club, looking to take the man out. I grew up occasionally hearing my mom cry herself to sleep because she was so sad. And I saw her work three jobs at a time—for the county, as a salesperson at a knife store, in security—sometimes up to ninety hours a week, so we could get Christmas presents.

But, as I said, I wasn't mad. I've always been glad he wasn't around. If he had stayed, I'd be a much different person. I'd probably be seriously messed up because I would have been raised in such a bad environment. Instead, I turned out remarkably well-adjusted. Seriously. In college I once kicked down a door that was stuck, and immediately the school put me into anger management (and made me pay $240 to fix the door). I spent one session with the counselor and explained that I just wanted to get on the other side of the door. After talking with me he told me not to come back. He didn't think I had an anger problem. I still don't. I'm not holding in any "Where's Daddy?" demons. I never step into the cage angry, trying to turn my opponent into my long-lost father. You can't win if you can't control your emotions; that's what my grandpa taught all of us when we were young. And he was my father figure, doing all the things that every dad does for his kids, and because of that, it's never occurred to me that I should be pissed my dad wasn't around.

We all benefited from living with our grandparents, and not just because they helped put food on the table, kept a roof over our head, and bought us equipment. They had already been parents and were more tolerant—and had a better sense of humor—when we kids made mistakes. When I was two, I watched Pops using a hammer to fix something outside the house. He turned his back for a second and I picked up the hammer, went over to the sliding glass door, and banged on it, the way he had been doing. The door shattered. And once everyone knew I was okay, his response was to laugh and say, "Well, he just wanted to get in the house."

He helped my mom relax, too. She was a single parent trying to raise four kids. It's hard enough for two parents to be sure of the decisions they make for their children. It's even more difficult when you're making all the parenting calls by yourself. My mom still admits she was harder on us at times than she would have liked because she was on her own. But when she was done doling out punishments or giving us a tongue-lashing, my grandfather would pull her aside and settle her down, asking her if she was being too harsh. He always respected her position, never challenged her in front of us, but most single mothers didn't have this kind of support and sounding board.

But plenty of times my grandfather did help raise the decibel level in the house, too. As you might have guessed by now, fighting, arguing, debating, cajoling, prodding, and any other form of confrontation were entertainment in our house. That's just another way we were a traditional Irish household: If something was bothering us, we didn't hold it in. And if we disagreed with someone, we were encouraged to share that with the family, too. My mom, especially, challenged us on everything. She'd use words we didn't know in the middle of a sentence and make us tell her what they meant by figuring out the context in which they were used. When she and my grandparents talked about politics at the table, she wanted to hear our opinions. The more we disagreed with her, the happier she seemed to be. No one considered it disrespectful to talk back to our elders when we were having this kind of discussion, which often escalated into an argument. A loud argument. My mom was teaching us a lesson: You had to know your stuff, because if you accepted what your teachers or your parents or your grandparents or the newspapers were saying without thinking for yourself, you were going to have problems.

And we all had plenty of those already.

CHAPTER 4

BE WILLING TO LEARN

MY MOM HAD DIFFERENT METHODS FOR PUNISH-
ing each of her kids. Laura liked to be the center of attention, so when she was bad, my mom sent her to her room.
It just killed her not to be in the middle of the action. Sean was a big
eater, so to punish him my mom would take away his favorite foods—
such as cheese—for a week. Danny, the baby of the bunch, well, he

Laura, me, and Sean. Just goes to show you can play with stuffed animals and still be
a badass.

was so worried about disappointing my mom that all she had to do was give him a disapproving look and he'd start to cry. But for me, nothing was worse than talking. And my mom knew it.

Every time I got into trouble, we'd have to sit down and have a conversation about it. I couldn't stand sitting still, evaluating what I had done, and trying to figure out why it was wrong. I knew the answers pretty well, usually before I did whatever I'd done. I didn't have the patience for long talks. Finally, one day after an argument I asked, "Why can't you just spank me? The talking takes so long." She answered, "I'm not hitting you, Charlie, because you need a punishment that is painful. And I know the talking hurts you a lot more than the spanking."

A lot of times we'd take what my mom liked to call "peripatetic" walks. That meant we were going to take a stroll around the neighborhood and she was going to lecture me. But we were both so competitive that neither of us would walk even a step behind the other. She'd be trying to tell me what I'd done was wrong, while I would try to walk faster than she was. Then she'd catch up, take a two-step lead, and keep going faster. Back and forth it went. It was hard to learn my lesson when both of us were so fixated on walking faster than the other. Mostly, the punishment my mom doled out taught me two things about myself: I didn't mind getting hit, and I didn't like to lose.

On one of these walks, I signed up for my first karate class. I was twelve and had gotten into the show *Kung Fu Theater*, which aired late on Friday nights. They put on demonstrations during the break that taught how to kick or throw a punch, basic moves, and I thought they were fantastic. It was something I wanted to try. A lot of people I knew were getting into jujitsu. But martial arts in general were a big deal in Southern California—the movie *Karate Kid* was a huge hit at the time—and I was such a big fan of all the different disciplines I started getting a subscription to *Black Belt* magazine.

I wanted to join one particular dojo in town. My mom and I went by it three or four times on our walks, but it was always closed. So, one day we walked into another place, Koei-Kan Karate-Do, which was

That subscription to *Black Belt* magazine paid off. I'd eventually earn my own black belt.

run by Jack Sabat. I was lucky the other dojo was never open, because Koei-Kan was perfect for me. There are dozens of different forms of karate. Some—such as tae kwon do—are more sports-oriented and focused on learning self-defense. But the style Jack taught, Koei-Kan, while still about discipline and concentration, was more combative. It concentrated on debilitating opponents, not just keeping them at bay. It utilized pressure points and emphasized good striking technique. Koei-Kan was about building fighters. And it perfectly fit with Jack's personality. He had grown up outside Detroit and served four years on an aircraft carrier during Vietnam. While in the military he wanted to find, he says, "the most hard-ass" system he could. And Koei-Kan was it.

The dojo was open seven days a week and I was a gym rat. During the school year I'd go to work out after football or wrestling practice. And during the summer, I spent every day there, sometimes until Jack locked the doors at midnight. For me, it was never about getting the next level of belt. I just wanted to learn. If you're going to be good at anything, you've got to be willing to learn as much about it as possible.

At first I was really good at roundhouse kicks, they just came naturally to me. But I still needed hours of practice to perfect them.

The instructors at Koei-Kan emphasized technique and being self-motivated. They'd show us something once and tell us to go off into a corner and do it five hundred times. Then they'd come over to check on us, point out a small flaw in our technique, and tell us to do it five hundred more times. We did high kicks, jabs, hooks, straight punches, reverse punches, roundhouses, side kicks, back kicks, elbow blocks, knee blocks, outside blocks. It was real Mr. Miyagi, wax-on, wax-off, *Karate Kid* stuff. I'd be there for three or four hours trying to master these precise and specific movements, and my body would ache, without ever taking a punch. But the repetition helped me understand what I could do with each different technique; the movements became a part of my muscle memory. We'd grind away, and pretty soon my body knew only one way to respond when I needed to use that move. The repetition helped us build seamless combinations and gave us a clear perception of what the move was, how it was used, and how to apply it. And, really, hitting is what I wanted to do more than anything else.

I couldn't get enough of sparring, which Jack let all of his students do almost as soon as they joined the program. At first, we were covered in protective gear, which allowed us to go full bore in as aggressive a situation as possible, without worrying we were going to get hurt. So many students begin sparring without any padding and get busted in the first week or two, then lose their incentive to practice. But your ap-

MY FAVORITE ACTION MOVIES:

1. *Best of the Best*—1989, starring James Earl Jones as a coach who takes a team to the world tae kwon do championships.
2. *Karate Kid*—1984, Ralph Macchio as a lonely kid who learns karate and finds himself.
3. *Rocky*—1976, if you don't know . . .
4. *Diggstown*—1992, Louis Gossett, Jr., an old boxer, fights ten men in twenty-four hours.
5. *Bloodsport*—1988, Jean-Claude Van Damme in the *Rocky* of martial arts movies.

preciation for the discipline, as well as the combat, is greater when you're not getting grounded every time you step on the mat. Once we were comfortable with being hit, the real merciless stuff began. We'd run at each other full speed from opposite sides of the mat to practice our defensive maneuvers. We'd use our knuckles as weapons. We'd spar for twenty minutes, and if either fighter was still standing, Jack would make us analyze what had happened and figure out why no one was hurt. We'd stand against a wall and learn how to fight off multiple people at one time when there was no escape. The only thing you can do is counter and move side to side, which helped us develop resistance and skill. We'd do that drill for ninety minutes some days. It got to the point where I became so comfortable that I liked having the wall behind me and three or four guys coming at me from all sides.

Accuracy was an important part of the program, so we'd punch stationary boards fitted with fake heads and chests. Then we'd punch moving targets, aiming not just for anywhere on the head or the body, but for specific points such as the lower jaw or the cheekbone or the

My early karate days. I'd take anyone on—no matter how old or skilled they were.

temple or the floating rib. We'd spend thirty minutes building up the strength in our shins by using them to kick sandbags in an alley behind the building. Jack had morning sessions and evening sessions, with about fifty people in each session, and it was holy hell for two hours.

The rest of the time, I was looking for someone to spar with. I wasn't bloodthirsty and I wasn't a thug. Then—and now—I was quiet and reserved and held back a lot of expression. But in the same way some kids love playing basketball and others never want to leave the baseball field, I always wanted to spar. I was still pretty thin, but I had strong legs. Jack used to call it tendon strength. But my greatest gifts as a fighter were internal. I never stopped moving forward. I fought with a single purpose: When I was on the mat, all I wanted to do was take the other guy out. It wasn't emotional; it was about the competition. It helped that I had no fear of getting hit. When someone is fearless, when pain isn't a factor, it's impossible to break his spirit. And a fighter with heart will almost always win out against a fighter with skill but no will.

When I was fourteen and had earned my green belt (the levels are white, green, brown, and black, with each belt having three separate classes), I joined my first national competition. Around fifteen of us from the dojo flew out to New Jersey and stayed in a Howard Johnson's. I came in second place nationally, winning a match with a roundhouse kick to the midsection and a hooking punch to the head—a move not all that different from the knockout punch I use now.

When I got back from Jersey, I sparred with anyone who'd take me on, not just kids my age. I didn't care how old they were or what their belt was. I was becoming so mature as a fighter that the guys I sparred with assumed I was older than I was. During the summer, people new to the dojo would offer me construction jobs. When I'd answer that I was still in school, they'd ask me what college I went to. I'd have to tell them I was still in high school, and eventually it became a joke around the dojo. I never looked at it as if I were better than anyone else my age—I still don't think of it that way. But I knew then that I could fight, and that I would want to do it for as long as I could.

CHAPTER 5

WHY? 'CAUSE SCREW THEM.

IF YOU WERE A KID LOOKING FOR ACTION ON THE weekends in Santa Barbara, you went to Del Playa Drive in the Isla Vista section of town. Three things could happen once you got there: You'd meet a girl, get in a fight, or get drunk—sometimes all three. But I didn't drink. In high school my friends told me there was no way I could wait until I turned twenty-one, so naturally I accepted the challenge. So for me the odds were fifty-fifty I'd get into a fight.

Santa Barbara is one of those idyllic towns that are perfect for attending college, and UCSB has a rep as a big party school. That means there were a lot of kids who wouldn't look at you twice while walking around during the week but found courage on the weekends, when the taps were flowing and the sun went down. Fights would start over anything, from the way one of the guys you were hanging out with looked at someone else, to some drunken college kid saying something stupid. When a lot of guys are drinking and looking to meet girls, there will occasionally be some aggressive behavior. Most of the time, we actually tried to walk away, such as the night I was with Dan and some young drunk guy bumped into us. He looked Dan up and down and said nothing, then looked at me and started mouthing off.

Before it escalated, Dan said to the guy, "Wrong choice." I started laughing so hard we just turned around.

But at times it was impossible to walk away. One night I heard about a friend who had been threatened. I took my friend to the guy's house and told him, "If my buddy gets touched in the next couple of months, I'm coming after you. I don't care who does it. I am coming after you."

A week later I was with that friend and some other guys and we were coming out of a Taco Bell. In the parking lot kids from another school started up with us. A bunch of my buddies scattered—including the jerk I had stuck up for the week before. The two who stuck around weren't worth much when it came to fighting. So this was the way it was going to be: me, two guys who couldn't fight, and some punks who wanted to take me on. I looked for a wall to cover my back—if you're outnumbered, you're always better off if you have one less side to protect—then practiced what I had learned in Koei-Kan. Street brawls don't look the way they do in the movies. They aren't pretty and choreographed. Guys don't wait to come at you one at a time. It's all at once. I used some spinning back kicks, side kicks, and roundhouse kicks to fend some people off. At one point, a buddy yelled, "Look out," just as I was about to get hit in the side of the head with a golf club. I did pretty well in the fight. I have a hard head, and I hit hard and did more damage than they caused. I just didn't lose many fights growing up.

I got home that night and told my mom and Pops what had happened. It was a stark lesson in learning who my true friends were. They reminded me that I'll always have friends when it looks as if I'm the toughest guy in the room, but when it looks as if that's no longer the case, people will scatter. I didn't hold it against him, but I knew if I was ever in a jam, he wasn't going to be there for me.

The truth is, though, with or without backup, no matter how much I practiced what my mom had preached when I was five years old about walking away, sometimes it was hard not to find excuses to fight. That's how it was in my family. One year, when Dan applied for a job, a question on the application asked if he had ever been in any fights and then gave him some options—1–10, 11–20, 21–30, 31 or more. Dan circled *31 or more*, and only when he was asked about it during an interview did it dawn on him that thirty-one or more fights are more than most people have in a lifetime.

Some people started with me because I had a reputation for being tough because of my karate. Hundreds of kids went through Jack's program every year, and hundreds more were a part of the karate community in Santa Barbara. Word spread that I liked to spar, and that I was pretty good at it. Normally it takes six to nine months to move up a class for each belt in karate. With three classes in each belt (white, green, brown, and black), a student could spend nearly three years at each level. But by the time I was sixteen—after just four years in his dojo—Jack felt I was ready to take my black belt test. The exam was a five-hour session that usually began before dawn and was so grueling, students would lose twenty pounds of water weight.

My mom had other ideas. She knew that when her kids went out, the night might end in a fight. She had a boys-will-be-boys attitude about the whole thing. If I became a black belt and had hands and feet that were actually considered lethal weapons, she worried that I'd be putting my future in jeopardy every time I'd get into a scuffle. I was never worried about that, but I didn't want to upset my mom, so I waited.

Which was fine. I found other outlets to satisfy my competitive urges. I had always been a good athlete. But because I was small, it seemed I had to prove myself whenever a new coach came to town or I went into a new school. When we changed school districts in junior high, we were playing a pickup football game one day on the playground. I was picked second to last, just before a girl, and that crushed me. By the time I had left my old school I was always one of the first guys chosen. Now people thought I was barely better than a girl, which is tough to take when you're eleven years old. Then, early in the game,

I picked off a pass and ran it back for a touchdown. I wasn't picked second to last anymore after that.

It was the same thing in youth football. We'd get a new coach, who'd take one look at my scrawny body and assume I'd be useless. I didn't give off the aura that I was especially tough or hardworking, and I'd have to fight to earn my position every fall. Then practices started. And I'd be flying all over that field, throwing my body around. I didn't care if I got hurt and didn't worry too much about hurting my teammates, either. Hey, you gotta commit. Even today, I still love the movie *Rudy*, about the kid who was too small to play but still walked on at Notre Dame and got on the field.

I may have looked scrawny, but I was an animal on the field.

In high school we all started on a level field, and during the tryouts I showed I was a pretty good athlete—and that hitting people wasn't a problem. I was a linebacker on a freshman team that wasn't all that good. Then, midway through the year we lost all three of our centers in the same week, one to injury, another to illness, and a third because the guy wouldn't do his homework. Coach Archer, the freshman coach, sat us down and asked if anyone had played center before. No one wants to play center when you're a freshman in high school. We all stayed quiet, avoiding eye contact with him, looking up at the ceiling. Then one of my buddies yelled out, "Hey, Chuck played center in Pee Wee." Because of that, I became a center for all four years of high school football. Between that and linebacker, I was on the field for every play except when we punted—some other guy did the long snapping.

I loved it, though. Even now, I can't sit still for more than a few minutes, even when I'm having a conversation. However, my coaches didn't always appreciate how eager I was to hit people. I was really fast as a kid. Covering the field sideline to sideline wasn't a problem. More than once my freshman season I timed my coverage on screen passes so I would collide with the receiver the second the ball arrived. It was obvious I could have been there earlier to pick the pass off, but I really just wanted to hit someone instead. Finally, Coach Archer pulled me off the field and yelled at me to make the interception.

After that freshman season, Coach Archer made us play another

With karate and football, it was no surprise I gravitated to wrestling. And it turns out I was a good wrestler.

sport to stay in shape. I chose wrestling, and while I knew I wanted to play football in college, I was a much better wrestler than I was a football player. I wasn't so technically sound, but I could scramble well and was in great condition. I was still doing karate nearly every day, and during breaks in school I would run the stadium steps to get in a good workout. And while I grew up and filled out between my fifteenth and sixteenth birthdays—jumping from five-nine, 155 pounds, to six-one, 186—I knew it wasn't my strength as much as my wind that would help me outlast any opponent. My junior year I finished third in the CIF Tournament, which is the California version of state regionals. At one point during a match I was close to finishing a guy when he scored a cheap point. My coach ran onto the mat and began arguing it. I yelled at him to get off the mat and not to worry; I'd finish the match if he'd stop fighting with the ref and letting the other guy rest.

I was a badass when it came to conditioning. That junior year the wrestling coach, who competed in my weight class in the local police league, challenged me to a match. If I won, the entire team could take off that day's conditioning drills; if he won, we had to do double the work: an extra set of sprints, an extra set of rope climbs, an extra round of wrestling without breaks. Everyone always felt sick to their stomach after one round of conditioning drills. Two would have been brutal. Then I pinned the coach in the first round, and while all my teammates were cheering, I yelled, "Screw it, we're doing the drills." That's how I was winning, and being in that good a shape didn't come easy.

The bigger and more painful the physical challenge, the more I want to do it. Or at least prove to someone that I can. In high school—and even now—when I've got a strength coach giving me a hard time, challenging me to get something done, acting as if he doesn't think I can do it, my response will be, "Why?" 'Cause screw him. Why finish the workout? Because screw him if he thinks I can't. If I'm told to do somewhere between five and ten lifts on a bench press—as if I'm being told to do whatever I can handle—I'll do the ten to spite anyone who doubted me. I know my coaches are just baiting me, but I couldn't, and can't, let them beat me or they'll have that over me.

One year John Hackleman, my trainer now, got me out of bed on New Year's Day to train. By the time I got to the gym, I think I was still drunk, but no way was he going to get the best of me. Fuck it if I'm hurt or tired; I do not want you to beat me.

CHAPTER 6

DON'T ALWAYS FOLLOW MOM'S ADVICE

HEADING INTO MY SENIOR YEAR OF HIGH SCHOOL in 1988, I was still hoping to play football in college. I knew I wasn't going to get a scholarship. But I was the best player and leading tackler—not to mention the most reckless hitter—on a team that improved every season we were together. The varsity team was 0-9-1 when I was a freshman. By the time we were juniors, after the core group of guys had been together for a couple of seasons, we had made the play-offs.

I had two great games to open my senior season. Then I rolled my ankle. I could barely run, I couldn't make it upfield with any speed, I couldn't make cuts or jump on those screen passes. It didn't take long for the coach to realize I was useless as a linebacker. I was moved to defensive end, but I still was just a split second slow rushing the quarterback. It was even hard to play center because we ran a slide-protection blocking scheme, which meant we were often getting out of our stance and moving laterally. Half the time, the guard to the right or the left of me would end up moving too fast—or I would move too slow—and my ankle would be stepped on. It hurt to get on the field, but if the options were watching or suffering, I'd choose the suffering. And even with a bum ankle, I was the best center option we had for the close combat of the offensive line. Besides, I still thought, Hey, maybe I'll get a shot.

Then reality hit home one weekend when I was invited to visit USC. I went down with my mom, got a tour of the campus, heard about how great the academic programs were and how much the students enjoyed living in LA. At the end of the visit I asked the guide when we were going to see the football coach. His response was, "Sure, we can go see the football coach if you want, but why?" When I answered that I thought this was a tour for football prospects, he laughed at me. I had been asked to visit because of my academics.

This is a good time to get something straight: People think "ultimate fighter" and immediately assume I'm some kind of knucklehead. I grew up fighting; I still like to fight; I'm not afraid of fighting. Automatically, people who like to fight get stereotyped as not having the brains to do anything better with their time. As if I don't have the good sense to walk away. Plus my voice is a little raspy and it's hard to understand me sometimes. When I was being recruited by Cal Poly San Luis Obispo to wrestle, I had a long phone conversation with the coach. I wasn't big on talking on the phone—I'm still not—and when we were finishing up, he told me he wasn't sure it would work out. If I didn't have the grades, he couldn't guarantee I'd get into the business college just because I was going to wrestle. I had a 3.6 grade point average at the time and had scored 1280 (720 math, 560 verbal) on my SATs. I told him that having the grades wouldn't be a problem. I thought to myself, I got into Berkeley, for Christ's sake. But he was still skeptical. So much so that he called up a high school wrestling teammate of mine whom he was also recruiting and asked, "Is Chuck slow?" My buddy answered, "No. I think he's pretty bright. He's just not that good on the phone." I had heard stuff like this from my teachers, too. One year an English teacher was passing back our papers. He looked at me, looked at my grade, then looked at me again and said, "You know, you are a lot smarter than you look."

I didn't do anything to try to stop perpetuating the myth that I wasn't the smartest guy in the room—at least other than getting good grades. For extra credit, I once had to make a visual presentation and a speech about things that interested me. I could have chosen karate or football or speed metal. But since Pops was a sheriff's coroner for a while, I thought it would be cool to bring in some pictures from his old cases. One guy in town had hanged himself in an old barn, and it was weeks before he was discovered. By the time Pops found him, the guy's body had turned black and his neck had stretched to the point that it snapped from the rest of his body. When they opened the barn door, the guy's head and neck were still hanging in the noose. But his body was slumped in a seated position on a chair just beneath him, the one he jumped off of when he hanged himself. Then I showed a shot of a man who had been knocked into the air by a train and impaled on a

Becoming a fighter was a choice for me. I had the brains to be what I wanted, and what I wanted was to fight.

nearby pole. I didn't need to show a third. And I got the extra credit. Very little work, a little more credit, nothing stupid or slow about that.

My mom had spent a year studying at Cal Poly San Luis Obispo after high school. While the coaches there weren't going to give me a football scholarship, when they realized I was going to wrestle, they invited me to walk on. I redshirted my freshman year and wrestled in the 177 weight class. But I didn't make it to my sophomore year as a football player. I had been in a motorcycle accident just before spring practice, and the idea of recuperating to play spring ball, then going to summer ball, then playing during the season—at 215 pounds—then losing thirty pounds and going back to wrestling was too much. So instead I focused on grappling.

Besides, I had become pretty tight with the wrestlers, while the football players probably saw me as some guy whose ass they could kick. A buddy from a rival high school in Santa Barbara, Seth Woodill, who wrestled with me at Cal Poly, introduced me to Eric Schwartz, from Soquel, California, who would eventually become one of my closest friends. The first time Eric and I met was at a dining hall on campus when we were all going to eat as a wrestling team. Seth leaned over to Eric and said, "That's my friend Chuck. He is seriously bad. He is tough." I looked real thin from always trying to make weight, had a short-and-tight buzz cut, and had my hands stuffed in my pants pockets. The only thing about me that said "bad" was my look. Eric leaned over to Seth and said to him, "This is the tough guy?" Then he just laughed.

Not too long after that, Eric got a glimpse of what Seth was talking about. We were hanging out on the beach relaxing one day when Eric started telling a joke. During the setup he waved his arm like a madman, the idea being that it would get the attention of the hot women sitting around, with the hopes they'd come over. A couple of them did. Which turned out to be a problem for their boyfriends, who had left them alone while they walked down the beach. When they got back to their blankets and saw their girls talking to some other guys, they started running right for us. I looked around and thought, Someone is going to get seriously fucked-up. Then I realized one was heading straight for me. Before I could get ready, he jumped up and threw an elbow right into my chest. It didn't hurt, but I was surprised. So I retaliated with three quick elbows to his chest, which dropped him into the sand. He popped up, got real close, and locked up my arms so I couldn't punch him. I got so tired of wrestling with the guy I gave him three quick head butts—boom! boom! boom!—and down he went again.

By now there was a crowd, and a friend of his jumped in with both arms swinging. Meanwhile, some guy came out of the crowd and punched me in the side of the head. After I dropped the second guy, Eric came over and asked, "Who was that guy that punched you in the head?" I was like, "Huh, what are you talking about?" I didn't have a concussion or anything; I just hadn't felt anyone hit me. After that I heard Eric whisper to Seth, "Damn, that dude *is* tough."

Eric was great at talking smack. He'd see a guy walking around who was bigger than all of us and tell me, "That guy can totally kick your ass," just to start up with me. Or, if I saw some guys who were acting like jerks or picking on someone, I'd tell him to go give them a hard time, so I could jump in and beat the crap out of them. And, as I said, I don't always follow Mom's advice. On a road trip to Oregon for a wrestling meet, we drove up in Eric's beat-up green Toyota hatchback with his brother and another buddy. Driving down the main drag in Eugene, we saw some guys screwing around in the street in front of us. When Eric was about fifty yards away, he pretended to veer into their lane, as if he were going to hit them. Okay, not the smartest thing, but we were just goofing off. When we passed them, they started flipping us off. Eric wanted to keep driving, but I said, "Stop the car." There were two guys, one about 260 pounds and another about 230. When we got out, they saw our Cal Poly wrestling shirts and started talking trash about us being wrestlers and losers. I had just had stitches put in my eye because of a wrestling injury, and Eric kept telling me to get back in the car because if I opened up the stitches, I wouldn't wrestle that weekend. He was right, so I started opening the door. Then the guy who was about 230 got in the face of Eric's brother, who weighed only around 160. I stopped, looked up, and said, "You're a dick."

The guy walked up to me and fake-head-butted me. I don't remember my reaction, but Eric says I didn't even flinch. Then I dropped the guy with an elbow. He went straight down, knocking his head on the bumper before crumpling into the street. We could actually see a little trickle of blood running down the gutter and into the drain. By now the bigger dude who was running with the guy I had just dropped had taken off his shirt. He had acne scars all over his back, as if he were mid–steroid cycle. He came at me, and I dropped him on his ass, too. Then he looked at Eric and said, "Why don't you guys just get out of here." And we did.

About a year later a teammate of ours who lived in that town was visiting home and was wearing a Cal Poly wrestling shirt. He ran into those guys we'd met on the street and they said, "Dude, there is a seriously crazy wrestler up there."

CHAPTER 7

NO COWERING, NO SCOWLING, JUST STARING

I DIDN'T DRINK AND I DIDN'T DO DRUGS. FIGHTING could have been considered my vice, although I've never viewed it that way. I don't know how to explain the sensation of being ready to throw down anytime and anyplace. But some people talk and act tough; then when you look closely, you see in their eyes that they are scared. I'm not. Friends have told me that I get a look in my eye when I'm about to fight, as if I don't even see the guy in front of me. I'm looking right through him. There's no cowering, no scowling, just staring. To me it's as if I've already knocked the guy flat on his ass.

Still, it's not like I had a rep on campus as some street brawler. I was actually pretty clumsy, often tripping over painted lines and landing in the push-up position. When it happened in downtown San Luis Obispo, I'd hear people whispering, "Man, that guy's drunk."

> **PEOPLE WHO SCARE ME:**
>
> Creeps on *To Catch a Predator*

If anyone knew me at all, it was as a decent wrestler. I wrestled at 177 until my senior year, when I moved up to 190. I was always really good at taking some of the best wrestlers in the country deep into a match, then losing by a point. I never gave up anything—which is why

As a wrestler, I'd try to pressure the guy until he'd break.

I was injured every season except freshman. I couldn't just let a guy beat me in a position, I had to try to fight my way out, which led to an injured shoulder, a hernia, and an injured knee. I was also still in great shape. In practice we did rope drills, sprints, and iron-man wrestling, which is when one man stays in the circle for several three-minute rounds while fresh wrestlers rotate in against him. And I had a lot of strength in my arms and hands. I would shoot on an opponent's leg, and if my fingers came anywhere near the back of his calf, I could suck that leg right in. My fingertips would creep around his calf, dig deep into the guy's muscle, and never let go.

But sometimes you make one change to your look, and it's as if people are seeing you for the first time. During my senior year, in 1992, Eric and I were going to see a Slayer concert with a bunch of our roommates. We loved Slayer and wanted to do something crazy and memorable for the concert. Matt Wilson pulled out a set of electric shears and said, "Hey, let's shave our heads." Everyone loved the idea—except for me.

My hair had been short and tight—just like my Pops's—since I was a little kid. But my senior year in college I had finally decided to grow it out. So shaving my head wasn't exactly a crazy notion. We started throwing out some ideas; then Matt suggested I get a Mohawk. I thought, Cool. That was the extent of the conversation. He shaved one side, shaved the other, and trimmed me down the middle so it was real low. I liked it. It wasn't one of those overgelled Mohawks reaching up to the ceiling. It looked clean, as if I were someone you wouldn't want to mess with. It definitely didn't look as if I were an accounting major. I

CHOOSING A TATTOO THAT'S RIGHT FOR YOU:

Make sure it means something to you. I always thought it was silly that people walk in and say, "I'll take that right there," and they are pointing to a little thing in a book. I'm not trying to stop people from making a living, but it should be something that means something to you. Put it wherever you want, but make it matter.

figured that it wouldn't be too long before I had to get a real job and grow it out, so why not enjoy it until I graduated?

That was my reasoning when I decided to get my head tattooed as well. I chose the Japanese letters that spelled Koei-Kan, my karate style, which means House of Peace and Prosperity. I wanted the tattoo to be somewhere everyone could see it without me having to take off my shirt, but also in a spot where I could hide it once I started interviewing. It took a lot of shopping around before I found a place that would tattoo my head. But putting it on the side of my skull made perfect sense. With a few weeks' notice, a full head of hair would cover it up.

Little did I know that interviews weren't going to be a problem, or that my signature look was born.

CHAPTER 8

PRACTICE WHAT YOU LOVE

HERE'S A SHOCKER: I DIDN'T WANT TO BE AN AC-countant when I was done with school, and not because I wanted to keep my Mohawk. Really, all I wanted to do was make a living as a fighter. This was before the UFC was created and before mixed martial arts became popular. Since I wasn't a boxer, my options were pretty much limited to beating the crap out of people in San Luis Obispo's alleys—which didn't pay at all—or becoming a kickboxer, which paid only slightly better.

Professional kickboxing had been popular in the United States for less than two decades when I left Cal Poly. And I didn't have any idea how to go about becoming a pro. Once school ended, I bartended around town and taught classes at some of the local dojos. I've never been a long-range planner or thought about how I was going to support myself. Until I discovered the UFC and dedicated myself to becoming a champion, making a living as a fighter didn't necessarily mean beating people up in the ring. It meant I was in a gym doing karate, practicing what I loved, every day, and getting paid for it. If I had never heard of the UFC, I'd probably still be teaching classes and bartending to make ends meet and would be happy about it.

But a former Cal Poly teammate of mine, Alfie Alcaraz, went out to Vegas after school, in 1993, to try to make it as a professional kick-boxer. (By the way, you'll notice a lot of kickboxers and UFC fighters are former college wrestlers. Unless we're going to the Olympics or the WWE [World Wrestling Entertainment], we've got no place else to turn if we still want to compete.)

Alfie was looking for places to work out and came across a gym called One Kicks, which taught Muay Thai boxing, run by a guy named Nick Blomgren. Muay Thai is the original form of kickboxing and al-lows competitors to strike from eight different points: the hands, el-bows, legs (shins and knees), and feet. It's actually called the Art of Eight Limbs. Most sport-oriented martial arts only allow two strike points, the hands and the feet. Muay Thai is as revered in Thailand as football is here. It's the national sport, is recognized by an official holi-day, and is treated with a respect by the combatants unlike any other sport. It's not just about sport to those in Thailand; it's about finding serenity and peace through the practice of an art. Fighters usually touch the rope three times. They always enter the ring from the top, rather than through the bottom, because the head is sacred and the feet are dirty. When in the ring, they perform a traditional dance called the Wai Kru, in which they circle the canvas to figuratively seal it off, meaning the fight is between them and them alone.

Here in the United States, the ritual is confined to the actual beat-ings. And Nick was a master. He had been a black belt in karate when he discovered the sport, then spent several years training in Thailand for three months every year. In 1992 he won the North American kick-boxing championship. Since Alfie knew I kept up with the sport, he called me and asked if I had heard of Nick and if the gym was any good. Nick's nickname was One Kick, because that was all he needed to knock someone out. So, yeah, I told Alfie, Nick was legit.

Nick was also becoming one of the bigger kickboxing promoters in town. At first, he was doing it just to get himself some publicity for his fights, but pretty soon he was putting together cards at casinos such as the Aladdin and Four Queens and the Orleans that drew as many as fifteen hundred people. Sure, these were the out-of-the-way, down-market casinos that the locals played at, not the upscale tourist traps such as the MGM and Mirage that drew fifteen thousand boxing fans for title fights. And, yeah, kickboxers made only about $500 per fight, rather than the $5 million or more that the boxers made, but the fights were sanctioned. They had refs, judges, and fans screaming for blood, and took place in a ring. For a kid like me, looking to fight someplace other than a bar, it was the pinnacle of combat sports.

Not too long after Alfie began training with Nick, Nick called me and invited me down for a visit. I told him I wanted to try a few matches, and without even seeing a tape, he started putting me in shows he was promoting. Pretty soon Alfie—who went on to win seven national titles—and I were Nick's headliners.

Nick said he liked my look—the Mohawk, my stare, my generally mean-looking disposition—and my style. That was the same as it was when I was wrestling or fighting in the street: aggressive, focused, and completely immune to the idea of getting hurt. Nick told me I was becoming a draw, that a lot of people were coming out to see me go on the attack when I fought. I had a pulse and energy when I stepped into the ring, mainly because I liked fighting so damn much.

But when I wasn't fighting, I was as invisible as a guy with a Mohawk and tattoo on the side of his head can be. I'd go out with Nick, sip on a Coke, sit by myself, and not say much at all. He'd take me all over town, trying to get me to open up, show a little life outside the ring, at least act as if I were having a good time. He wanted me meeting people, elevating my profile, increasing interest in the sport. Really, he just wanted me to lighten up and have a good time. But that wasn't me, at least not then. I was all about fighting. Everything else was not only secondary, but not all that compelling.

It wouldn't be too long before I realized that would have to change.

CHAPTER 9

NEVER UNDERESTIMATE ANYONE

I SETTLED INTO A NICE RHYTHM AFTER COLLEGE: I'D fight in Vegas for Nick, bartend during the week, teach karate at a couple of local dojos nearly every weekday. I made good money—a lot of it in cash—and between winning a few kickboxing matches and my teaching, I developed a rep as a good fighter in SLO's karate community. Then, one afternoon, I got a call from the sensei at my dojo asking me to stop by. A new fighter had moved to town, and he was looking to spar.

Going a few rounds in the afternoon is no different for me from playing a pickup basketball game for anyone else. And I'm always eager to take on someone new, try out my moves, and see if they've got anything I can pick up. When I arrived at the dojo that day, I noticed the new guy, John Hackleman, right away. He was shorter than me and stocky, with a barrel chest and thickly muscled arms. At first glance you might wonder how he moved those things with any speed. Then you get on the mat with him and you realize how smart it is never to underestimate anyone. Because your question is quickly answered.

John was born in New York and moved to Hawaii when he was four years old. He picked up judo when he was nine, mainly because, as a white kid living in a Samoan neighborhood, he was tired of get-

John Hackleman is an amazing trainer and a great friend.

ting his butt kicked. By the time he was a teenager he was a kickboxer, a Golden Gloves boxer, and on his way to becoming a tenth-degree black belt. His style of fighting was called Kaju Kenbo, which was created by a group of Hawaiian martial artists in the mid-1940s. It was hard-core. The guys who started it weren't looking for some kind of inner peace. They developed Kaju Kenbo because they wanted to become better street fighters. And it wasn't long before John perfected the form.

He was—and still is—a master at all the combat sports. After a three-year stint in the army in the late 1970s and early 1980s, he was signed by Don King and had twenty professional fights. He then became the number-one-ranked kickboxer in the world during the mid-1980s, when he moved to Southern California and opened his gym, The Pit, which was for hard-core devotees of martial arts. Then he realized owning a gym called The Pit and having a rep for teaching what was essentially street fighting didn't exactly invite the widest swath of customers. That was when he tweaked the Kaju Kenbo style and created his signature form of karate, Hawaiian Kempo. It had all the striking and fighting techniques of Kenbo, along with conditioning drills that made it more mainstream.

John was moving The Pit to SLO with his wife, who was from the area, and he came to spar that day to get a feel for the local talent. We didn't do any serious fighting. The instructor ran us through some drills; I'd run at him and he'd defend; then he'd run at me. Both of us would do wall drills, with our backs to the wall and multiple people coming at us. It was the first time in a while that I'd sparred with someone who was better than me. He was great at landing powerful punches and kicks from different angles, and I was impressed. As he was leaving, he handed me his card and said, "If you ever really want to train, give me a call." After the workout he had given me already, I was intrigued. And later that week I rode my motorcycle out to his house for a session.

John had bought a place—it looked like a compound, really—about twenty minutes outside San Luis Obispo. It was on three acres of woods, halfway up one of the foothills that surround the town. His house and a garage were on one plateau, and behind that, farther up the hill, was another house. This was where he had relocated The Pit.

It was raining when I drove up the hill. I was soaked, and my motorcycle wheels were spinning to get traction on the dirt driveway. I had barely had a chance to dry off when John led me up a set of steep steps made of pebbles. John was a registered nurse who was working at a jail at the time, and the scene at the top of the hill looked like something out of a prison yard. My buddy Eric, who trained with me there, joked that it looked like one of those bunkers people have when they're expecting the apocalypse and have a basement full of machine guns. With all the modern technology and exercise equipment available—even back then—John's program was decidedly old-school. The single-story house—which had a covered deck—was empty, except for several heavy bags. Hundred-pound tires were lying around, which John's trainees used to flip up the hill to improve their explosion. People filled wheelbarrows with weights and then pushed them up and down the hills. A thin pad wrapped around a metal pole holding up the roof of the deck was used as a punching bag. Dumbbells, free weights, medicine balls, and benches were lined up around the place. John had those working out do Black Jack drills, which were a push-up, then a body-weight squat, then a push-up, then two body-weight squats, until you reached twenty-one total. All the exercises ended when John rang an old-time boxing bell.

The holiest place at The Pit was the ring, which was set up along the edge of the woods that abutted John's property. It was four-sided and made of fraying rope, with an even greater incentive to staying upright than not being embarrassed: The entire ring was surrounded by poison oak. If you got knocked on your ass at The Pit, you'd be feeling it long after the pain of the punch went away.

Before John had me lift a weight, climb a step, or punch a bag, he wanted me to spar. With him. This time, no instructor was blowing his whistle and calling out drills. John decided when we started and when we finished. In an all-out fight session, we went at it for nineteen straight minutes. UFC rounds last for only five minutes, and boxing rounds last for only three, because fighting for even that long is exhausting. Even if you're in shape, your legs and arms start to shake from all the adrenaline pumping through your body. Sparring for nineteen straight minutes felt like running a marathon. My whole body was burning. And hurting, too. Because John handed me a beat-down like I'd never had. My roommate at the time was Eric, and when I got home, I looked at him and said, "That was awesome."

But I must have shown Hack something. When I left that day, it was still raining, and it was expected to keep raining for several days after that. As I hopped on my bike to leave, John tossed me the keys to his truck. I gave him a look as if to ask, "What's this?" But he answered with a question: "You coming back tomorrow?" I said yes. He told me to take the truck so I didn't kill myself riding my bike up his hill in the rain. I told him I couldn't do that, and he just asked me again, "You coming back tomorrow?" When I said yes again, he turned around and walked away. That was the end of the discussion. I was taking the truck, and I was becoming a member of The Pit.

I was proud to become a part of John's team of Pit Monsters.

CHAPTER 10

BEING MENTALLY TOUGH IS NOT A SOMETIMES THING

THE UNDERLYING THEORIES OF HAWAIIAN KEMPO are the same as they've been since the Kempo form was first created by a Buddhist monk in A.D. 525. While visiting China to teach Buddhism to villagers, the monk saw them being robbed and beaten by bandits. He didn't believe in fighting, but he believed that not being prepared for a fight was a graver sin. For several days he fasted, until a vision of a new fighting style came to him. He taught the villagers how to defend themselves using an open hand and their feet, knees, and elbows. They would not always stop the marauders, but at least they could now defend themselves.

The tenets John preached were the same. If you couldn't pay for workouts, he didn't care. Most of the guys he trained weren't paying a cent. John was always saying, "I never let lack of money come between you and Kempo. All I ask is that you give Kempo and The Pit the respect and loyalty it gives you. Confidence, loyalty, and humility are what I expect from all Pit Monsters."

It wasn't easy to come by that confidence, but the humility was no problem. You couldn't just sign up for a trial membership to The Pit and decide if it was the right gym for you. You had to be invited by someone who was already training there. After my first few times, I

There's no better—or harder—place to work out than The Pit.

would bring Eric. We were so close that he was once accused of being in a fight in college—while he was sitting at home watching TV—just because I was there. He knew how much I wanted to be a kick-boxer and made himself miserable trying to help me. He used to wince when we'd do drills that strengthened our shins. When we'd be driving over, his head would start hurting and I'd hear him whispering, "Please no sparring today, please no sparring today." Eventually, though, he'd become a black belt. He was one of the few who survived the program.

Even with an invite from someone on the inside, there was no guarantee you'd become a lifetime member of The Pit. Every day you came to work out, you were going to be pushed to agony. Not just on the weights or the tires or the heavy bags, but in the ring. Sparring was a constant, and the sole purpose was for you to get beaten until you decided you'd had enough or John decided you were ready. It may sound extreme. Hell, it *is* extreme. But John's purpose was clear: He wanted to separate those who were strong from those who were weak. And not just physically strong, but mentally strong.

Being mentally tough is not a sometimes thing. You don't turn it on and off. If you're not mentally tough in the gym while you are training, then when you're challenged in a fight, you will fold. It doesn't mean you have to be balls-out every time you work out. But, when you are being pushed in training, you can't just fold a couple of times because you feel that you've done enough that day. Before you know it, when you get in a fight and are tired and beat-up and in a bad position, you will give up, too. That was the point of the beatings. If you were going to fight, you'd better be prepared—for everything.

CHAPTER 11

SIZE DOESN'T MATTER

FITTINGLY, THE HISTORY OF MIXED MARTIAL ARTS and ultimate fighting began at the circus. Or, more accurately, in a booth next to the big tent that held the main events. It was in Brazil in the 1920s, and these fights were sideshows, no different from seeing the bearded lady or the man who swallowed knives. They held bouts the organizers called Vale Tudo, Portuguese for "everything allowed." And it was. The more insane the matchup, the more popular the show. One Brazilian newspaper in the 1920s wrote about a large black man fighting a tiny Japanese man. The crowd expected the little guy to be pummeled—in fact, that was what they had paid to see. He was thrown to the ground by his opponent, an expert in the South American fighting style of capoeira, and was vulnerable. But as the looming giant readied to kick the man in the head, he was suddenly brought down. The Japanese man had used a deft jujitsu move to lock his opponent's leg before he could finish his kick, then rendered him unconscious with a few other deft maneuvers. After the short struggle, the fight ended with the Japanese man sitting on top of his felled opponent's chest.

This style of fighting was especially popular in Brazil, where Mitsuyo Maeda, a former Japanese boxing champ, had immigrated. When he arrived in Rio, Maeda found a benefactor in Gastão Gracie, a wealthy businessman. He took Maeda in, helped him get established, and became a leader in the movement to bring Japanese immigrants to Brazil. In exchange for his help, Maeda taught Gracie's sons the ancient art of jujitsu. Only he added a twist.

The Japanese jujitsu learned by Maeda when he was a boy in the late 1800s focused on using an opponent's force against him, which often led to throws and flips. But Maeda emphasized grappling and defending yourself from the ground. He taught submission holds, joint locks, and choke holds, making it a more violent, aggressive, and combative form of jujitsu than that taught in Japan. Three of the Gracie boys—Carlos, Carlson, and Hélio—took to it instantly. It wasn't long before they opened their own academy, Gracie Jujitsu, and became known as the founders of Brazilian jujitsu.

The sport's popularity quickly spread across the country. Children practiced in the countryside, and the circus made it a regular part of its traveling road show. Everyone loved the choke holds, seeing men spasm as they became unconscious, and the joint locks that twisted elbows into gruesome angles. The Gracies were confident that their form of martial arts was superior to all others. They believed that when it was practiced properly and the right technique was used, size didn't matter. No matter how small they were and how big the opponent, they could not be beaten. Shortly after perfecting their sport in the 1920s, Carlos inaugurated what became known as the Gracie Challenges. He challenged anyone throughout Brazil to battle him or his brothers in a fight to submission. The challenges became legendary within the country and lasted for decades. In 1952, Hélio, then thirty-nine, participated in what is still the longest recorded fight in history, a three-hour, forty-minute loss to Brazilian judo expert Valdemar Santana.

Then in 1959, the original form of Vale Tudo fighting first appeared on Brazilian television, on a show called *Heróis do Ringue* (Ring of Heroes). Hosted by the Gracie boys, it featured no-holds-barred fights between competitors from all different disciplines. On the first show a Brazilian jujitsu expert named João Alberto Barreto battled a nationally known wrestler. Barreto quickly locked his opponent in an armbar, but the wrestler refused to tap out. Barreto slowly applied more pressure, expecting the match to end or the wrestler to give up, but he never did. Not until the arm snapped like a twig, leaving an exposed compound fracture for all of Brazil's television audience to see, was the fight stopped. The violence was so shocking—and the complaints flooded in so quickly—the show was immediately pulled off the air.

At the end of the decade, in 1969, Hélio's son Rorion left Brazil as a seventeen-year-old for a summer vacation in California. For three months he roamed around SoCal, sometimes working odd jobs, sometimes just spending the night on the streets. He loved it and had a vision of bringing his family's style of jujitsu—and its academies—to the United States.

Nine years later, armed with a law degree and a lifetime of martial arts training, he moved to LA full-time. To make ends meet, Rorion cleaned houses, worked as an extra on such shows as *Hart to Hart* and *Fantasy Island*, and choreographed fight scenes for movies (such as that choke hold Mel Gibson uses on Gary Busey at the end of the first *Lethal Weapon*). He also set up a mat for training in his garage. The friends he made walking around Hollywood's lots as an extra became his students, spending afternoons, mornings, and evenings in his garage in Hermosa Beach, learning the arts of submission holds and choking people. Word about this Brazilian badass teaching jujitsu out of his garage began to spread—one of those in-crowd secrets that so many Hollywood poseurs wanted in on. It helped that Rorion would challenge any dojo sensei to an anything-goes fight, right in front of the sensei's students, to prove how powerful Brazilian jujitsu could be. By the mid-1980s, classes became so large Rorion needed one of his younger brothers, seventeen-year-old Royce, to move from Brazil to help out. Hundreds of students were learning Gracie-style jujitsu, filling thirty-minute classes from seven in the morning until nine at night, seven days a week.

In 1989, Rorion opened the first Gracie Jujitsu Academy—finally getting out of his garage—in Torrance, California. And within twenty years there would be Gracie academies in nearly every major town in the country. The Pentagon would hire Rorion's jujitsu experts as consultants to teach hand-to-hand combat. (Thanks to *Black Belt* magazine for letting me crib Rorion's history from one of its stories. As I said, I've been reading that magazine since I took my first karate class.)

Rorion produced Gracie jujitsu videos that developed a cult following among martial arts and combat sports fanatics. And to cement his rep and build his business, he brought the Gracie Challenges to the United States. Only now the winner didn't just get bragging rights that his form of combat was the best. Rorion also threw in $100,000 to whoever beat a Gracie jujitsu expert. He never had to pay up.

In 1991, Gracie met Art Davie, a Southern California ad exec who was researching martial arts programs for a client. Davie eventually became a student and friend of Gracie's. He saw the popularity of the Gracie videos and often heard about Gracie's quest to constantly prove Brazilian jujitsu was the most dominant form of martial arts in the world. So in 1992 he proposed an idea to his teacher: an eight-man, single-elimination tournament in which any fighting style was allowed. They'd call it War of the Worlds. Gracie loved it, and he and Davie took it to John Milius, another student of Gracie's, who wrote *Apocalypse Now* and directed *Conan the Barbarian*. He loved it, too, and within a year they had sold the idea and had a show on pay-per-view.

Newly titled the Ultimate Fighting Championships, UFC 1 debuted on November 12, 1993, from McNichols Sports Arena in Denver. The show featured two kickboxers, a boxer, a karate expert, a shootfighter (the original term for mixed martial arts), a savate black belt (kickboxing with shoes), a sumo wrestler, and a small—by comparison—frail-looking jujitsu expert named Royce Gracie. Among all his brothers and students, Rorion actually chose Royce for UFC 1 because he was the least physically threatening. He was the pawn to prove, if he won, that Gracie jujitsu was the most dominant martial art in the world.

The promoters knew how to create some drama. They billed the event as "no holds barred," which was essentially true. They flew in João Alberto Barreto, the Brazilian jujitsu master whose breaking of an opponent's arm in a 1959 fight got the sport thrown off Brazilian television. They had a Hollywood designer design the Octagon. And they offered prize money of $50,000. The first UFC fight attracted nearly one hundred thousand pay-per-view buys.

It didn't take long for Royce to prove Rorion right. His first fight that night was against Art Jimmerson, the lone traditional boxer in the competition. Jimmerson was so mismatched, he used a boxing glove on one hand only, unsure of what exactly he was getting himself into. Royce needed just a few kicks to Jimmerson's lower body to take him down and mount him. Jimmerson didn't even wait for Royce to put him in a choke hold or any other submission move before he tapped out.

Royce needed even less time against Ken Shamrock in the semifinals of UFC 1. In this fight he proved how powerful the Gracie jujitsu style could be. Shamrock had an early advantage in the right, getting the dominant position. But with a few deft moves, Royce got the upper hand, literally. Fifty-seven seconds into the first round, he had Shamrock in a choke hold and forced him to tap out.

In the finals that night, Royce left no doubts that he was the world's ultimate fighter. He faced Gerard Gordeau, a boxer/kickboxer from Amsterdam. In his first match that night, Gordeau had hit his opponent, Teila Tuli, so hard that Tuli's teeth were knocked not just out of his mouth, but out of the ring, winding up beneath the announcer's table. The force was so strong it also broke Gordeau's hand, but it didn't matter. Gordeau won easily in the semifinals. But he was no match for Royce. Gordeau was at such a disadvantage at one point, the legend goes, he bit Royce on the left ear. Royce allegedly showed the bite mark to a camera crew covering the fight. One minute and forty-one seconds into the fight, Royce caught Gordeau in a rear-naked choke. He held on a little bit tighter and longer after Gordeau had submitted.

The win was no fluke. Five months later, at UFC 2, in a sixteen-man tournament with a $60,000 purse, Royce earned the title again, winning four fights in a row one night. In the last one he was punching his opponent so often and with such ease, the guy submitted just seventy-seven seconds into the fight. Royce bowed out of UFC 3 after an injury, but proved the power of Gracie jujitsu all over again in UFC 4. Fighting for $64,000, Royce made it to the finals of the tournament against Dan Severn, a 275-pound wrestler. Severn had been a four-time all-American at Arizona State and once held the U.S. record for most victories by pins.

That night he was clearly the stronger fighter. The match lasted a UFC title-fight record of 15:49, with Severn keeping Royce flat on the mat for most of it. But the ground moves the 180-pound Royce had been perfecting his entire life—the types of moves his grandfather insisted could be used no matter how small he was or how big his opponent—were eventually too much for Severn. From his back Royce maneuvered his legs so one of Severn's arms and his head were caught between Royce's thighs. It was a picture-perfect triangle choke. Slowly the blood flow to the hulking Severn's head was constricted, until he was forced to submit. For the third time in less than two years, Royce Gracie had won a UFC tournament. He had proven once and for all that his family's style of jujitsu was incomparable.

CHAPTER 12

TAKE IT TO THE NEXT LEVEL

ONE NIGHT BACK IN 1995, I WAS TENDING BAR ON A busy Saturday night in San Luis Obispo. The place was pretty crowded with regulars and college kids, but it was still early, so there was plenty of room for people to move around. Suddenly the bar's doors flew open and this huge black guy burst through. He was built like a tank, legs practically bursting through his pants, chest the size of a beer keg, and shoulders that seemed to merge with his neck. Seriously, this was one of the few guys who would make me hesitate in a dark alley. There just aren't a lot of African-Americans in SLO, so when someone as big as this guy throws open the doors, the crowd is going to part, just as this one did. Imagine their relief when he yelled out, "Where's Chuck Liddell?"

I felt everyone's eyes turn toward me. I had been getting some good local coverage for my kickboxing fights. Between that and the occasional scuffles that I had to deal with when I was bouncing or working the bar, I had built my reputation around town as a tough guy. It was no different from my days in Santa Barbara. Still, if you just looked at the situation, you'd think this couldn't be good for me. My girlfriend at the time was working with me as a bartender, and she just gave me a look that seemed to say, Do not jump over that bar. Out loud, however, all I could hear her say was, "Oh, shit."

Of course, I couldn't stop myself from jumping over the bar and wading into what most people assumed was going to be a serious beat-down. But I couldn't let them think I was going to back down. So I answered the guy, letting him know I was the man he was looking for. Then I asked him, not too politely, "What the fuck do you want?"

He didn't talk back. Instead we slowly began walking toward each other, all the eyes in the bar watching us, waiting to see how badly I was going to get my ass kicked. It was like the shoot-out at the OK Corral. Then, just as it looked as if neither of us had any more room to walk, when it looked as if the next move we made would have to be one of us throwing a punch, we each threw open our arms and gave each other a huge hug. It was Lorenzo Neal, now a Pro Bowl fullback for the San Diego Chargers. He was also a good friend of mine from our days as college wrestlers, his at Fresno State. When we finally let go of each other, and when the crowd caught its breath, let out a sigh, and started laughing along with Lorenzo and me, I turned around toward the bar, told my boss I was done for the night, and took a seat with Lorenzo. Then we got seriously messed up.

Lorenzo asked me if I had been watching these Ultimate Fighting Championship shows on pay-per-view. Of course I had, I told him. These fights had been going on for two years, and in the world of combat sports that I lived in, they were impossible to ignore. Not to mention they were getting more and more viewers with every battle. Ken Shamrock, Royce Gracie, Dan Severen, they were revolutionizing the fight game. This seemed to be what boxing had stopped being a long time ago: a tough-guy sport that combined science and form and heart and, most important, pure ferociousness. In the end, that was all that counted in these fights. They were no different from bare-knuckle brawls in Isla Vista in Santa Barbara—or any other town where kids who liked to fight were going at it. It was all about who was the best fighter—not who could score the most points or who could line up the best deal or who would make their promoter the most money.

We talked about these fights at The Pit, mimicking their moves, trying to incorporate some of the moves we saw in UFC into what we did in kickboxing, making mixed martial arts training a regular part of our workout regimen. Not only was I watching, but I was wondering, Should I be doing that instead of kickboxing? Lorenzo was thinking the same thing and told me I was so right for the sport that he'd sponsor me if I decided to do it. And he wasn't the only one pushing me. My brother Dan wanted me to do it, too, as did most of my friends who knew my background. They weren't wrong. I knew more than one style of martial arts, and I had begun studying jujitsu. I had wrestled in college. I loved fighting, wasn't afraid of getting hurt, and in every fight I had one purpose, and that was to knock people out. Nothing less. In a sport that usually ended only when one of the guys was either knocked unconscious or was forced to tap out because he was in so much agony, nothing mattered more than wanting to lay a guy flat on his back.

Nick used to constantly tell me that I could thrive as a UFC fighter. He thought the combination of my grappling ability and that I was hard to take down and even harder to keep down would make me nearly impossible to stop. "No one can take you down, and if they try to stand up with you, they will be in trouble," he used to tell me. Then Nick did something that, considering the way things turned out, was pretty selfless. Not to mention that he wound up looking as if he could see into the future.

We were at a gym in Las Vegas working out. I was getting ready for my next kickboxing match, which he was promoting. I wasn't Nick's meal ticket by any means, but I was a good draw for his fights and didn't cost much. I would wind up with a 10-2 record as a kickboxer. I'd win two national titles as well as championships in the USMPA (an American Thai boxing association) and the WKA (World

Kickboxing Association). Even when I was the main attraction, I still wasn't making more than $500 a fight. While there was more dough in the UFC—and trying to make it in that sport had been something I was thinking about—I wasn't exactly pursuing it as a lifelong dream. I didn't know anyone, and I certainly wasn't the only person fighting—in the ring or in the alley—who thought he was the toughest guy in the world and deserved a shot in the cage. It wasn't a fantasy. I just didn't spend time scheming and worrying and planning how to make it happen. I've always let things like this come to me. If they work out, great; if not, I don't worry about what I'm missing. I just wanted to fight—kickboxing, MMA, in the bar, it didn't matter.

Nick, however, was thinking more about the rest of my life than I was. And he laid out the scenario in pretty blunt terms. Nick was a great kickboxer, a champion, one of the best in the world at what he did. But he couldn't make any real money. He had other jobs while he was training and competing. He started his own promotion company to get himself more publicity, only he became so busy trying to put together exciting cards and negotiating for venues and making sure he had the dough to pay out purses, he couldn't keep up with his fighting career. Pretty soon he wasn't kickboxing anymore. Instead he was just promoting.

I thought his life looked pretty good. I was twenty-five, making money fighting, getting some publicity, teaching classes, and training at The Pit. But Nick thought I had potential to be bigger, to do more, to be a champion. That day at the gym in Vegas he told me that no matter how much of a badass I looked like with my Mohawk and the tattoo on the side of my head and a cold, hard stare in the ring, I'd never make any serious money kickboxing. There'd never be more than fifteen hundred people in the stands for my fights. I'd never be able to focus solely on training and not have to bartend or teach. It wasn't the future. "Don't be like me," he said. "Don't be sitting around one day saying there isn't enough money in this sport to be beaten up this bad. It hurts too much for just five hundred dollars a pop." It was time, he said, to make a career move. Either move on with my life, get into accounting, and forget fighting, or make getting into the UFC a priority, improve my combat skills, and take it to the next level.

Nick had been dispensing advice to me for a few years by this point. One lesson had always been that if I wanted to become a bigger name, I had to show more of a personality. But this was different. It wasn't about me doing better so he could make more money. It was just about me. He thought I had a huge future in the UFC. "You could be a world champ," he told me. "When opponents see how easily you get back up, if they are lucky enough to get you down, they will no longer be able to fight. They'll get weaker. They'll be worried about keeping you down, not your hands and your kicks. You will break their spirit."

That was what I wanted to do. And Nick was going to help me.

CHAPTER 13

YOU'RE NEVER TOO TOUGH TO SHOW THE LADIES YOUR SENSITIVE SIDE

I HAD OTHER REASONS I WAS A BIT ANXIOUS TO GET MY career going.

During the summers my brother Dan and I used to work at the California midstate fair, which was held about half an hour outside San Luis Obispo. Most nights the fair put on a concert at which Dan and I worked security, while girls from groups such as the Future Farmers of America worked as ushers. One of the guys I trained with at The Pit was dating one of those girls, so she and I would carpool together from San Luis Obispo to the fair every day. She always brought along a friend of hers, Casey Noland.

Casey was a cute blonde who lived in a tiny country house outside town. Since she was seventeen and between her junior and senior years in high school, she still lived with her parents. At first there was nothing between us; we were just two people with a mutual acquaintance sharing a ride to the fair. But after a few weeks, I became interested. I wasn't thinking, Oh, man, she's seventeen and I'm twenty-five and this is a bad idea. I definitely did not think about the ribbing I would take from my mom, sister, brothers, and friends if I started dating a teenager. One night, I was supposed to go back to SLO after the fair

All dolled up for the prom.

because I had a date. Next thing I knew I had blown the date off and was spending two hours sitting in a car talking to Casey.

Honestly, she thought I was a little nuts. I told her about growing up with my grandfather, about my mom, about getting in fights as a kid, about high school football and college wrestling and about training and kickboxing. I wasn't thinking, Why am I opening up to this kid? But she was definitely wondering, Why is this twenty-five-year-old talking to me so much and telling me all this? Of course, the one thing I didn't do that night was ask her for her number. I still don't know why. Instead I asked my buddy's girlfriend.

Soon after that, we were dating. Or at least trying to. Her parents weren't high on the idea. She was a nice girl living a conservative life in San Luis Obispo, and I was some Mohawk-wearing thug whom they saw as corrupting their daughter. One night her dad sat me down and said, "I don't like you dating my daughter, but I'm not about to threaten you. So just be nice." And I was. Half the time we got together we wound up watching movies with her parents in their house. Other times I'd drive my blue Ford Ranger—on the days it was actually working—to the school, pick her up when she got out for lunch, and we'd cruise around together or find a place to eat. Once I even surprised her with a romantic picnic. Because, really, you're never too tough to show the ladies your sensitive side.

We started dating in August of 1995 and were still together as she neared the end of her senior year. Her prom was approaching fast. Now, I had been getting made fun of because I was robbing the cradle for most of the year. And I had been able to handle it. But when Casey asked me to go to her prom, and I said yes, it took on a whole new dimension. My mom was particularly brutal, telling me, "Well, Charlie, I hope this is the last senior prom you're planning on going to."

If I was going to go, I was going to embrace it. I even decided to grow out my hair on the sides and fill out my Mohawk. Then Casey saw what was happening and made me shave it down again. That night we took a horse-drawn carriage down the main drag in town that went past all the bars. I worked at a place called the Library with my brother Dan. And when the horse pulled Casey and me past it, we saw a sign that read, CHUCK'S NOT WORKING TONIGHT. HE'S GOING TO THE PROM. Standing beneath it were my friends, the people I worked with, and Dan, who were waving at us. It was hysterical.

I thought I could marry Casey. I even told her so. But at that moment in my life I wanted to commit to fighting even more. I didn't have the time or the energy to focus on a serious relationship. So we broke up that August, after a

HOW TO IMPRESS YOUR GIRLFRIEND WITH YOUR SENSITIVE SIDE:

Be nice, be a good person, remember things like birthdays and anniversaries, little things that she is talking about that make it look as if you are paying attention—or I should say show that you are paying attention. Bottom line is, as my daughter says, I'm not always very sensitive.

Me and Pops. He was always there to support me. If he could only see me now.

year of dating, as she was getting ready to go to junior college. But we stayed friends, and every so often I'd see her around town. One night I had a kickboxing match in Arroyo Grande, a town just a few miles from San Luis Obispo. For most of that fall we were on and off, dating each other, getting together as friends, never as serious as we were before, but not quite ready to completely sever ties.

Also, it was a good time to have someone I was comfortable with around, because that Thanksgiving Pops passed away. We're not the most emotional family, and a lot of that came from Pops. He had been a coroner in the sheriff's department for a while, and from the time we were young, both he and my mom taught all us kids that death was a part of life. Before he retired, Pops had befriended a man who had tried to commit suicide by blowing his head off with a shotgun. It didn't work, and instead the guy shot off half his face. The point of the story, Pops told us, was that if it's not your time, it's not going to happen and then you have to live with it. But when it is, there's no use in everyone who is left behind shedding tears. We did a lot of internalizing when it came to that. Although, to this day, I'm sad he never got to see me fight in the UFC. It's a huge regret for me. He had told me since I was a kid I could be the best in the world at whatever I did. Sure, that's what everyone's parents or grandparents say, but Pops made you believe it.

Casey and I were in one of our "off" phases, as our situation seemed to change week to week. But we'd still talk and see each other regularly, so I could tell when something was wrong. And she did not look healthy. Her face was flushed, as though she had a fever, and she seemed tired and irritable. I kept asking her, "What's wrong? What's wrong?" Finally she told me, "I'm pregnant."

You'd think I'd be freaking out. My eighteen-year-old girlfriend whom I'd just taken to the prom was pregnant. Meanwhile, I'm twenty-six, working in a bar, making nearly nothing as a kickboxer, teaching at the Y, and training to become a professional fighter in a league a senator who had been a prisoner of war thought was so violent and repulsive he called it the equivalent of "human cockfighting." No state wanted to host a UFC fight, and to make matters worse, there was a good chance this league might go under any day, before I even had a chance to make my professional debut.

Casey was sure I'd be mad when she told me she was pregnant. But I wasn't. After I heard the news I just stared straight ahead for a few seconds. Casey tried talking to me to snap me out of it, but I could barely hear her. Eventually I slowly felt a smile creep across my face. I was going to be a dad. I was thrilled.

If you're the kind of guy who stresses about how to support a family, then my life wasn't—and still isn't—for you. But I never worried about that. My mom worked hard and she loved us. My grandparents worked hard and loved us. I grew up in a house where making ends meet was a challenge, and I don't think I suffered because of it. I don't think I even noticed it. In fact, if we were any more comfortable, I'm not sure I'd be who I am today or doing what I'm doing today. I may have lived in a nicer neighborhood, gotten in fewer fights, had more space to avoid my brothers, or not moved in with my grandparents. I would have missed out on living under the same roof as the single greatest male influence in my life, my grandfather. So, no, stressing about making money wasn't my biggest concern. I knew what it took to raise a child, and being comfortable had little to do with it.

That night I called my mom and told her the news. I couldn't have played it straighter, saying, "Mom, Casey is having a baby and it's mine." It's not that I wanted to downplay it for her sake, or downplay it at all. I was actually just calling her to find out if how bad Casey was feeling was normal.

Needless to say, my mom was shocked. She thought we had broken up. And we had. Casey and I weren't going to get married; we both knew that. But my mom didn't want us rushing into anything, either. When I was growing up, she and my grandparents had always made it clear that the children in the family came first; they were the priority. The grandparents were considered the past, the parents the present, and the kids the future. The generations past and present knew that if they didn't take care of the future, there'd be no one to take care of them.

So later that night, after I told my mom the news, I called her again, this time to talk about the impact of it all. This is a woman who had four kids and raised them all without a partner. She had a life's worth of experience in relationships and parenting; she understood how hard it was for people to stay together when one person was giving more than the other; she knew how it impacted the kids when someone walked out of the house for good. When she doled out advice, it wasn't necessarily to find a way to get Casey and me together so we could live happily ever after. She actually wanted to make sure that Casey and I didn't make any rash decisions about our future together, which, if they were wrong, could cost me a lifetime with my kid. My mom asked me straight up, "Can you be faithful to her forever?" I wasn't sure, I answered. After all, we had been broken up. "Well, if you get married and you're not, there will be hard feelings and it will compromise your ability to be in your child's life. That's how couples work. But if you don't marry her and still support her while she's pregnant and take on the responsibilities of a parent, you'll be able to retain a relationship with your child."

More than anything else, that was what I wanted. And while the thought of having to help raise and support a kid didn't fill me with dread, I'd be lying if I didn't say that at least a small part of me thought, Okay, I really need to get a UFC fight.

CHAPTER 14

THE MORE YOU MOVE, THE MORE SOMEONE HAS TO TRY TO KEEP YOU STILL

LATE IN 1996, NOT LONG AFTER OUR SIT-DOWN ABOUT my career, Nick sent me to see his buddy John Lewis, who was already one of the most respected names in the nascent world of the UFC. Like Hackleman, he was raised in Hawaii and was a street fighter turned martial arts expert. He began studying kickboxing, then picked up a Japanese style called sho kwan do—which is like Thai boxing—and then earned his black belt in judo and Brazilian jujitsu. In one of his early mixed martial fights he battled Carlson Gracie to a twenty-minute draw, in a fight between two of the best Brazilian jujitsu masters in the world. John had tattoos all over his body and a shaved head and looked like a seriously hard guy. But while he could take anyone down in less time than it took to say hello, he was incredibly generous. He normally charged around $200 an hour for his time as an instructor in Brazilian jujitsu, but if you were a fighter, he took you in and made you great (he still gives 15 percent discounts to anyone from Hawaii). He knew how exalted his stature was in the UFC world and also knew that if you trained with him, chances were good you'd get on the radar and get a fight. But he wasn't interested in guys who wanted to come in, work out for two weeks, get a fight, and then disappear. He wanted guys to practice their craft for six months and build their career. He was training people for a lifetime of fights, not just one.

Close to a dozen UFC guys were already training in his Las Vegas gym, called Jsect. It was a single room with one huge mat where everyone worked out. It was all about perfecting moves. He created a completely pure technical environment where we watched each other, trained against each other, and learned from each other. It wasn't the kind of place where you had to worry about getting hurt while you were working out or guys getting jealous of your skills or someone holding out when it came to sharing information. John wouldn't allow it. His place was known for guys helping each other. He studied martial arts because of the discipline it instilled, because he wanted to be well-rounded, and because he wanted to learn as much as possible. Kicking people's asses was secondary. And he brought those same principles to his school.

> **HOW TO PROTECT YOURSELF WHEN YOU'RE ON YOUR BACK:**
>
> The best way to protect yourself from your back is to duck your head and hold your opponent. But the main thing is to be working to get up and be offensive on the bottom. That is your best defense. Because if a guy is trying to stop you from getting up, he is not hitting you or setting you up for submission. Always be moving from side to side and hip to hip.

John had seen me kickbox and remembered me taking out a guy with a straight kick to the head in one of my earliest fights. He told me he thought I was tough and skilled—and definitely looked nasty. But we both knew why I was there. I was scrappy and fearless and mentally ready to take it to the next level as a fighter. But when I decided to make the transition from kickboxing to UFC, my ground game was just too one-dimensional. I was hard to take down, and because of my wrestling experience and understanding of a lot of maneuvers, I was equally hard to keep down when I fell. But I knew nothing about the intricacies and dangers of making someone submit while I was on the ground. I didn't know about joint manipulation or maintaining my guard. I could get out from under someone, but I could never win a fight from my back. And John was better than anyone else at teaching me how to do that.

At first, he wanted to teach me how to get off the ground if I was taken down. We worked on a lot of technical ways to maneuver my body and my arms and my legs so I could get up. For example, if I'm lying on my back and my opponent is on top of me, he is controlling my chest. But if I pummel him and get my arms under his armpits, I can begin to control him a little bit. It's all a matter of making space when you're on the ground. If someone is on top of you, they are naturally leaning over while punching you. So I learned how to get some room. I take my forearm across an opponent's face and then try to wiggle my body, getting him lower on my chest and toward my stomach. I keep wedging my hand between his face and mine, pushing him farther back every time I buck my body, even if it's less than an inch. Eventually I can drop my elbow inside—between my shoulders and his—and then I can get his arm under my arm. If I can hook him from underneath, then I've got the leverage and can practically throw him off me.

Even if I can't, the distance I've created now forces his punch to travel farther before it can actually cause any damage. Which means by the time it reaches me it's losing force. That's if the guy can even punch me. Because the more I'm moving, the more someone has to keep me still. And he can't hit me if he's working to make me into a target.

John and I worked for a month on groundwork, perfecting how to get off the mat when someone was on top. Then we spent time on submission moves and joint manipulation, and then on takedowns from the mat. Slowly, I was building up my glossary of moves, becoming more comfortable with Brazilian jujitsu and the concepts of the ground game. There are so many disciplines in the UFC: kickboxing, wrestling, and a variety of martial arts. For me, once I started training, it wasn't enough to be able to get off the ground. I wanted to dominate from the ground. I wanted to be as well-rounded a fighter as possible, eliminating any weaknesses.

As soon as I decided to fight in the UFC, I knew I wanted to become the light heavyweight champion. Getting a push from Nick was the first step. Training with John was the second. And getting a fight was the third.

I couldn't just call up the UFC and say, "Hey, I'm ready." First I needed to get at least a little experience in an MMA fight. Luckily, Nick was promoting his first MMA fight and invited me to be on the card. He set it up at the Orleans, which held around fifteen hundred people. But just before the fight, the Nevada State Athletic Commission kept making Nick change the rules. Like a lot of state commissions, Nevada's was spooked by MMA's perceived violence. It objected to closed-fist punching because our bare knuckles were hardly covered by padding. Instead, they allowed us to do only open-palm hitting, which was essentially slapping.

Some other, more minor, rules changes watered down the event, too. But it didn't seem to impact the enthusiasm of the crowd. They were curious about the sport, and no doubt anxious to see some guys get their heads caved in. I, of course, was happy to oblige. Nick told me some big guy from Ohio—neither of us can remember his name—kept asking to fight me. He was always in Nick's ear pleading, "Gimme a chance with Chuck, gimme a chance with Chuck."

Nick decided this MMA fight was the right time. For the first couple minutes of the first round, the guy kept trying to go low and engage me in some judo moves. But I wasn't having it. I may have come up as a wrestler—and after training with John I may have been even more comfortable on the ground than before—but my most basic stance is aggressive. That's when I'm comfortable and confident. The only time I'm going low is when I have no other choice. But this guy gave me plenty of other options, including just kicking him in the head every time he made a move to wrestle me to the ground. So that's what I did. Twice. Hard. Before the first round was over, I had knocked him out.

And my MMA career had officially started.

CHAPTER 15

APPRECIATE RISK

IT WASN'T JUST UFC GUYS IN JOHN'S GYM. ANYONE who loved combat sports and wanted to learn about martial arts was welcome. And in Vegas, that's a lot of guys. Not another town in the country loves a tough guy more than Las Vegas. Every night the casinos, the strip joints, and the clubs are packed with alpha males throwing around money, gambling fortunes, taking the kind of risks that scare most people. It's a city that appreciates the most basic and gluttonous instincts in all of us. And it rewards them, too. I think that's not only why big fights are drawn more to Vegas than other cities that sanction boxing or UFC, but also why the fighters themselves are so revered there. These days I'm recognized in a lot of the cities I visit. But for the first seven years I fought in the UFC, in most towns I was just a scary guy with a Mohawk. In Vegas, however, where a lot of the fights took place, I felt I was approached as often as Siegfried and Roy. People there love their fighters.

And it's not just the tourists who come to town for a big fight. The natives are the ones who truly appreciate risk. After all, a lot of them had moved out there to chase big dreams—just like a lot of the people who were working out at John's gym. They were the ones who approached him when he was walking through a restaurant just to shake his hand and tell him they liked watching him compete. They're the ones who wanted to learn how to do what he was doing and learn it from him. That's how Dana White and the Fertitta brothers—Frank and Lorenzo—wound up in John's gym studying Brazilian jujitsu alongside me.

The three of them had been friends growing up in Las Vegas. They weren't just fans of boxing, but amateur boxers as well. Dana was a wild kid who loved the fight game. In 1988 he was living in Boston, working as a bellman at a hotel near the harbor, and trying to decide if he had the right skills to become a professional boxer. He trained at a club in town with a guy named Peter Welch, who now coaches UFC fighters. Welch let Dana know that although he might love it, he'd never be a pro. "For a long time it really messed with me that I hadn't fought a pro fight," I once read in an interview Dana did with *Playboy*. "But to fight pro is a lot of work, a lot of money, and a lot of sacrifice. I didn't take that step. I've always felt I didn't have the balls to turn pro. It wasn't that I was afraid to fight. Fighting is what I loved more than anything. But I used to see guys at the gym who were thirty-five or thirty-six years old who hadn't made it. I would look around and think, damn, I don't want to be that guy."

Instead he joined Welch as a boxing coach, and they started doing classes for inner-city kids as well as a fitness program for people who didn't know anything about boxing. Dana was making about $50K a year working as a bellman and had a good life doing the boxing stuff on the side. But, like most people from Vegas, he had a notion that life had more in store for him than carrying someone else's bags. He had big ideas, and he had the guts to go after them. He moved back to Vegas and started his own boxing gym. If you've seen Dana on TV hawking the UFC, you know the man can sell. He's a no-BS, fast-talking, great-storytelling pitchman. And, as a native, he had plenty of contacts in the area who would listen. He was still as wild as he had been as a kid. Only now his energy was focused on more than just getting into trouble. He didn't know it at the time, but he was putting together the connections that would make him the most important new sports executive of the twenty-first century. He convinced a lot of high-profile businessmen to come by his place. That included Lorenzo Fertitta, who was vice chairman of the Nevada State Athletic Commission.

One night Frank, Lorenzo, and Dana were at the Hard Rock and saw John Lewis walking through the lobby. Frank pointed him out. This was around 1995, and all three of them had been keeping up with this new sport that was just a couple of years old, the UFC. It was particularly big in Vegas, since that is where so many of the fights took place. It had piqued their interest in MMA, and right before John walked through the hotel, they had been talking about how they all wanted to learn new forms of combat sports, such as submission fighting. So Dana, who knew John because they both ran gyms in town, asked if he and the Fertittas could come by Jsect and do some training. As Dana says, "We became completely addicted to it." Pretty soon they were working out with John three or four days a week. They'd practically rip each other's arms off and do other nasty joint manipulation and submission moves that most people wouldn't dare try if they weren't doing this for a living. But they loved it, and they loved the sport. It was impossible to see at the time, but this is essentially how, where, and when the modern version of the UFC was born. Dana and the Fertitta brothers started training with John, fell in love with the sport, met a lot of UFC fighters, and eventually bought the UFC and turned it into what it is today.

Of course, in the mid- to late 1990s the revitalization of the UFC was still a long way off. In fact, in 1996, before I had ever had a fight, it seemed more likely that the sport would disappear rather than beat Major League Baseball and the NBA in television ratings. The idea that it could become the next NASCAR was insane. That year Senator John McCain, a longtime boxing fan, called UFC bouts the equivalent to "human cockfighting." Not long after that, George Pataki, then the governor of New York, had his state's athletic commission ban the sport. In time the sport became even more marginalized. The founders of the UFC had always marketed the extreme angle of the sport. They pushed that it was "no holds barred" and liked the idea that the fans were tuning in to see men go at each other with such unbridled ferocity. The original intent may have been to find out which style of fighting was the best in the world, but it quickly became obvious, to the men who ran the sport, that selling the blood and gore was the best way to go. But the problem with this strategy was that it reduced the fights to what they had been back in the 1920s in Brazil: They were circus sideshows. The fighters weren't considered athletes. Instead they were treated like badass bar brawlers who had a lust for violence; nothing more than hard-core weekend warriors. No one saw the training that was involved or the fighting science that was practiced or the skills that were exhibited. Tens of thousands of fans were buying the fights on pay-per-view and knew what the sport was all about. But to the vast majority of people, ultimate fighters were eye-gouging, head butting, biting freaks who liked to hurt other people. This was what the owners were selling, much more than they sold the competitive nature of the sport or the skill of the guys in the cage. And it backfired.

The original owners of the UFC didn't worry about ticket sales. They didn't see filling stadiums as the best way to make money off the fights. They weren't even that interested in selling DVDs and sold off those rights to another company. For them, the clearest path to cashing in on the sport was through lucrative television deals.

But after McCain did his rip job and Pataki banned the sport in New York, state after state refused to sanction UFC fights. The commissions called it too violent, barbaric even, and they caved in to community activists who complained about having fights in their states. And when that happened, the TV execs couldn't help but be concerned. Before long, cable companies refused to put the UFC on pay-per-view. By the late 1990s, when I was finally ready to fight, the only way to see the UFC was on satellite TV. And if that revenue stream dried up, there was virtually nothing to keep the sport going.

For me, the politics didn't matter. I understood what was happening, but didn't care all that much. And I definitely didn't worry how it would affect my future. That's not how I think. It's not how I've ever thought. I don't plan; I just do. I was bartending, kickboxing, teaching, and training. To me, that was making a living as a fighter.

But that would change.

CHAPTER 16

NEVER LET A LITTLE THING GET IN THE WAY OF MAKING A BIG THING HAPPEN

CASEY GAVE BIRTH TO OUR DAUGHTER, TRISTA, IN September of 1997. She was a beautiful little girl whom I fell in love with immediately. And while her mom and I weren't together anymore, we stayed close. I would probably always have had some kind of relationship with Casey. Now that we had a kid together, it was a no-brainer. Although, even she'll admit that she was brutal to me during her pregnancy. Partly because the chemistry in her body was constantly changing, partly because she was getting bigger every day, and partly because I'm the one who got her pregnant at eighteen, right when she was about to leave home to go to college. But I never took it personally, never got angry. I was always saying, "You bet, whatever you say, if that's what you need." Having been raised by my mom, I've got nothing but respect for other mothers and how

Me and my daughter, Trista. I fell in love with her immediately.

hard they have it. When Casey was having a difficult time adjusting to life after the baby, I bought her the book *Don't Sweat the Small Stuff*. It was advice I lived by, and I think it helped her prioritize her new life. Years later she was still telling me how much she appreciated my getting her that book.

She'll always be my little girl.

In February of 1998, when Trista was just four months old, I got some more news: No, I didn't have a UFC fight yet. But now my girlfriend, Lori, whom I worked with at the Library, was pregnant. Lori and I had known each other for a long time before we started dating. I first noticed her when I was bouncing and she was a customer. We had a lot of mutual friends and, through them, started hanging out regularly. She told me she was impressed that, despite my rep, I seemed to be a guy who had control at the door. I wasn't starting fights; I was usually trying to keep things pretty mellow.

At first we kept things pretty casual. But I'm a romantic guy, and when her birthday came around early in our relationship, I decided to step it up. I surprised her with a night in a hotel in town. I had called ahead and had music playing in the room when we walked in. Then I took her to a nice dinner and made her think, Wow, this guy is really sensitive.

Lori was five-four, had dark hair, and was a knockout. People always liked her; she was one of those girls who was so sweet, customers just gravitated toward her end of the bar. The truth is, when I found out she was pregnant, part of me was like, Whoa, this happened fast. What did I do here? We were together and things were going well. But I was worried, too. Trista was so young, I had barely gotten used to the idea of being a father. I was a little nervous about money. Now I was going to have two kids just thirteen months apart.

But you get over that fear fast; at least I did, because I loved being a dad. From my perspective, between Trista, a new kid on the way, and my training, things were going pretty well for me. Then I got the call I had been waiting a year to get: The UFC wanted me to fight.

Nick had set me up with a couple of managers named Al Davis and Charlie Angelo. He told me that if I signed with them, a fight would come my way sooner rather than later. And he was right. I had sent the UFC a tape of one of my MMA fights, my kickboxing matches, and my training sessions with John Lewis and requested a chance to fight. Plus, because I had been working out at John's and knew so many of the guys who were already UFC fighters, I figured, naively, it would just be a matter of time before someone tapped me to take on the UFC's light heavyweight champ. But a few UFC shows went by after my MMA debut and after I had sent in my audition tape, but no one called. Not until I aligned with managers who were connected did I become a legitimate candidate to join the rotation. When Al and Charlie called me in April of 1998, they might as well have told me another girl I knew was going to have my baby. That's how excited I was.

In mid-May I flew down to Mobile, Alabama, with Nick, Scott Adams, John Hackleman, and some other friends to make my Ultimate Fighting Championship debut. It may have been the top rung of the mixed martial arts world, but it was still pretty bush-league stuff. Only a few states—such as Alabama and Mississippi and Louisiana—would even sanction these fights. And even then they often took place in the middle of nowhere, as far from big cities and the rest of civilization as possible. That is, if they took place in the United States at all. You were just as likely to see a UFC fight happen in Japan or Brazil as you were to catch one in Bay St. Louis. People acted as if just having a UFC fight in a major stadium in the middle of Atlanta or Charlotte would corrupt the entire town. So we fought in such outposts as Dothan and Augusta or, in the case of my first fight, in Mobile, Alabama.

When Charlie and Al called, it wasn't exactly the most enticing offer I've ever had. I was the sixth fighter invited to square off in a four-man middleweight tourney for UFC 17: Redemption. Essentially, I was an alternate, a part of the undercard, but not a draw for the tournament. The only way I could advance in the tournament was if one of the top four guys won his first-round fight and was hurt, then the winner of my fight took his place. I was fighting only so I wasn't fresh if I needed to fill in. That would have been an unfair advantage.

They paid me $1,000—including expenses—and put me up in a Marriott or a Sheraton or someplace like that. When we had the weigh-ins, they used a bathroom scale, which made me laugh. If you knew how to shift your weight right, the balance on the scale would change, and you could come in just over- or just underweight. It wasn't exactly a science.

This was the UFC I had been training for? This weigh-in on a bathroom scale represented years of boxing lessons with my grandpa, karate lessons, getting in street fights in Santa Barbara, wrestling at Cal Poly San Luis Obispo, kickboxing, teaching. All of it led to this chance, to the Mobile Civic Center for a one-shot, $1,000 fight against a guy named Noe Hernandez in front of a couple thousand people. The operation had such a shoestring budget that Scott had to call around town finding me gym times so I could stay loose in the three or four days I was there. So much for dreaming big.

I weighed in at 199 pounds, one pound under the 200-pound weight limit. But when Noe stepped off the scale, he was two pounds overweight. Apparently he didn't know the secret about tilting your body. Just like that I could have won my first UFC fight without ever stepping into the Octagon. But I didn't travel all the way across the country to win by forfeit. I wanted to go at it. I wanted a knockout. I was not going to let two pounds come between me and the fight I had been waiting to have for years. I would never let a little thing get in the way of making a big thing happen. So when they told me Noe didn't make weigh-in on that piece-of-crap scale, I said, "Screw it. Let's fight."

Noe was a strong guy with a buzz cut who had already had five UFC fights. He'd won three, including one after a doctor stopped the bout because Noe was hurting the guy so badly and another because he had literally beaten his opponent into submission with punches. There wasn't a lot of tape on fighters in those days, but I had heard from friends such as Nick and John that he had a wicked right hand that had knockout power, so I should be on the lookout for that. I made a note of it.

While Nick and John were getting me prepped in the Mobile Civic Center's locker room, I got a visit from John Peretti, who was the UFC's matchmaker. He'd been a kickboxer and had been around MMA for a while promoting fights and working in corners. He also decided which fighters were invited into the cage and which ones were always stuck looking on the outside in. If you're a first-time fighter—especially one who is just an alternate—you want to keep him happy.

I thought he was going to wish me luck, tell me to have a good fight, and maybe give me a few words of advice. That wasn't the case. John knew I came from kickboxing, but had heard I wrestled in college. Have you ever been to a college wrestling match? It's not exactly WWE excitement. No throwing chairs or jumping off the top turnbuckle or chicks in bikinis fawning over the guys. It's just grappling. A lot of times the wrestlers aren't moving so much as pushing against one another, trying to tire each other out. And while going to the mat and getting a guy on the ground might be a good way to win a fight, it's not going to bring the crowd to its feet.

John wanted to make it clear that they wanted knockouts in their fights. He reminded me that I should be aggressive and stay off the ground if I wanted to get invited back. I had to take what he said seriously if I wanted a career in the UFC, so I nodded my head earnestly, told him it wouldn't be a problem, and went back to prepping for the fight. In truth, he didn't have anything to worry about. I had every intention of coming out striking.

I don't fill up with nervous energy waiting for my fights to begin, which I think goes back to my wrestling days. Getting too pumped up was only a waste of energy. And I wasn't really nervous waiting for the fight to start or walking out to the cage; it's not as though it was my first fight in front of a crowd. Although, it wasn't the way it is today, with the music, the lights, the crowds hanging over and trying to give me high fives. More people were in the stands than I'd ever seen for one of my fights, but it was pretty quiet. It seemed as if half of them didn't know what to cheer for, as though they had heard about this violent sport and wanted to come check it out for themselves. They weren't quite fans; they were curious. I didn't mind the peace. I could think, focus, and go over my game plan, which was essentially to go beat the crap out of the guy.

I didn't feel any real butterflies when I walked into the ring either. But maybe I should have. I had been telling myself to look out for that big right. My friends had warned me about it. And yet, ten seconds into the fight I let my guard down, and *bam*, he popped with that powerful punch of his. I said to myself, "Damn." I wasn't worried; I just couldn't believe I got caught by that. I felt my eye starting to swell up; I knew it was going to be black-and-blue within minutes. I couldn't believe I had done something so mindless so early in the fight.

But it was good. It knocked some sense into me, reminding me I was in a fight and not just baiting some chump I had thrown out of a bar. After that, I settled down and used some of the strategies I had been working on through years of training, from my days at Koei-Kan Karate-Do to John Lewis's gym in Las Vegas.

I got in a good pop right at the bridge of Noe's nose, which sent blood gushing to the canvas. For the rest of the fight, whenever we locked up or stood still for too long, you could see drops of blood forming a pattern at Noe's feet. While it looked bad, he clearly wasn't hurt, because he came at me as much as I went after him. I'd give him a low kick to knock him off balance, then follow that up with a sweeping right. Then he'd get low on me, flip me over, and make me use some energy to get off the ground.

It was a tense, tight fight. Years later Nick described it as electrifying. And it had that feel of whoever was in the crowd and whatever fight they were waiting to see after we were over actually began to enjoy it. We were both so desperate to win—me for reasons more than just my competitive nature—the crowd could sense it. Even with a minute left in the fight, we were showing no signs of letting up, throwing as many punches as possible as quickly as possible. Pretty soon the entire crowd was on its feet, cheering the effort as much as they were rooting for one guy or the other. I remember Nick and John screaming, partly encouraging me, partly instructing me. They wanted to make sure I kept Noe moving in a half circle around the ring. The last thing they wanted was for me to give him a chance to set up and take a straight shot with his right hand directly at my eye again.

That was what I did for most of the fight: I moved around in the shape of a moon, as if we were dancing with a little bit of space between us. I looked for my shots, high and low, and tried to protect myself as best as I could. Was I a kickboxer, street fighter, wrestler, jujitsu expert? To tell you the truth, I didn't know at that point. I was just discovering what I was all about as a mixed martial arts fighter. I wanted to survive, win, and get invited back. I could worry about style points the next time around.

I must have done something the judges liked, because after twelve minutes of fighting with neither of us getting knocked out, the folks at cageside had to declare the winner: Chuck Liddell, by a decision.

My right eye was practically swollen shut. But the first thing I did after the fight was find the matchmaker. I wanted him to know I was ready if someone went down. One eye or not, I could fight anyone who was still standing.

CHAPTER 17

A FIGHT'S A FIGHT,
NO MATTER WHERE IT IS

I WANTED ANOTHER FIGHT. FAST. MUCH SOONER THAN the UFC was going to give me one. But I did have an offer to fight that August, two months after my UFC debut, in São Paulo, Brazil. It was truly a Vale Tudo fight in the tradition of Brazilian fighting that dated back to the beginning of the sport in the 1920s. The bout was a no-holds-barred, bare-knuckles brawl called IVC 6: The Challenge. My opponent was already a Brazilian MMA legend named Jose Landi-Jons, also known as Pele.

If you're going to have the balls to answer to the same nickname as the greatest athlete your country has ever produced, you'd better be great at what you do. And Landi-Jons, who had been called Pele as a boy because he never missed one of the soccer star's games, was as good as it got in Brazil. He had been a member of the country's Chute Boxe Academy, which was one of the few fighting-oriented gyms that didn't focus on one type of martial art over another. The fighters there studied everything from Muay Thai kickboxing to Brazilian jujitsu. It became known throughout the country for producing the best, most well-rounded, and toughest Vale Tudo fighters in the sport. They're energetic, can punch and kick from anywhere, have no problems taking you down or being taken down, and learn a dozen different submission holds.

By the time we fought, Pele had been in fifteen fights during his five-year career. He'd won thirteen of them, all by knockout, technical knockout, or submission. Nearly half of his fights had ended with him victorious in less than four minutes. And the two that he lost? Those were decisions that went the distance—all thirty minutes in the world of Brazilian Vale Tudo. This was how eventual mixed martial arts legends such as Wanderlei Silva and Rickson Gracie had made their reputations and sharpened their skills. The fights were a barrage of head butts, elbows, kicks, and viciousness. If Senator McCain had seen how brutal these fights were, he'd have dropped his objections to UFC immediately and declared it the most regulated sport he'd seen.

Going into the fight, I had heard plenty of horror stories about no-holds-barred fights. And the only bare-knuckle brawls I had had were in the streets of Santa Barbara and San Luis Obispo. Our gloves barely covered our fists and left our fingers bare, but having no gloves at all would be an entirely different sensation. Another factor I had to consider: I'd be fighting a five-year vet and a Brazilian legend in front of his hometown crowd. That should have been enough to throw an experienced fighter, let alone someone like me, who had had just one professional fight. Yet, none of it bothered me. A fight's a fight, no matter where it is. Whether it's in the backyard, an alley, a dojo, or the middle of São Paulo. You've still got to strap your game on and brawl.

I went down to Brazil with Nick, who organized the fight. And I had plenty of reasons to be pumped, despite all the circumstances that seemed to be lining up against me. I had my first sponsor, the magazine *Full Contact Fighter*, which was paying me $500 to put its logo on the shorts I wore into the ring. Even better: Not only was I getting $1,000 to fight, I'd get another three grand for a win as long as I actually won the fight—that was more than what Nick would pay me in two or three kickboxing fights combined.

Not that I ever had any doubts, but right away, Nick and I knew this was a different rumble from what we were used to seeing in Las Vegas, San Luis Obispo, Mobile, or anywhere else we'd thrown down in the United States. The venue was a nightclub. When we walked in through the back door, we could see fighters bleeding from their noses, mouths, heads, and eyes getting stitched up in the kitchen. It was pretty crude, even for me, and looked like a butcher shop. Then these guys with nothing but fresh stitches and a high tolerance for pain were being sent back out to fight. And those were the winners. There was no sign of the losers, but a lot of blood was everywhere you looked.

Nick kept telling me before the fight that the key to winning—not just lasting the full thirty-minute fight, but winning—was to make Pele stand up with me the entire time. If I hit the ground, with his expertise in Brazilian jujitsu, I might find myself in trouble. But if I stayed up, Nick and I both felt Pele and I were evenly matched in our striking ability with our hands and feet. In some ways, it was to my advantage that I'd had just one previous MMA fight. There was very little to know about me. That first bout was a slugfest; it didn't show a lot of technique. So Pele might as well have been blind coming into the fight.

Nick also kept telling me I had to take the fight into "deep waters." I had yet to train with a fighter who could go toe-to-toe with me for a twelve-minute fight, let alone thirty minutes. I was in as good a shape as I was in high school, when I used to make the team do extra conditioning drills. I could punch and had natural power, but I had no idea yet how strong I was or what my best attributes as a fighter were. But conditioning has nothing to do with natural talent. It's all about heart and determination and want, wanting to train longer and harder and better than anyone else so you can stand in the middle of that cage for as long as possible. Wanting to win because the alternative is so goddamn embarrassing. Losing a fight because you ran out of steam is cowardice. It means you didn't have the guts to push yourself when no one was watching, when the foundation was laid for what would become your legacy as a fighter. Mine will never be: He gave up before the fight was over.

Walking toward the cage was the complete opposite of what the stroll had been in Mobile. It seemed as though 80 percent of the fans were wearing Chute Boxe Academy T-shirts, in honor of Pele. And nearly 100 percent of the fans were cheering wildly for him and either booing or ignoring me. When the fight started, I wanted to take it slow, make him work, and get him tired out. But he had other ideas.

The crowd was electric, and clearly energized; Pele came right at me. Early in the fight he caught me with a kick to the head that brought me down to one knee. Before I could catch my breath, he was on top of me, trying to wrestle me to the ground. No matter what kind of shape you are in, trying to catch your breath, slow your heart rate, free yourself from a Brazilian combat-fighting expert while thousands of fans scream for your head, and then stand back up is going to take a lot of energy. Fortunately, being the aggressor in that scenario wears you down, too. When I was able to get back on my feet, it did a few things: It tired out Pele, made him lose a little confidence, since his opening gambit had failed, helped me slow down and focus after the initial blow to my skull, and, most important, gave me a boost, even if I didn't know that I needed it.

After that, the fight settled into the kind of pace I wanted it to. We were on our feet, trading lots of bare-knuckle blows. Nick was right: The deeper the water Pele and I waded into, the more dangerous I became and the more Pele tired. The crowd seemed to be turning my way, too. Vale Tudo isn't like the UFC. The sport has such a long history in Brazil, fans are educated and understand when an epic battle is taking place. It is not just about the blood and gore for them, although they don't mind when they see it. And as our fight progressed, fans began to recognize that I wasn't going to quit, that I had a strategy, and that Pele was fighting exactly as I hoped he would. Midway through the fight, you could hear the fans cheering whenever I connected or escaped from a vulnerable position. Slowly, they started chanting my name. It was straight out of *Rocky*. I was just some onetime fighter, an underdog who should have lain down for this superstar. But not only was I going toe-to-toe with the guy, I was whipping him. Like, really whipping him.

It got so bad late in the fight that I couldn't believe the ref, who was Pele's manager, wasn't stopping the match. My fists were dripping with Pele's blood; it looked as if I worked in a meatpacking plant. A net surrounded the ring so no one could get out, and Pele was just falling into it, but the ref wouldn't step in, so I had to keep hitting him. He had a cut so bad above his eye that a huge piece of skin was just flapping around.

I started talking to Nick while the fight was going on, asking him, "They ain't going to stop this fight, are they?"

"No, man," he said, "they're not."

With five minutes left, Nick was yelling at me to just tap the guy in the face or in the body or gently kick his lower leg. But don't kill him. It was a mercy match by the end, but this guy was not going to tap out; he was an absolute warrior. I think he would rather have died than submit to punches. I saw Pele the next day and his face looked like the Elephant Man's.

When the ring announcer was getting ready to declare me the winner after the fight, Nick gently nudged me behind him. He was afraid people were going to start throwing things at me. But instead, the fans cheered. All of them. The people of Brazil were great to me and had accepted me. Afterward I got stitched up in the back, right next to a bunch of guys who were doing the same and going right back in to fight. Nick had to go to the hospital with a guy who had broken his jaw, and when he got back, he told me, "Thank God you didn't have to get stitched up there."

Winning that fight earned me my first magazine cover. Naturally, it was *Full Contact Fighter*. It also put me on the international map as a mixed martial arts threat. Most important, it helped me realize what I could do in the ring. I knew I had the talent to go far in this sport.

CHAPTER 18

BE ABOUT BEING THE BEST

L ET'S FACE THE FACTS: NO MATTER HOW MUCH MY star was on the rise as a mixed martial arts fighter, I was standing knee-deep in a whole lot of life-changing stuff at this point. Cade was born in October of 1998, and unfortunately, Lori and I broke up two months later. So by the end of the year I had two kids, both less than a year and a half old, with two different women, neither of whom I was with anymore. (Casey and I would give it another try after Lori and I broke up, but it wasn't meant to be. We were better as friends than we were as a couple. Realizing that back then is probably why we are still so tight today. I'm close with Lori, too, who is happily married and living in Denver with Cade, her husband, and their three kids.)

I wasn't stressing about any of it. That's just not me. One of the things I love most about being a fighter is the lifestyle. Fortunately for me, these were all the same things that, until my fight career took off, made being a bartender great, too. I like to stay up and stay out late. Some nights I want to split a bottle of Jameson's with a buddy. Some nights I want to drink the bottle of Jameson's myself. There are nights—and days—I want to bring more than one girl home. I don't really like to get up before ten a.m. I don't get to sleep until midnight, at the earliest. The way I'm wired, I've always known I'd find a way to

Me and my son, Cade. I've been asked if I'd let him become a fighter when he grows up. Absolutely.

live this way. I'm pretty carefree, and little in the world has ever made me stay awake at night worrying.

Which is why, after Cade was born, it seemed like the perfect time to take on even more risk—as if having two young kids and trying to become a full-time MMA fighter at twenty-eight wasn't enough. My buddy Scott Adams—who had wrestled with me at Cal Poly—and I had been debating opening a kickboxing gym together in San Luis Obispo. Scott had been a freshman when I was a senior. Traditionally at our school, during our first practice, the upperclassmen would square off against the underclassmen and give them a lesson in what college wrestling was all about. Scott was a hotshot prospect from Ventura, California. But I figured he couldn't know much. He was too green. Turns out he was ridiculously quick, too. We got on the mat, and before I could get low, he was diving for my ankle. He took me to the mat in a single-leg takedown, which made me furious. A lot of the all-Americans I wrestled couldn't take me down. And this freshman punk had done it on his first try. For the rest of the year, I chose to wrestle against Scott in practice. And he never took me down again.

Scott became interested in MMA fighting when he graduated, and he wanted to build on his wrestling background by expanding his grappling skills. He focused on Brazilian jujitsu and spent a lot of time commuting to Los Angeles for workouts at Beverly Hills Jiu-Jitsu. We went together once, but mostly he'd go down, pick up some technique and some moves, and spread them around to the rest of us who were hanging out in SLO.

Billy Blanks's Tae Bo training was big back then, MMA was getting popular, I had kickboxing skills and students from teaching in town, and Scott had jujitsu skills from his training. That December we decided to open up SLO Kickboxing in town. We put $10,000 into the business, found a location, and by January 1999 we were open. I handled most of the stuff in the front of the house—teaching and business—and Scott worked on the marketing and publicity. We had a big mat that Trista used to crawl on, medicine balls, a weight room, and heavy bags. R & B from SLO's local station was constantly coming through the loudspeakers. A lot of the people who came by were students of mine, but plenty more came to get a good workout and just hang. Even today, some of the people I met there are still my closest friends.

Within a year the gym was packed. It felt as if we were doing something different from a lot of facilities because of the combination of weight training and kickboxing and martial arts we were offering. Our workout didn't feel like exercise, but instead you felt as if you were playing a sport. Before you knew it the workout was over and you were healthier, too. Scott and I were each usually earning between $4,000 and $5,000 a month. That was enough for me to quit

MY FAVORITE DRINKS/SHOTS:

1. Patrón
2. Wild Turkey
3. Jameson's
4. Cactus Cooler
5. Grey Goose

bartending and focus just on the school and, of course, my training. Developing my UFC career was never far from the forefront of my mind, especially not after that first fight. When we opened SLO Kickboxing together, I told Scott that the business would always take a backseat to my goal of becoming a world champion. I always wanted to be about being the best. Luckily, the business did well, and I was always there. Which meant I was working out and training every single day.

The MMA world had been around for only six years when we opened the gym. It still felt brand-new and, in a lot of ways, experimental. New techniques, new styles, new forms of combat were being invented right before our eyes, every time we saw a fight. The sport had a real pioneering spirit, from the way business was done to the way it was marketed to how the fans treated it. It was almost like a cult. The enthusiasm from those who followed it was boundless, but still, only a small group of people knew anything about it.

San Luis Obispo, and especially our gym, felt like an incubator for UFC. We were in the middle of nowhere. Whenever we trained, it seemed as if we were creating something, setting new precedents. There was no money in the sport then. We were doing it for the same reasons people had been practicing martial arts for thousands of years: the discipline, the challenge, the way it made you concentrate. In my case, I still absolutely loved fighting. I would tell Scott this all the time. I couldn't get enough of it.

I was getting better, too. I did round-robin training with Scott and another guy we worked out with named Jeremiah Miller. I really never wanted anyone to force me to submit, so Scott and Jere-

MY TYPICAL DAILY MEAL:

Cottage cheese and fruit for breakfast

Sandwich for a snack, turkey and cheese in a pita

Pasta with chicken and mixed vegetables for lunch

Protein/carbohydrate shake

Chicken with rice and broccoli for dinner

miah focused on making me hone the Brazilian jujitsu techniques I had learned with John Lewis. I also began to take myself more seriously as an athlete. I started doing plyometrics regularly. Brett Hamlin and Pat Hopkins worked out a strength and conditioning plan for me. I started eating more fish and chicken and vegetables.

Now that I had won my UFC debut and beaten Pele in Brazil, I was a legitimate Ultimate Fighting Championship fighter. I was someone the matchmaker could slot into a tournament and know he was going to get a good fight. He didn't have to worry about me trying to grapple my way to a win. The fights would be coming now. I had to be a professional.

CHAPTER 19

TURNS OUT MOJO DON'T PAY THE BILLS

GOT HOME FROM BRAZIL FEELING GOOD. GOING THIRTY straight minutes with Pele and pounding his face literally into the ground was huge for my career. I had the gym. And I was tapped to fight in UFC 19: Ultimate Young Guns, which took place in March of 1999 at Casino Magic in Bay St. Louis, Mississippi. The promoters even put a picture of me on the poster that touted the fights. My fee now that I was gaining such exalted status in the mixed martial arts world? A couple grand. Turns out mojo don't pay the bills.

Naturally, with all the momentum going my way, I did the one thing all fighters who are early in their careers are not supposed to do: I went out and got my ass kicked. One of my greatest skills as a fighter is that I have no fear. I don't back down from fights and never worry about the implications a potential loss may have on my career. Some guys might line up against soft competition, but I take on whomever the UFC matchmakers want me to take on. And, in this fight, they matched me up against Jeremy Horn, not an easy battle for someone with as limited experience as I had at this point in my career.

Jeremy was five years younger than me but had already fought twenty-nine times before we met, including a championship-bout loss to Frank Shamrock in UFC 17. Jeremy was a badass country boy from Omaha who started doing martial arts at thirteen just to hang around his older brother. By seventeen, he had earned his black belt, and after his first couple of MMA fights, Pat Miletich, one of the original UFC superstars, tapped him as an up-and-coming star and began training him. Jeremy was an expert at submission moves, so much so that all but a handful of his wins early in his career were from armbars, rear-naked choke holds, guillotine chokes, triangle chokes. You name the submission move, Jeremy not only knew it, but he had perfected it and used it in a match. One reason he had such success with all these body-twisting holds was because he was so damn flexible. He'd actually been nicknamed Gumby for the way he could move his body, although he didn't exactly love the label. It wasn't the most intimidating nickname he'd ever heard.

Despite the cartoon name, I knew not to take him lightly. And we had some great exchanges early on. I actually felt that I was winning the fight through the first couple of minutes. He went for a high kick quickly, then made a nice, low shoot move for my leg and tried to bring the fight to the ground. But I wouldn't give up my position. I heard the guys in my corner reminding me not to let him get square, to keep him moving in a half circle so his shoulders were perpendicular to mine. Soon I had him in a headlock and was able to get a couple of blows with my leg and my knee to the top of his head. Then I maneuvered my way back to my feet while keeping him pinned against one of the cage's posts on his knees. While he had his arms wrapped around the backs of my legs, I delivered shot after shot to his head. This was all in the first one minute and forty-five seconds. Then, for the next several minutes, we both caught our breath. While he was lying on his back and I was standing, he pulled me down to the mat while wrapping his legs around my chest. It was a powerful move. Even though I had been working on my jujitsu and grappling, I still felt like a novice in that part of my game, especially compared to so

Most of my fight with Jeremy was on the ground. I'd rather strike, but I was still trying to stay on top.

many of the fighters, such as Horn, who specialized in that art. But, even on the ground, I didn't feel that he had much of an advantage, as we wrestled to a standoff.

Then as I tried to get up, he snaked his legs around my right thigh. It felt like a vise as he locked down on my limb and got his hands on my heel. They say that when a snake wraps itself around you, it suffocates you by squeezing a little more every time you exhale. That's exactly what was happening to my leg. The more I tried to wriggle myself free, the harder he held on. He had me in a heel hook, which puts a lot of pressure on the knee. I was comfortable because I knew how much I could take, since Scott used to put me in those kinds of holds all the time. But I must have grimaced pretty badly, because the announcers made a point of mentioning it on the broadcast. I could hear Pat Miletich, who was in Jeremy's corner, yelling, "Hook, hook, hook," because he thought Jeremy had a great shot at making me submit. But no way was I going to tap out. He had me twisted around and down on my stomach, and for a full minute my leg was his plaything, but I was able to squirm out and regain the top position so I could pound away at his midsection.

The entire match basically took place in front of one post. We barely moved. If it had been my first fight, John Peretti would never have invited me back, because we hardly threw any punches or kicks while we were standing. It was just me on top of him, him on top of me, back and forth. Finally, with nine minutes left in the match, the ref pulled us apart, sent us back to our corners, and told us to come out fighting. That lasted about a minute before Jeremy dove for my midsection and we were back on the mat, grappling. Then people actually started booing because we weren't fighting enough. I couldn't blame them. While we were both exhausted and fighting hard, all of the action was taking place in a corner of the cage, and most of the punches were thrown while one of us was on top of the other. There weren't any roundhouses or front kicks, just hard-core wrestling and jujitsu. A challenge as a fighter, but a pretty boring show for a fan.

With a minute left in the fight I was on my back and Jeremy slowly moved his way to my chest, so we were face-to-face. Then, with about fifteen seconds left in the fight, he let me flip him over, which caught me by surprise. Then he went for a submission move that I had never seen before, called an arm triangle choke. I had watched guys use a triangle choke, where they get an opponent's neck caught between their legs and squeeze them out. But this was entirely new to me. He got my neck caught between my shoulder and his arm and then used my body against me. It would have been nice if someone had taught me about this move before it was being used to choke me out.

I couldn't move, and he was locked in on the hold so he couldn't move. We were just on the ground, lying there perfectly still, my body flat on top of his, my back to his chest. He wasn't hitting me or letting go. I wasn't hitting him, nor was I trying all that hard to maneuver my way out and get back to my feet. I still don't know exactly why. That the blood wasn't rushing to my head may have had something to do with it.

I'm usually cool as ice before a fight, but I still like to warm up with some taps.

But, with both of us on the ground, this was not the nonstop, rough-and-tumble action the UFC wants and expects from its "young guns." The ref pulled us off each other and told us to stand back up because it was the end of the round. Jeremy got up with no problem, but I was just lying there, motionless. I started out resting during his submission move. I didn't want to tap out, and I thought I'd be able to hold on for the last few seconds and send the fight into an overtime round. But I must have blacked out. No one in the arena—not Jeremy, not the ref, not my corner, and not the fans—had any idea. I'm not even sure I knew what had happened. One minute I was on the mat waiting for this thing to go into extra time, and the next minute I see that Jeremy is being declared the winner because of his arm-triangle-choke submission move. Jeremy was so surprised to see me down and out that, after he got up and the ref called it and he walked back to his corner, he rushed back to make sure I was okay.

If you think I was crushed after the fight—after losing badly in my first fight after making a name for myself, my first chance to prove that I wasn't a fluke—it's obvious you've only been skimming this book.

My pulse rate rarely goes up or down, no matter how tense or relaxed the situation. In fact, that's how I got my nickname: the Iceman. Hackleman gave it to me around my third kickboxing match. We were hanging out in the locker room before the fight, and he noticed that I wasn't breaking a sweat or shaking out my arms to release some of the jitters and didn't have any other nervous tics. He told me he had been in countless pro fights and was anxious before every one of them. Meanwhile, I looked as if I were going for a stroll in the park. He thought I had ice in my veins.

I don't get overly euphoric once I leave the ring after a win, and I don't crawl into a shell after a loss. What's the point? I knew I'd get another fight. I knew I'd get better. I knew I'd find a way to win the next time Jeremy and I faced each other in the cage. And I damn sure knew it'd be a long time before I got beaten by an arm triangle choke again. It's not that I am overly confident or arrogant. I just don't worry about the long-term impact of decisions I make or things that I do. I have never been the guy who maps out his future; I just live my life. When Casey had just given birth and Lori was pregnant with Cade and I was trying to get my fight career going, I never felt that it was too much to handle. It's not like I'm unloading this stuff on my friends and having some kind of pseudotherapy session, either. I think I offhandedly told Scott that Casey was pregnant when we were driving to Beverly Hills for a jujitsu class. Even then I mumbled it so casually he could barely understand me. When I got my first UFC fight, I didn't spend all day calling friends and family to tell them. Good or bad, news has a way of trickling out and finding its way to the people who need to know. That's fine by me. I've got better things to do than to keep everyone in my life up-to-date with what's happening to me.

Instead of sulking that night after the fight with Jeremy, a bunch of us went to karaoke in Bay St. Louis. I was having a great time, although my friends knew better than to get me up on the stage and make me sing. It's not that I wouldn't have. It's that I'm horrible. Really horrible. Instead I sat at the table, relaxing, while I watched Nick belt out a heartwarming rendition of Jimmy Buffett's "Margaritaville."

And I knew everything was going to be fine. Eventually.

CHAPTER 20

IF YOU DON'T FIGHT, YOU DON'T TRULY KNOW IF YOU CAN WIN

I WON MY NEXT MMA FIGHT THREE WEEKS LATER—A Neutral Grounds tourney—and then won a TKO on punches against Paul Jones four minutes into the first round of UFC 22 that September. I wasn't anywhere near being famous yet, although my last two UFC fights—against Horn and Jones—had been on pay-per-view. And some people had seen them. Including my father.

He had found a new life, with new kids. I hadn't heard from him in twenty-five years, and neither had my mom. None of us were particularly upset about that. He was a stranger. A guy who, when he'd left, told my mom he'd check in years down the road and see if the kids were worth claiming. My mom had been working for the county for a couple decades when I started my UFC career, and anyone could find her if he wanted to. It hadn't even been two years since she had moved out of Pops's house and gotten a new home number. Now, all of a sudden, late in 1999, there was contact.

Not from him, though—from his kids. They called my mom and said they wanted to meet their brothers and sisters. None of us thought they had done this on their own; we were convinced he'd put them up to it. But my mom is so damn sweet and open and willing. She never once took out her anger toward him during that first phone call with his kids. She was what she always is: a woman who thinks about her kids above all else. And she didn't want to get in our way—or theirs—if any of us wanted to have a relationship.

I wasn't interested in seeing my dad, and my mom had to convince me to go meet his kids. So we all met at a restaurant. It was tough from the start. One of my dad's boys tried convincing my mom to let our father back into her life, but she was having none of it. Then he asked why they had gotten divorced, and she replied, "That's between me and him. But if you love your father, that is all you need to know." She's classy.

Then the boy turned his attention to me and Laura and Sean. He asked each of us, "Do you want your father in your life?" All of us answered no, as easily and unemotionally as if the waiter had just asked if we wanted coffee. Sperm donors aren't fathers. None of us had a relationship with the guy. But one of his kids kept pushing the issue until, finally, one of them said I really only knew my mom's side of the story and I should hear his. Then I lost it. I said, "Fuck you. I remember her crying herself to sleep at night. I remember her working three jobs at Christmas. I guess I could say thanks to him for donating the sperm that created me, but if he wants more than that, he has to be around. And not just come by after twenty-five years, when he sees me on TV." Then I just turned around and walked out. From the looks on their faces before I left, it seemed my new siblings were pretty much saying to themselves, Okay, let's leave the caged animal alone and get the hell out of here. Which they did.

And while I've seen them at fights the last several years—I might nod their way, and my mom will actually say hello—the subject of meeting my dad has never come up again.

Meanwhile, I had other issues to deal with. Even after I'd beaten Paul Jones in an upset in UFC 22, my star had definitely fallen in the eyes of the UFC matchmakers. With a 2-1 Ultimate Fighting record, I wasn't the draw I had been before UFC 17. And their offer for me to fight after I won in UFC 22 wasn't all that appealing. They wanted a three-fight deal. I'd get $1,000 to fight the first match, plus another $1,000 if I won. Then $2,000 and $2,000 for the next fight, and $3,000 and $3,000 for the third fight. Honestly, I would have done it. But that's because I'd fight for free, like Michael Jordan's love-of-the-game clause. But Dana wasn't pleased. He told the UFC bosses, "Screw you. I wouldn't let Chuck off of his couch for one thousand dollars."

Dana didn't wait for a counteroffer. That was the end of the negotiation. I wasn't going to fight in the next UFC tournament, or any UFC tournament, until Dana felt that I was getting my due. It felt good to have Dana on my side. He loved the sport, he loved fighters, and he loved fighting. He was as confrontational outside the ring as any of his clients were inside it. And he was also fiercely loyal, especially to me. When he was making his case to the UFC on my behalf or telling me to sit out, it never seemed that he had a hidden agenda. Plenty of promoters will sell one client out to get another client a better deal. But Dana didn't do that. He had an innate sense for calculating the value of a match, what his fighters were worth in that fight, and how much the entire UFC enterprise was worth. And then he squeezed every penny he could out of the UFC suits to make sure my real payday equaled his theoretical payday.

Instead of taking a guaranteed payday of $6,000 up front from the UFC for three fights, Dana found me a one-fight deal from the IFC (International Fighting Council) for $4,500. The IFC wasn't as big as the UFC yet—at just four years old it was an even younger league than the UFC. The fights weren't as high-profile either. But, five fights into my career, I wasn't that picky. A fight's a fight and money is money. Plus the fight was in July of 2000, ten months after my previous fight, and I was anxious to get back into the cage. Some mixed martial artists were fighting every three months. Some had a match once a month. Jeremy Horn fought twelve times the first twenty-four months of his career. He was racking up valuable experience. Meanwhile, my first fight was on May 15, 1998. Two years later, heading into my IFC fight, I had been in the cage just five times. I needed to get some action. Because if you don't fight, you don't truly know if you can win.

Dana kept telling me this was going to be the most important fight of my life, that I had to win it. But he said that about every fight. If it wasn't about proving to the UFC they should have paid me, it was about proving to the UFC I should be on track to fight for a title. There was always something to keep me motivated. Although Dana knew I didn't need to hear it as much as he did. Whenever I was training, he'd call me every day to check in and remind me how huge whatever match was coming up was going to be. On fight days, he'd call me practically once an hour until the moment I left my hotel for the arena. The guy is driven, no doubt, but a little anxious, too.

My opponent in IFC 9 was a guy named Steve Heath, who had learned Brazilian jujitsu from one of the Gracies. Steve's record was 6-1 when we faced off. He'd won his first four fights by forcing his opponent to submit in a choke hold. I knew, like Horn, he'd be great on the ground, if he was good enough to get me down. But I didn't think that could happen. I'm six-two, 205 pounds (although I weighed in at 195 the day of that fight, after dropping 19.5 pounds in eighteen hours). Heath is five-nine, 184 pounds. The strictest followers of jujitsu are always saying that, in their sport, a size advantage means nothing. But in mixed martial arts, when your opponent is usually at least equal if not better as a fighter, that kind of logic gets thrown out the window. I knew, with my size advantage, it would be hard for him to get close enough to take me down. And when he did try to shoot for my legs, he'd have to lead with his head, which meant I'd have a clear shot to take him out. And that was exactly what happened. With 5:39 left in the second round I kicked him in the head. It was lights-out, fight over, declare me the winner, and let's go have a good time, because my kick had knocked him out.

Then the UFC took notice. Again. Now I had a three-fight offer on the table, with all three fights set to take place either in late 2000 or early 2001. The terms were $5,000 guaranteed for the first fight, plus another $5,000 for winning; $7,500 guaranteed for the second fight and $7,500 more for winning; and $10,000 guaranteed for the third fight, with another $10,000 if I won. That was $22,500 just for walking into the cage, probably more than I had made combined in my previous seven years of professional kickboxing and MMA fighting. This was a deal Dana and I could live with. I'd have no problem getting off the couch for this kind of money.

The people who owned the UFC were playing hardball, and not because they were cheap. In fact, by the end of 2000 they were broke. Every dollar they gave me was another dollar they lost. The arenas weren't filling up. And when UFC 29 took place in Japan in December—my first fight back under my new deal—it was the sixth straight tournament that wouldn't be televised on pay-per-view or released on DVD. The campaign to choke out mixed martial arts that had begun in 1996 was nearly complete—just as my career was getting ready to explode.

I've never been uncomfortable in a fight—on the mat, in the street, in the cage. These may actually be the situations in life in which I feel most at home. But, as I began my climb toward a UFC title, I didn't necessarily know everything about myself as an MMA fighter. It's easy to be confident in your abilities, but greatness is believing you can win while being humble enough to understand you don't know everything. In that respect I was still learning every time I trained at The Pit with John or got into the Octagon for a match. And that's part of what I love about the sport. As much as its competitive nature, I love the chance to constantly broaden my horizons as an athlete. Ask any martial artist and he'll tell you he doesn't do it so he can kill people with his hands; he does it because he wants to keep being challenged and learning. Being in the UFC did that for me.

So while the league itself careened toward bankruptcy and shutting down, I focused on getting ready for Jeff Monson and UFC 28 in Atlantic City in November of 2000. Monson was another of those

Brazilian jujitsu grappling experts. And he was a compact, strong motherfucker. The guy was only five-nine, weighed 240 pounds, and was nearly as mean-looking as me, with a shaved head and chiseled frame. They called him Snowman, a nickname he earned while fighting a tourney in Brazil. They said he was like a snowball—white, compact, rolling, and getting bigger and stronger as the fights went on. He was completely unknown at the start of the tournament, but then rolled through four Brazilian jujitsu experts with no problem.

John trained me as hard as he had for any fight to that point. John and I were back together after a year of going our separate ways. He had tired of the fight game and just wanted to teach and train people who wanted to get in shape. And I spent most of my time training at SLO Kickboxing. It was good for business, but bad for me. The people working me out were either my partners or my students; none of them were inclined to tell me when I wasn't working hard enough or what areas I was starting to slip in. I won some big fights, but I wasn't nearly as sharp as I could have been—as I would have been—if John were putting me through the ringer.

We both wanted to avoid a Jeremy Horn situation, where I was building some career momentum and moving up the UFC ranks only to get taken down by a move I wasn't prepared for—or just taken down, period. If the UFC was going under, I wanted to have enough appeal to keep fighting anywhere else in the world. At the same time, if some moneyman was going to step in and save the league, I wanted to be in a position to make the new bosses see me as a marquee talent. Either way, losing couldn't be part of the equation.

When Jeff and I weighed in for UFC 28 in Atlantic City, I came in two pounds overweight. The good news was, so did Jeff. We had an hour to lose the extra baggage before we were checked out again. It was easy for me to shed that kind of weight. I used to do it all the time when I was wrestling in high school. I ran back up to the hotel room, jogged around for half an hour, and sweated out the two pounds. But

Jeff couldn't get down. They actually asked me if I wanted to fight him at heavyweight, and I said sure.

Then they found another problem. Every UFC fighter has a pre-match brain scan to make sure everything is functioning normally before a fight. But Jeff's scan showed an abnormality. There is no negotiating that. The fight was postponed for thirty days, until UFC 29, in Japan.

Things would get worse a couple days after the weigh-in. My buddy John Lewis fought in UFC 28 and got knocked out by a guy I thought he could have beaten. Then my other good friend Gan Mc-Gee, a heavyweight, gassed out in his match and lost as well. Between those two losing and me not fighting after training for months, I still count it as the worst night of my UFC career.

Part of the frustration was because of the training I had put into the fight. No one likes to work that hard and not get the reward. And leading up to a fight there's a pattern and a rhythm to your workouts. You don't want to peak too soon. The ideal is to be at your strongest, fittest, and sharpest just as the fight approaches. You can feel if you're there when you're sparring. Is your timing right? Is your breathing right? Do your legs feel strong or do they get weak easily? It's not like a *Rocky* movie, where one second you're sparring and connect on a great hit, and then next thing you know you're in the ring. But you know when you're ready. And I was ready for that fight.

At least they rescheduled for a month later, so I could maintain my pace in training. John had me stay in Jersey for the week, doing some light workouts, working on timing, before I went home for two weeks and then flew off to Japan for UFC 29. And the fight, after all the drama putting it together, wasn't as exciting as I would have liked. I kept kicking him and wanted to catch him in the head, but he wouldn't give me that opening. He's a grappler. I'm a striker. So we spent three full rounds circling each other. He tried to bring me to the mat. I wanted to stand him up and punch. In the end, I won by decision after three rounds, but it wasn't because I dominated the fight.

I had more fun carousing around Japan after the fight than actually being in the cage. We hung out in Roppongi, which is a district in Tokyo where all the Americans go when they want to have a good time. Walking around, you'll see the rich ex-pats, the guys in finance, and salesmen all looking to unwind. There are dozens of nightclubs, restaurants, hostess clubs, strip clubs, cabarets, and anything else you might be in the mood for. The whole section of town used to be run by the Japanese Mafia, and their influence is still pretty heavy there. Enough so that, if you drop the right name, you'll be treated really well. And we dropped a name that night. We were hanging out in a club with my buddy who lived there. When he left, he told the waiter and the bartender to make sure they took care of us. We got hungry and ordered a pizza. In twenty minutes we had a pizza, only to find out they didn't actually serve pizza there. The waiter had run across the street to get it. When I tried to leave a tip in a glass, the bartender took it out and handed it back to me in a rush. He waved me off and insisted that he couldn't take my money.

I didn't realize it, but in Roppongi, there are people who are scarier than ultimate fighters.

CHAPTER 21

ALTITUDE TRAINING IS BULL

THAT SAME NIGHT I BEAT MONSON IN JAPAN, TITO Ortiz had defended his UFC light heavyweight title against Yuki Kondo. He beat him with a neck crank less than two minutes into the fight.

Tito and I were both repped by Dana at the time, so we often found ourselves training together or sparring against each other. We had similar backgrounds, both having wrestled in high school and college before getting into MMA. I'd stayed over at his house a few times and hung out with him every once in a while when a group of us went out, but he wasn't a confidant or close friend or even a guy I'd want to call to hang out with one-on-one. But since he was the champ and we were occasional training partners, if he needed help, I went to help him out.

A lot of MMA guys—John Lewis, Tito, Tony Desouza, Rico Rodriguez—went to train at a compound in the mountains in Big Bear in Southern California. This was one of Dana's ideas, and the UFC picked up the tab. A lot of the guys felt that they'd get in better shape by training in the higher altitude. I never bought into that. Altitude training is crap. Two days back at sea level and any benefit you gained from being up there was gone. But it was a cool environment for training. All the guys stayed in these huge cabins that had multiple rooms. We had people cooking for us and taking care of whatever we needed while we were there. We had masseuses who kept us loose when we got tight running up and down the steep mountainsides. All we had to do was work out, train, and get whoever was gearing up for his next big fight in shape to dominate.

I went up there after UFC 29, in the winter of 2000–2001. Tito was going to fight again in UFC 30 that February, so were all trying to keep him sharp. It was snowing a lot at that time of the year in the mountains, so it would get cold. Which meant the workouts took on more intensity because we'd be working that much harder to stay warm. This was fierce stuff, like back in my karate days. The guys who were getting ready for the fights would stand in the center of the mat, and people would just come at them for iron-man drills. One after another, we'd move forward with a kick or a punch, or try to get low, take him out, and apply a submission move. All of us were doing it to make the guy who had the fight—in this case Tito—a better fighter and more prepared for his title bout. But we all are competitive. Each thought he was the world's best fighter, and no one wanted to let anyone else one-up him.

Then one day we decided to spar, one-on-one. And I gave the "Bad Boy from Huntington Beach" more than he could handle. To be honest, this was usually the case when we were training together. He was the more high-profile fighter because he had been doing it longer, had a bigger personality, and had already won a UFC title. All that would be enough to make me want to kick his ass every time we sparred, to prove he had nothing on me. But none of it bothered me. I knew my success would come as long as I was fighting hard and fighting right. When we sparred, I wanted to beat him up because that was how I sparred. We didn't go hard to the head, but full-contact body shots were fair. If it had been one of my best friends—such as Eric or Scott—I would have tried to drop him, too. But on this day in this session I was sparring with Tito. And while he may have been the champ whom we were supposed to be getting ready, it didn't mean I had to coddle him. In fact, I leveled him with a shot to the body. He doubled over in pain. He got up and I threw another punch to the body. He fell again. It happened a few times. I finally put my hands down, looked at Dana, and said, "I am not going to hit him anymore. He drops every time I hit him." Dana was so mad that Tito was so soft he started screaming at him, "Get back on your feet, motherfucker." But he wouldn't.

As far as I was concerned, that was the end of the session. I didn't think about whether he took it personally. But I also knew I wouldn't be giving this chump any more help trying to be the champ.

REGULATION IS GOOD

I BARELY KNEW WHAT WAS GOING ON WITH THE UFC AND its business. Sure, I saw signs that things weren't great. That it had been a couple of years since our fights had been on pay-per-view or were released on DVD was one. But I was always getting paid, and the checks were clearing. As a fighter, that was all I was worried about.

But I wasn't shocked when Dana called me in January of 2001 and told me he and the Fertitta brothers were buying the UFC, and that I would need a new manager. The deal happened fast. Dana saw the league was in trouble, told the Fertittas, and within a month they were the bosses. There weren't three more passionate UFC fans than those guys, and if anyone knew how undervalued the league was, it was them. Before they bought the league they went to a fight in New Orleans just to talk about what they were doing and make sure they weren't crazy for doing it. They sat in the crowd and thought about what they would do differently. "The old owner didn't care about the in-house show," Dana told *Playboy* in July of 2006. "All he cared about was the pay-television event. He didn't care about selling tickets and building up the in-house show and making it exciting. Lorenzo and I sat there saying, 'What if we dim the lights when they walk in, play some cool music, and get the fight shows going?' We knew the first thing we needed to do was make the in-house show cool. We believed a lot of revenue could be made from ticket sales, which the old owner didn't care about. We figured we'd start the business from the live show. It ended up being the perfect plan for us. In the early days, when we were just getting this thing off the ground, ticket sales saved our ass."

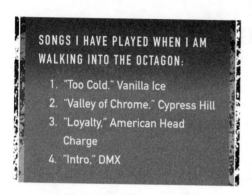

SONGS I HAVE PLAYED WHEN I AM WALKING INTO THE OCTAGON:

1. "Too Cold," Vanilla Ice
2. "Valley of Chrome," Cypress Hill
3. "Loyalty," American Head Charge
4. "Intro," DMX

They paid $2 million for the rights to the UFC name and the Octagon ring from the owners. They got a sport that was banned in most states; a sport that had been kicked off freaking pay-per-view, which meant TV execs were so afraid of the mixed martial arts they wouldn't even offer you the option to buy it; a sport that had no merchandising rights, DVD rights, or video game rights. It had image problems, economic problems, competitive problems, and management problems. Basically, Dana and the Fertittas bought an idea they believed in. And they'd have to work their asses off to turn that idea into something everyone else believed in, too.

The Fertittas were used to taking plenty of risks. Their father had come to Vegas in the 1960s and started working as a bellman at the Tropicana. Less than two decades later he had built his own casino. The brothers could have had a nice life working in their dad's shop, but instead they struck out on their own and started a vending company, first renting out pay phones, then selling poker machines to bars, then finally just buying the bars themselves. (Since I studied business, I'm always impressed by guys who built their own empire. I read all this about the Fertittas in *Business 2.0*.) Eventually they combined their business with their dad's casino, renamed it Stations Casino, and took the company public. Now they had serious money. To them, the UFC was a hobby. Although it was one they didn't intend to lose money on.

Dana once told *Boston* magazine that he spent the first three years as president of the UFC telling everyone he spoke to, "Screw you," and threatening to sue them. He was working so hard to get back some of the moneymaking rights—DVDs, video games, merchandise—the other owners had sold away. But he had other ideas for making the UFC worth his investment—making the world perceive it as a respectable mainstream sport instead of a no-holds-barred freak show. For a guy who was as big a wild child as Dana, the idea was downright revolutionary: He was going to make the UFC embrace rules and regulation.

When the sport was banned by nearly every state and relegated to outposts such as Birmingham and Puerto Rico, the old owners acted as if they were badasses. Their sport couldn't be regulated, they said; it was truly no holds barred. Biting, head butting, and gouging were part of the allure. If a guy wanted to come into the ring with a boxing glove on one hand and nothing on the other, that was fine, too. They didn't see the value in instituting rules just to appease a few state athletic commissions.

Dana, however, did. He likes to joke that when he and the Fertittas bought the UFC, the first thing they did was run to regulation. He'll tell anyone who will listen that John McCain saved the sport. If he hadn't come after the UFC the way he had, it would probably be out of business. Dana recognized that regulation is good and courted the state athletic commissions like some kid looking to get laid. Eye gouging was banned. Head butting was banned. Kicks to the groin, banned. Biting, banned. The size of the gloves became standard. The refs were given discretion to stop a fight. A scoring system similar to boxing's was instituted. Doctors were put cageside. The weight classes were realigned. Dana made the safety of the fighters paramount, to the point where we can't even spar for forty-five days after we've been knocked out. Then Dana went on a road show, pitching the new, safer, rule-friendly UFC to every member of every state athletic commission he could find.

He started with Nevada, of course. And it helped that Lorenzo was a former member of the NSAC. Pretty soon the commissioners around the country started buying into what Dana was selling. When the politicians and their appointees came on board, it became more palatable for the public interest groups, and when they were happy, suddenly it was easier to get on TV again. The UFC finally got back on pay-per-view for UFC 33, which was broadcast from the Mandalay Bay in Las Vegas. This was just eight months after Dana and the Fertittas had bought the league. It didn't go off without a hitch, unfortunately. The fights ran beyond their allotted time. The show was kicked off the air in the middle of one fight and before the rest of the card could be finished. It cost the UFC $1.5 million. As Dana has said in the past, "It was a very bad start. And it took us a long time to rebuild."

The UFC, however, had moved beyond the days when Ken Shamrock was debating the merits of mixed martial arts fighting with John McCain on *Larry King Live*. Not only was Vegas in our corner, but so was New Jersey. And soon Dana would bag Florida and Massachusetts, too. It wouldn't be long before more than twenty states were willing to sanction UFC fights. Now we had ring girls in booty shorts sashaying around the Octagon. We had bold entrances set to music and lights, and prefight interviews with the ring announcers. Over those first few years, Dana and the Fertittas spent $44 million promoting the UFC in ways big and small. They were taking it mainstream, turning it around from a sport that used to be the movie equivalent of NC-17 and was now a more commercially friendly R rating.

The UFC always had hard-core fans. Even when we weren't on television and you couldn't buy our DVDs, people recognized us. One night shortly after Dana and the Fertittas had bought the UFC, I was at an autograph show with Dana. I was, as usual, amazed at how committed our fan base was. And I showed my appreciation by telling Dana, "I hate this stupid sport. Every guy on the planet wants my autograph but there is not a chick in here who knows who I am."

I was kidding, mostly. The best thing about UFC fans is how committed and connected they are to the sport, in a way I don't think is possible with football or baseball or basketball. Most people don't have the talent to make it in one of those leagues professionally. And while most UFC fans know they're not qualified to fight professionally, everyone can relate to wanting to be tough, to being able to knock someone out, and sometimes, just as important, being able to take a punch. It's a visceral, innate feeling that we pick up as kids and never really let go of. When someone challenges you in a bar, your first instinct isn't, I can take that guy in a game of one-on-one, or, I can throw a football farther than he can. You're thinking, I can take that guy out, or, He can't take me down. By watching our fights, a lot of fans see themselves in the ring. It's why they are jumping up and down in front of their plasma TVs or in the stands and throwing haymakers in the air. As often as fans ask me for an autograph, they ask me if I'll punch them. Seriously. I was at a bar one night talking to a friend when a drunk kid came up to me and asked me for my autograph. I said, "Sure, just give me a minute to finish my conversation." He turned around, then came back a couple of minutes later, again yelling my name. He didn't want my autograph anymore. He didn't want to fight me either. He was begging me to punch him in the chin for his birthday. He just wanted to see if he could take it. My buddies said to him, "Dude, how about if I punch you in the chin?" But this is what I mean by the connection fans have to our sport. Everyone thinks he's a tough guy. And I'm glad. Otherwise no one would be watching.

That desire to constantly expand our fan base is why, in the same way Dana and the Fertittas were trying to win over one state athletic commissioner at a time, we were also trying to win over one fan at a time. Sellout matches were keeping us all in business, which meant we were on the road a lot, pimping the sport as much as possible. It didn't matter if we were on the local television news, or trading smack talk with a loudmouth shock jock, or, as was the case one night in Boston, winning over fans in the basement of a hotel. Our job was to connect with our old fans and reach out to new ones.

Those first few years no one knew us on the East Coast. I toured

Ibiza, Spain, with Dana and was stopped every five feet. But in Boston or New York or Philly, I was just some guy with a Mohawk people crossed the street to avoid. One night we went out after a day of pushing the UFC and wound up at our hotel at around two in the morning. It was a fancy place, not the kind of joint where you'd try to take someone down in the lobby. But the basement, that's another story.

While I went straight back to my room that night, Dana got into a conversation with one of the hotel security guards, who wanted to know what was up with Dana's buddy with the tattoo on his head. Dana told him I was a UFC fighter. The guy's first response was, "This is all crap. None of that stuff is real."

Dana answered, "I got five grand in my pocket, and I guarantee that you can't last five minutes with Chuck Liddell."

The guy took the bet. Then Dana called me down into the lobby. He told me he had five grand riding on me to beat the crap out of this hotel security guard, who used to be a high school wrestler. But I couldn't just beat the crap out of him. I had two minutes to make him tap out. Anything less, and Dana was out five thousand bucks.

Within a few minutes a large portion of the hotel staff and some of the guests were in the lobby of this four-star hotel at two in the morning to see the ultimate fighter take on the hotel security guard. It was like the old days of Vale Tudo fighting in Brazil—we were all part of the circus, just looking to entertain the masses, make a few bucks, and win a few fans. And, in less than two minutes, just as Dana asked, it was over. Before the guard could make a real move, I put him in a neck crank that was so fierce he started yelling, "I can't see, I can't see." I let him go and he was writhing in pain on the ground. Afterward Dana and I went out for cannolis.

Dana saw the guy the next day and he looked to be in so much pain Dana felt bad and gave the guy some money anyway. Part of him probably did it so we wouldn't get sued. But at least we had bought ourselves another fan.

CHAPTER 23

WITHOUT ANY SUBSTANCE, YOU CAN NEVER HAVE ANY STYLE

I WAS ON A ROLL WHEN DANA AND THE FERTITTAS bought the UFC. I had won my last two fights of 1999 and my two fights in 2000, the second being that win over Monson in Japan. But, while Dana was rebuilding the UFC, I clearly wasn't going to be a marquee name. At least, not at first. As Dana put it, I was known within the UFC community and by hard-core fans as a great fighter. A real fighter's fighter. But that didn't sell tickets or attract TV cameras. Tito, however, was known for being a loudmouth. And that garnered a lot of attention.

Dana was straight with me. Tito was the champ. He was the biggest draw in the UFC, which needed all the money it could rake in. He bad-mouthed opponents. He wore into the ring T-shirts that taunted the guys he was about to fight. For UFC 18 against Jerry Bohlander, his shirt read, I JUST FUCKED YOUR ASS. For UFC 19 against Guy Mezger he had on a shirt that said, GUY MEZGER IS MY BITCH. When he fought MMA legend Frank Shamrock, he wore a Frank Shamrock T-shirt. Plenty of guys need to disrespect their opponent to pump themselves up. And everyone uses some form of mind game before a fight. I stare, a cold, icy stare that makes you feel as if I don't even see you. I don't really need to work on it. It's just natural. I've always had a menacing look.

It's part of my charm. But I've never been big on talking a ton of trash leading up to a match. A little something like, "I'm gonna knock him out," is fine and good for promoting the fight. But most talking is a waste of time and energy. Tito, however, built his rep on it. And the new version of the UFC was banking on it.

I could be patient, though. I wasn't going anywhere. I knew back then that I was going to be fighting in the UFC until they dragged me out of the ring. More than I needed to get a title fight or to be one of Dana's name brands, I needed to get better as a fighter. That happened every day in training, not just in the Octagon on a Saturday night in Las Vegas. And the trappings that came with celebrity weren't as important to me as that improvement. It's a substance-versus-style thing. And I knew that without any substance, you can never have any style. Stuff like that was fine for Tito, but I preferred to come in under the radar, build a fan base and a reputation first, then get what I deserved. The more mature I was as a mixed martial artist, the more I'd be ready to handle being a champion.

My first fight in 2001 was in Atlantic City at UFC 31 against Kevin Randleman, who was a serious fighter—and not just of the MMA variety. He was an Ohio state champion wrestler in high school, a three-time all-American, three-time Big 10 champ, and two-time NCAA wrestling champ at Ohio State. When he got into MMA in the mid-1990s, he didn't join the UFC. He went to fight Vale Tudo style in Brazil. He fought in three matches in one night in his first tournament, winning all three, and the tourney. He was built like a tank, and he just beat up on people, making guys submit after landing a barrage of punches. He was great at the kind of no-holds-barred fighting that scared off

> **HOW TO PROTECT YOURSELF WHEN YOU'RE STANDING UP:**
>
> Elbows in, hands up, chin down.
>
> **HOW TO LOOK MENACING:**
>
> I never had to try to do this. If I'm not smiling, everyone thinks I'm mad at them. But it's natural: If I look at someone seriously, I look mad.

people like John McCain. He had been a world-class wrestler, and you could do little to him on the mat that he couldn't find a way to get out of.

In 1999, three years after beginning his MMA career, Randleman won the UFC heavyweight title, only to lose it to Randy Couture a year later. His fight against me, in May of 2001, was his first fight after losing the title. I wanted to fight him. In fact, I had asked Dana if we could set up the match. Randleman was coming down from heavyweight to light heavyweight, and he was a former champ. I may have been winning fights, but I still needed the kind of match in which I could earn my stripes. This one would do it. Going into it, I was a 4–1 underdog.

If he won, Randleman was in line to take on Tito in a UFC light heavyweight title bout. Everyone knew this. So Dana asked me, If I won, would I be willing to take on Tito for the title, since I would be the top contender? Otherwise they were going to have Randleman fight someone else. I still don't know why the hell he'd ask me a question like that. What was I doing this for? It wasn't to keep myself from getting into fights on the street. I was fighting to become a champ. Maybe Tito was already telling Dana we shouldn't fight because we were friends. Or maybe he was coming up with some other excuse. But whichever the case, Dana felt compelled to ask me because Tito and I used to train together. He wanted to make sure I could fight against a guy who, on the surface, was a friend of mine. I told Dana that fighting Tito wasn't going to be a problem. At all.

But a funny thing happened in the Randleman fight. You'd think having lost the title, he would have been raring to go and that I should have been on my guard. But I had studied him pretty well. I had seen him get knocked out and knew, if I could sneak a punch in there, he was susceptible to going down. But I wasn't concerned about his ground game, either. He had a great résumé and deserved his rep, but the more I watched him, the more I thought I could not only handle myself against him on the ground, but actually score some points. I

I went in for the punch and knocked Randleman out.

was always working on the jujitsu, and I knew my ground game was getting better with every fight. I felt I was getting to the point where I could handle almost anything that someone could throw at me.

When the fight started, it was a good twenty seconds before either of us made a move. We danced around each other in a circle until we finally locked up and grappled against the side of the Octagon for about forty seconds. Then we pushed off each other and squared up again. I'm not sure how I saw it, but as soon as we both had our feet set, I leaned in with a left hook. I think it was actually the only time that he wasn't protecting himself. His legs buckled, and as he started to fall, I pounced. I got off two or three punches while he was on his back; then the ref swooped in, pushing me off and calling the fight. Randleman protested afterward that the fight had been stopped too soon, but he didn't even remember being hit. As Hackleman said, I would have been happy to stand back up and finish it. But it would have ended the same way.

The whole thing lasted one minute and eighteen seconds. It was stunning to the MMA community not only that I had won, but won by a knockout so early in the fight. At this point, I'd won five straight matches since my lone career loss to Jeremy Horn. Four of those five were by knockout or submission, and one was by decision. I had won with power. I had won on my feet, on the ground, and I had won by endurance. Now it wasn't just backroom dealings in the UFC that were going to get me a title shot. There were plenty of rumblings among fans, too, that Tito should put his crown on the line against me. But he wasn't biting. And he didn't have to, at least not yet. He was on top and had some marquee fights that would be bigger draws. I was a contender, but still an up-and-comer. I could have called him out and pushed for the fight, but that wasn't my style.

Instead, I had business to take care of, in and out of the ring. I had another fight against another top-name MMA fighter scheduled for three weeks after Randleman. And I also had to negotiate my new UFC deal with Dana.

The timing of the Randleman win, my streak of good fights, and my new status as a contender for the title helped put some money in my pocket. My new contract guarantee went like this—$25,000 / $25,000 for the first (that's $25K to fight, another $25K for winning), $30,000 / $30,000 for the second, $35,000 / $35,000 for the third, $40,000 / $40,000 for the fourth, and $45,000 / $45,000 for the fifth. This was big-time money.

I had already made $20,000 for beating Randleman. And I had another $40,000 on the line ($20K for showing up, $20K for winning) in my fight against Guy Mezger at the end of May. I fought Mezger in a Pride tournament—which is a Japan-based mixed martial arts league—on a one-fight deal. Mezger was a wily fighter. He had had close to forty career fights when we faced off, his first in 1994. He was an MMA pioneer, winning kickboxing titles before moving over to the UFC while it was in its infancy. He had had fights for a title, but could never close the deal. But he did have some big wins, including one against Tito in UFC 13. Late in that match Tito nailed Guy with several knees to the head, and it looked to a lot of people as if Guy had tapped out. But the ref saw it differently. He ruled that Guy was actually blocking the blows to his head with his hand, and when Tito shifted his weight, Guy's hand naturally fell to the mat. He declared there was no tap, checked both fighters for cuts, then put both men on their feet. The announcers, the fans, and even Tito thought the fight was over. So Tito was loaded to finish the job after the ref restarted the fight. When Tito immediately went in for a takedown, Guy protected himself and instead got Tito in a guillotine choke. That was the fight; Tito submitted.

Naturally, Tito felt robbed. Tito was yelling, and the ending was so controversial it was a rematch perfect for TV. They battled again in UFC 19. This time Tito dominated, never giving Mezger or the ref any choice about who should be declared the winner. At one point Tito was repeatedly throwing punches at Mezger's head, and Mezger wasn't responding or trying to protect himself. Tito was just laughing for the whole crowd to see. When the fight was finally stopped, Tito pulled out his GUY MEZGER IS MY BITCH T-shirt. I'd like to say that Tito is a good guy, and that his stunts are just to draw a little attention to himself, make himself a little more money, and play to the crowd. But even now Dana says the two biggest pains in his ass as UFC president are policing steroid users and dealing with Tito. Every sport needs a punk you want to root against. And Tito's ours.

Ken Shamrock, one of Guy's mentors, was in his corner that night. Seeing Tito laugh and then put on the T-shirt sent him over the edge. Without even planning it, Dana now had a new grudge match for the future that was going to knock me off to the side: Tito versus his new enemy, Ken Shamrock.

Mezger was the kind of opponent who fought the way I wanted to fight. His background was similar to mine—he had come from karate and kickboxing—which meant we both wanted to be on our feet and striking. I wouldn't have to spend a lot of time and energy grappling with someone against the ropes or trying to fight my way off the mat.

Right away the fight had a quicker pace than the last few I had been in, which were all against jujitsu grapplers. We were kicking low and flowing around the ring looking for openings to hit, not plodding so we could find a way to grab each other's waist. Early in the fight he connected hard with a left hook. It surprised me, but I was able to shake it off before he could add any kind of combination. Then he actually knocked me down with a kick late in the round. It was only the second time in my career—and the first since my fight with Pele in Brazil—that I had been knocked down.

Throughout the first round I felt that he was scoring more points, but I was getting in more hits that actually hurt. I could see it in his eyes—after all this time you know when you're hurting a guy with your punches, and I was definitely beginning to wear on him. This whole fight I felt different from in any of my other fights. My timing finally seemed right and I had completely made the adjustment from kickboxer to mixed martial artist. I knew I was doing well.

My goal in every fight is to take the guy down, just knock him out. It's more satisfying than a well-executed submission hold or a kick to the head and definitely better than winning a fight by a decision. It's the most visceral joy you can get from fighting, and it's why I was doing it in the streets twenty years ago and why I got into the cage. It's like hitting the perfect golf shot or making the perfect tackle or hitting a clean line drive in baseball. It just goes, with a little bit of a thud in your hands, a little push back, as if you were breaking through a piece of paper. Then it just gives. You can feel it in your legs, your waist, your torso, and your arms when you connect on the perfect punch, but you barely feel it in your knuckles, where you actually make contact. By then, so much force and power is leaving your body that the guy's chin or the guy's cheek is absorbing all of the blow. It's an incredible sensation. It's something everyone dreams about doing—just walloping a guy—and so few get to actually do without getting arrested.

The fight with Mezger was the kind of bout—high energy, a couple of strikers—that ends in a knockout. And it wasn't going to be me.

Late in the second round, I had an opening. As he was backpedaling, I caught him with a combination of three punches to the head and face. He staggered, which gave me an even bigger opening to deliver some punishment. I set up, stepped in with my left foot, and threw a right hand that hit him square on the cheek. His neck gave way and his head bobbed back and then forward as he fell to the ground. It was over. Guy wasn't just knocked down; he was knocked out, with his left leg twisting at an ugly angle underneath his ass and back.

I screamed at the top of my lungs, hugged my corner guys, jumped on the turnbuckle, and pointed to the crowd. Winning a fight never gets old. The payoff is never less than what you expect after months of working. And in the euphoria of all that, it's easy to forget about the guy you just pummeled who's lying on the mat. For those guys, you never know how bad the damage is, when they'll recover, when they'll fight again, or if they'll fight at all. After that night, Guy Mezger would fight just four more times in his career. It happens to everyone.

But it wasn't even close to my time. I felt that I was just getting started. And I celebrated. I had made more money in that month—between the Randleman fight and the Mezger fight—than I had in my entire UFC career. Now I had a contract guaranteeing even more than I could fathom getting paid as a fighter. So I splurged. I had been driving a 1988 Ford Ranger that was in bad shape. It was leaking clutch fluid, and I felt that I was replacing the clutch nearly every month. The car was such a beater it was hard just to keep it together, and I was afraid to drive long distances. I took $14,000 in cash and got myself a 1997 Expedition.

Now I was rolling.

CHAPTER 24

TO LEAVE NO DOUBT, YOU'VE GOT TO KNOCK A GUY OUT

NEW CONTRACT, NEW CREDIBILITY, NEW CAR. MID-
way through 2002 I was thirty-two years old and a legitimate
pro fighter, making a living at what I did best, probably better
than anyone else in the world. I felt that I was peaking, too. The Mezger
fight just flowed and gave me a confidence I didn't have before. I had
always felt I could beat anyone in a fight, a knockdown, drag-out brawl.
But I was feeling now that I could beat someone in a test of talent. The
original intent of the UFC, of all the mixed martial arts competitions,
was to find the most skilled fighters in the world, whether it was in
wrestling, karate, boxing, jujitsu, or any other form of hand-to-hand
combat. While some people thought the UFC had veered off the path
and become nothing but a tough-man contest, it was viewed that way
less and less now. And I knew I could compete. I was proving time and
again in the cage that I was among that top tier of warriors.

Most athletes, when they reach their midthirties, start to show
signs of slowing down. Their reflexes aren't as quick, their timing suf-
fers, their body takes longer to recover from training, let alone a game
or a fight. Boxers especially find themselves in a steep decline. By that
point in their careers they've probably been fighting for twenty years.
Between sparring and actual matches, they've taken thousands of

blows to the head. Whether they are punch-drunk or not, a lot of them can't help but have lingering effects from all those shots. But we UFC fighters, despite all the controversy surrounding the brutality of mixed martial arts, seem to get stronger as we get older. For starters, we don't take countless hits to the head. So many other disciplines are involved in our sport that we spend as much time grappling on the mat and trying to twist each other's limbs as we do trying to knock each other's brains out. A boxer probably takes more hits to the head in one round of a twelve-round fight than a UFC fighter will take in three rounds. Which means, despite some of my media appearances (more on that later), our heads are pretty clear as we get older and we can keep fighting longer.

I'm not trying to keep people from being boxing fans. I loved the sport when I was growing up. Guys like Marvin Hagler and Sugar Ray Leonard were great to watch, but I think the sport has run itself into the ground. There are too many divisions, too many promoters more interested in making a buck than in making a good fight that will keep fans interested. One reason I think the UFC is doing so well is that lots of boxing fans are fed up with the way that sport is run—and the lack of exciting fighters—and are crossing over to watch MMA fights. But you don't see a lot of our fans getting all that pumped up to watch a boxing match. We're gaining new combat sport fans and enticing the boxing lovers, while boxing's followers are getting older or switching over. It doesn't help their cause that the more well-rounded athletes are going into UFC. People always ask me, Who would win a fight between a boxer and an MMA fighter? I'm pretty sure I could handle my own in the ring if all we were allowed to do was box. I am a slugger and I like to land a punch. But if you let an MMA fighter go against a boxer, it's no contest. MMA fighters have too many skills. Remember UFC 1? The boxer didn't last long against Royce Gracie.

Boxing will also always be about speed and strength. A fighter's ability to strike with power, elude punches, and take advantage of openings quickly are the keys to his success. While some wily guys can

Winning a fight—there ain't nothing like it.

last on talent and wits, boxing is a young man's game. But in the UFC, leverage plays just as important a part of success as punching. Learning jujitsu for me was as much about longevity as it was improving my ground game as I began my career. Randy Couture is a heavyweight champ at forty-three. And he is not slowing down. That comes from his ability to dominate on the mat. I know I won't be the most powerful striker in the sport forever, but that doesn't mean I won't be able to compete. That's the beauty of mixed martial arts. Multiple disciplines mean multiple ways for fighters to evolve during their career.

In 2002, however, I was just thinking about beating the crap out of people the best way I knew how, with pure striking power. After the Randleman bout I didn't get the title fight against Tito, because he was going to fight Ken Shamrock. Still, I wanted to stay sharp. I was in too good a rhythm not to challenge myself against topflight challengers, even while Dana was telling me I shouldn't take fights against guys like that in case I slipped up once and lost. Then I'd have to fight my way back into contention for the Ortiz fight. But I fight to prove I'm the best, every time. And that means standing toe-to-toe with the strongest guy willing to challenge me. In UFC 33 in September of 2001, that was Murilo Bustamante, a Brazilian who, naturally, was a jujitsu expert and had been schooled in the Vale Tudo style. Basically that meant he was impossible to hurt and would never tap out. Bustamante was actually a founder of the Brazilian Top Team, which had been established to come up with entirely new styles of fighting in mixed martial arts. Bustamante was at the top of his game when we fought, so much so that four months later he would actually win the UFC's middleweight title. This was what Dana was warning me against: Why take a fight I didn't have to? Why risk a loss when a title shot was mine if I were patient and strategic about my choices? Well, because I don't ever want to waste a fight. It's an insult to whatever gifts I'm lucky enough to have.

Besides, if I lost the bout, I didn't deserve the title shot in the first place. Then whomever I lost to would obviously deserve the title shot.

I am a fighter. The belt was just a symbol of being the best. The only reason I wanted the belt was because I wanted to beat Tito. People considered him the best guy out there at the time, so he was the guy I wanted to beat.

But for now, I had to beat Bustamante. To be honest, I didn't train well for that fight. I had gained too much weight the summer after beating Mezger and I had to rush to cut pounds. I normally like to fight at 205 pounds. I walk around weighing between 212 and 222 pounds. I was 220 pounds just days before that fight, which left me feeling sluggish. That cost me some stamina and power. Even worse, I underestimated Bustamante, especially stupid considering his experience and that he was peaking toward a title shot as well.

When the fight began, I was the aggressor, on the balls of my feet, leaning in, looking to strike quickly. I knocked him down in the first round, and the crowd started chanting, "U-S-A, U-S-A." Then I nailed him again at the end of the first round with a huge right to the side of the head. He started swelling up just as the bell sounded. I was hoping I had hurt him and could pummel him a bit more in the second round.

But then my lack of training caught up to me. He went for an ankle lock early in the second round and I escaped, but I was winded from that. Then he nailed me with a huge right-left combination. I had let the fight slip away a bit, mainly because he was getting more confident that he could stand. He was throwing some quick, stinging jabs, which I didn't expect, since even he had described himself as 100 percent Brazilian jujitsu. Late in the second he shot for my legs again and tried to lock me up, but I was able to slither away. Still, I was not being assertive. I did a lot of dancing in that second round and wasn't looking for openings—or taking advantage of the ones that I saw—nearly as much as the first. Sometimes, when I did make a move, I was reaching and didn't have great form. He took advantage when I opened myself up.

In the third we were both pretty tentative, partially because we were wary of each other and partially because, by now, we were both winded. If either of us got in a big hit, it might have ended. And, with 2:13 left in the fight, I thought I had done that. I caught him with a big right that knocked him onto the mat. Normally I'd go for the ground and pound, but he was such a dangerous grappler I didn't want to get caught up with him. So I hovered over him while he lay on his back, kicking his thighs and making it tough for him to get up. We were like that for thrity seconds until the ref backed me up.

With about 1:15 left, I think we both felt that to guarantee a win, we had to go for a knockout. Putting it in the hands of the judges would have been too close a call. I landed a nice combination to his head. Then he popped me in the face with a shot I wasn't expecting. But neither of us went down for the count. It was an exhausting, well-executed fight. I'm not sure either of us had the power to finish it by the end.

You never want a fight to go into the hands of the judges. It's too subjective. I may have thought I outpointed Bustamante, but the judges could have downgraded me for being kept on my heels in the discipline that is supposed to be my specialty. The punishment of a fight is easy compared to the torture of waiting for judges.

Luckily, they saw the fight my way, unanimously. Not that there wasn't a little controversy. Plenty of UFC fans debated the judges' call and believed that Bustamante deserved the win. I could see their points, so I went back and watched the fight twice. Both times I thought it was close, but I had still won. The fight did teach me two things: Listening to other people's scouting reports about fighters is a waste of time, and to leave no doubt, you've got to knock a guy out.

In UFC 35 in January of 2002, I fought Amar Suloev, an Armenian kickboxer. I had a five-inch height advantage on the five-nine Suloev, but he was an aggressive fighter who, while he had a wrestling background, liked to stay on his feet. He had also won twelve straight mixed martial arts matches.

Hackleman worked me hard for that fight because I was so sluggish in the Bustamante fight. And it paid off. I went after Amar right away and I hurt him early. But he didn't really reciprocate. I expected a different fight from him, honestly. He is so aggressive, and because of his experience as a kickboxer, I thought he would stay close and try to trade punches. But he backed off for most of the fight once I had connected. I won the first two rounds easily, and I kept chasing after him, but he would just take a punch and then run. There was nothing I could do about that. In the third round I threw fewer punches, partially because I couldn't get close, but also because I moved into kickboxing mode. I was kicking his legs and expecting to get a head kick in. I just didn't get it in before the bell sounded, and again it went to the judges.

Unlike with Bustamante, there wasn't a question about this fight. I could have pressed harder—I didn't throw much more in the third than an overhand right—but I was out there in control, just throwing my attacks. If he came at me a little bit, maybe I could have landed one. However, it is really hard to knock a guy out if he is running away from you. Fans didn't love that fight—a second straight decision after I had been knocking people out—but a win is a win.

In the UFC world, I was on fire. I had won eight straight fights against strong competition. I was becoming a name, a potential draw, developing a fan base, and doing it all the way I thought it should be done: not by bragging about myself or ripping opponents, but by being a powerful striker who was feared as a fighter.

And my timing couldn't have been better.

CHAPTER 25

LOYALTY IS EVERYTHING

THIS WORLD WAS GETTING KIND OF CRAZY NOW. The money was bigger. The fights were bigger. I was getting more popular. And thanks to my sperm donor, I had seen what kinds of people can come out of the woodwork when you start getting attention. It makes you nervous. How can it not? I'm an open guy; I trust a lot of people. If you walk down the street and want to start a conversation with me, then I'll stop and chat and take a picture and sign an autograph. But, at the same time, I needed to surround myself with people who didn't care if I was on the way up in a growing sport or bartending back at the Library.

In 2002 I had bought a house—a perk of the job and something I had never thought about doing. Because of my training and travel schedule (it seemed I was always on the road either pimping the sport or fighting), I needed help managing stuff in my life. My brother Dan lived with me for a while. And I invited my friend Antonio Banuelos to move in, too.

Antonio loves to fight. He grew up in a big Mexican family in Fresno with gangster cousins, and every weekend one of them was beating the crap out of another. As Antonio says, "You get boozing and see your cousins fighting in front of you, then something is going to go down."

The dude's only about five-three, which means, as a brawler, he's perfectly built for wrestling. He was a stud in high school, then wrestled at Cal Poly San Luis Obispo about ten years after I did. I met him through a bunch of friends there. He wanted to train with Hack and then get into the UFC, and I offered to help him out. The guy is intense. One of Hack's drills is swinging a sledgehammer into a tire. He'll have you do it close to two hundred times in one session, switching arms back and forth. Afterward, it's difficult to lift a toothpick. Your arms are burning, your back is tight, your shoulders feel as if they were carrying anvils, and your forearms bulge like Popeye's. It's nasty. But Antonio doesn't let up on that tire. He's a punk-rock kid at heart, and a sound track of that stuff must be playing in his head all the time, because he'll be pounding the tire harder at the end than he was at the beginning, pushing the guys he's working out with to finish as strong as he does.

Antonio's an animated guy, literally. He's got tattoos from his neck to his back to his legs. He gets one after every one of his fights. Hack and I had to make him stop getting them above the shoulders in case he wants to open a gym one day. Tats on the forearms don't scare away customers as much as snakes wrapping around your throat. And he doesn't just tell a story; he's usually jumping a few feet in the air to get his point across. He finishes off with a lot of "Bam!" and then the sound of his fist punching his open palm. He's also fiercely loyal—a scary, wouldn't-hesitate-to-take-someone-out-and-go-to-jail-for-me-if-he-felt-I-had-been-wronged loyal. To me, loyalty is everything. You can get away with saying and doing a lot more to me than you can to one of my friends. You've got to do right by the people closest to you. My mom can remember back in fourth grade watching me run across the playground when I saw a bully picking on one of my buddies. I stood up to him and said, "You can't do that. If you've got a problem with him, you've got a problem with me." My brother Dan is six-five and knows how to hurt people, but if I see someone starting with him, my first instinct is to be protective.

I know I can handle myself in a fight and that I don't mind getting into one. But that's not true for everyone. And if someone I'm close to—someone I know isn't all that interested in throwing punches—is getting into some trouble, I'm going to step in. I'd like to settle things down. But if I can't, so be it. That doesn't mean you can't tell friends when they're being idiots and asking for trouble. But if things go down, you've got to be ready, too.

Not that you can't make exceptions. When I was around twenty-six, a buddy asked me and Dan to drive with him to Bakersfield so he could confront a guy he thought was dating his ex-girlfriend. On the way there Dan and I realized our buddy had lost it; he was basically stalking her. When we got out of the car to knock on the guy's door, I looked at Dan and said, "I can't do this stuff anymore." So we turned around and left. The point is, if your buddy is stalking a chick, don't help him beat up the guys that she's dating. You've got to know where to draw the line.

> **HOW TO BEHAVE LIKE A GROWN-ASS MAN**: You've got to take care of yourself. I'll look for my buddies when it's time to go, give them fifteen or twenty minutes to come back to where we were hanging out or for me to find them. But that's it. After that, you're on your own. You're a grown-ass man, okay? Get home by yourself. We're not holding your hand.

Seriously, though, who wouldn't want a guy as loyal as Antonio on his side? I needed people around I could trust, who had known me before the UFC started going mainstream. Since I was starting to take off and Antonio was just getting his career started, I made him an offer: Come live with me and Dan in my new digs, help me out as my assistant, and you can focus on training and fighting. He accepted. And then his fight career started rolling. He won nine straight mixed martial arts matches. Now when people deliver pizza to the house, he answers the door and gets recognized as a fighter.

That's as rewarding as anything I can do in the ring.

Of course, no one knows me or Antonio if they don't see our

fights. Dana has always liked to say that the Trojan horse for the UFC, the one thing that would knock the door down and turn this from a fringe sport with hard-core fans into a mainstream event with the pageantry and hype of boxing in the old days, was television. And not just pay-per-view, which we were on and doing well with in just the first year Dana and the Fertittas had owned the sport. He was talking about the stations you get whenever you sign up for cable. Finally, in June of 2002, he got the interest that he needed.

Lorenzo and Dana had been working David Hill, the president of Fox Sports, to get UFC fights on the air. Hill is one of the most innovative and risk-taking execs in sports. He carries around a notebook that only he is allowed to touch that has every idea he has ever thought of for television, beginning with his days working for Rupert Murdoch in Australia. I'm pretty sure he never had an entry in there that began, "Sign up mixed martial arts." Yet he did just that. At first it was taped shows with UFC highlights and fights. But the numbers were through the roof, something they hadn't expected. It gave Dana the balls to push for bigger and better exposure.

Fox's *The Best Damn Sports Show Period* had been building the exact audience that loves UFC fights: young guys in college who like to tell raunchy jokes, get messed up, and see guys beat the snot out of each other. The show had Chris Rose and a bunch of jocks and comedians mixing it up. They riffed on everything from the day's scores to the pros who were acting like jerks. And it was the first show to really embrace mixed martial arts. While ESPN and other networks ignored it for years, *The Best Damn Sports Show Period* was airing UFC highlights, the best, most cringe-inducing ones they could find. The show treated ultimate fighting like a legit sport, talking about the winners and losers and contenders with the same seriousness with which they talked about the Patriots winning the Super Bowl or the Yankees contending for the World Series.

When the producers were putting together their *Best Damn Sports Show Period* "All Star Summer Celebration," they decided to try something different. They hadn't been losing viewers with UFC highlights, people hadn't been complaining, and they had hours of programming to fill. Besides, Dana was in their ear 24 / 7 about putting some fights on the air and making an event out of it. Dana is the kind of guy I would hate to fight in the ring. He'd never stop coming. You could rip his arm off and start beating him with it and he'd still keep trying to take you down. That's the kind of energy and passion he was bringing to those early days of his reign in the UFC. He was a man obssessed with making this thing happen. The network execs had been happy to run the highlights because they knew it played to their audience. But they were skeptical about how an actual fight would play on TV, not just with people watching who knew only of the UFC's brutality, but with skittish sponsors. In the end, they took the shot to make it a part of the show, but I think it was partially just to get Dana off their back.

The fights came together at the last minute, which was why it was called UFC 37.5. But, even though most of us had less than five weeks to train, we all wanted in on the showcase. The card for UFC 38 in London had already been announced. Even the posters for UFC 38 had been printed. UFC 37.5 is not the greatest name in the series, but promotion isn't a pretty business. UFC 37.5 was a six-match card in which me taking on Vitor Belfort was the main event. Dana had been told when he bought the UFC that it would never get back on pay-per-view. When it did, they told him he'd never get on basic cable television. Now they were showing taped fights on Fox, and they told him he'd never get on live TV because the UFC was too unpredictable—you could never know what was going to happen. Only now, it was about to happen. Free TV reaching millions was the opportunity the sport had been waiting for.

Leading into our match, Vitor had already made his name internationally as a fighter. He was Brazilian, of course, and had earned his jujitsu black belt at nineteen training under Carlson Gracie. He was one of the best grapplers in the world because he had learned from one of the best grapplers in the world. In his first MMA fight he knocked his opponent out twelve seconds into the first round. In his first UFC tourney he had such an easy time taking guys out he was nicknamed the Phenom. By 2001 he was considered the top light heavyweight contender, ranked ahead of me even, and was in line to fight Tito in UFC 33. But an injury prior to the fight knocked him out. Now he was trying to make his way back into contention. And beating me in UFC 37.5 would put him there.

As usual, I got a lot of calls from Dana heading into the fight, reminding me how huge this fight was, how important it was for me. As much as I tend not to get too hyped up about these things, he was right. If I won, it was one more way for me to make sure Tito couldn't avoid me in a title fight. Heading into it, a lot of people had me as the underdog.

It was also the last deal of my contract with the UFC. I was getting $35,000 guaranteed just for stepping into the cage. Winning earned me another $35,000. I can live with $70,000 for one night's work that won't last any longer than the fifteen minutes it's sanctioned for. But Dana was also reminding me how huge this was for the sport. It had never been this close to being accepted by the mainstream media. Less than two years earlier, pay-per-view broadcasters weren't even giving fans the option of buying the fights. Now we were going to be on for free. I know—and I knew—my success is only as great as the UFC's. We are tied together, and I wasn't about to let this chance slip by. This had to be done right.

Because it was such a last-minute deal, the fights were held in a freaking hotel ballroom. But it didn't diminish the atmosphere. We came out washed in a crisscross of white, green, and pink lasers dissecting the room. Close to four thousand fans were packed in there, and we walked in on ramps that were raised above the crowd, like models on catwalks. Vitor was a few inches shorter than me but was just as heavy. He was pretty cut, and unlike a lot of jujitsu guys, he wasn't afraid to stay on his feet and punch it out. He liked to box, had terrific hand speed and a big left, and was good enough to win fights

Belfort and I traded kicks, but I got him in the end.

without ever hitting the ground. I expected him to be aggressive and come at me, which is exactly the way I want to fight. I'm not a guy who sets up combinations to knock you out. I've got a lot of power coming up from my legs and through my hips. The torque I can generate to throw my punches is unlike that of most other fighters. I want guys coming at me aggressively and leaving themselves exposed as they get closer so I can surprise them with a devastating overhand right.

One thing opponents rarely try to do with me is kickboxing. I've won national championships as a kickboxer. It's just not a strategy I often see. But Vitor came out looking to kick. He actually caught me with a couple of head kicks, which surprised me. And thrilled me. If a guy wants to stand and kick, I'll do it all day. Even though he caught me with a couple, it didn't really impact me. I train against that all the time; I come from that background. Kicks in the head clear out the

MY THOUGHTS ON HOW TO THROW A KNOCKOUT PUNCH:

Knockout punches are about timing and accuracy as much as power. Knockouts happen from catching a guy in the right spot at the right time. But, if you do that and don't have any strength behind your punch, you're wasting an opportunity. It's all hips and snap, a lot of practice and twisting. I've been working on it since I was twelve. Some say knockout punchers have it in their genes. I do think it's a fast-twitch muscle thing, but you have to practice. It starts with a good stance. You need staggered feet so you can stop takedowns and kicks, too. You have to stand wider than a typical boxing stance, which gives up a little on the power, but if you are on your back and can't throw punches, what's the difference? Then twist your hips as much as you can; imagine if you didn't have a spine and were trying to twist all the way around. The arm means nothing; it can come from any angle. It's all about the power you generate in your hips.

cobwebs; they're not about to knock me down. Besides, with him kicking, it gave me the chance to kick. And I caught him pretty good, especially one spinning kick that landed right at the top of his ribs, which made him buckle for a minute.

I thought Vitor was going to be more aggressive with his hands, but instead he kept his distance. When the kicks weren't working, he tried to take me down. And that seemed to be his strategy for the rest of the fight. We danced around each other for most of two rounds, occasionally connecting on a kick or a punch, but then we'd hit the mat. I thought I hit harder than him, and I really wanted to test his chin, but I wasn't getting the chance. Instead, I'd try to throw everything I had in the few seconds we were both close enough to exchange some shots.

It was another of those fights that, as the third round ended, I was afraid was going to be left up to the judges. And this was way too big a match for something like that to happen. Vitor's corner was yelling for him to make something happen. And then I decided to take the fight to Vitor. With about a minute

UFC 37.5 vs. Vitor Belfort. He took me off guard with a nice pop, but in the end I nailed him with some major blows and won by unanimous decision.

left, I caught him with a strong right that knocked him down. He wasn't knocked out, but I was able to pummel him for the last minute of the fight. It left little doubt that I was the unanimous winner, and the judges agreed.

I wanted that shot against Tito, but I knew I was going to have to wait. Dana had told me before the fight that he had a chance to set up an Ortiz-Shamrock match for UFC 40 that November. It was a grudge match, with one of the UFC's most respected statesmen taking on its resident bad boy. Shamrock was still pissed about the way Tito had treated his protégé, Guy Mezger. This was going to be a boon for the sport. Ken had wrestled in the WWE and brought along an entirely new audience because of it. It could be the fight in which the UFC and MMA took one more step toward becoming mainstream. And because

Dana asked me to, I told him if I beat Vitor I would step aside and let the Ortiz-Shamrock fight happen. I'd been patient; I could continue to be patient.

I would have been content that night to walk out of the ring a winner and collect my $70K. Tito was sitting in the front row for my fight with Belfort. But I didn't feel the need to point to him with national TV cameras rolling and tell him that he was mine or that I was going to kick his ass.

He felt different. Maybe he couldn't handle that someone else was getting attention. Or maybe he wanted to prove to himself that he wasn't afraid of me. Whatever the case, he jumped into the ring and started talking. As soon as he was done fighting Ken, he said he was coming after me. It was going to be in his home, and he was going to kick my ass. Before that, neither of us had ever talked publicly about a fight. It was always something bubbling under the surface. I wouldn't bring it up because it's not my style. And he wouldn't bring it up because he wanted to avoid it. But that was impossible now. Other than Shamrock, there was no one left for Tito to fight except me.

I was just hoping to get the chance.

CHAPTER 26

FORGET PLANS AND EXPECTATIONS

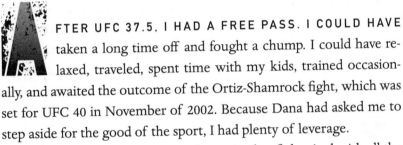FTER UFC 37.5, I HAD A FREE PASS. I COULD HAVE taken a long time off and fought a chump. I could have relaxed, traveled, spent time with my kids, trained occasionally, and awaited the outcome of the Ortiz-Shamrock fight, which was set for UFC 40 in November of 2002. Because Dana had asked me to step aside for the good of the sport, I had plenty of leverage.

But I didn't want to sit around. I wanted to fight. And with all the hype surrounding Tito and Ken's fight, it got me anxious to get back in the cage. Of course, Dana was adamant that I not do it. As my friend, he was thinking about my career. I didn't need to take on a fight, to put my number-one-contender ranking on the line just because I wanted to hit somebody. It was a stupid risk. As the boss of the UFC, Dana definitely did not want me getting into that Octagon. UFC fans were ready to shell out top dollar for a fight between me and Tito or me and Ken. The pay-per-view revenue for either fight would be astronomical. By the time UFC 40 happened, it would have been more than three years since I had lost a fight. I had become a fan favorite by dominating opponents. If I dropped a meaningless fight, all that goodwill and hype would go away, and so would my shot at the title.

But screw it. Screw plans and expectations. When you start

worrying about them, you stop doing what put you in a position to be great in the first place. I wanted a fight in UFC 40. And I didn't want some bum. That would just be a waste of time. I wanted a challenge, someone who could keep me sharp, because I expected to have a title fight soon after. I called Dana again and told him to get me a fight. The matchmaker came up with Babalu.

Babalu's real name is Renato Sobral, a Brazilian. But everyone calls him Babalu because that's what kind of bubble gum he likes to chew. Shocker, this Brazilian was an expert in jujitsu, the Gracie style, and loved getting opponents on the ground. He'd won with armbars, key-locks, and rear-naked chokes. But as much as for his fighting, Babalu had a rep for his serious workouts. He didn't just go for jogs; he sprinted through the mountains of Brazil. He didn't just bench-press at the gym; he used training partners as dumbbells and lifted them. He didn't just swim; he swam two thousand meters in less than an hour. This was an appropriate challenge. I liked this fight, and when I told Dana, he said, "Screw you. Screw you because you are not fighting, and screw you because there is no way you are fighting Babalu. That is a danger-ous fight. Sit back, relax, watch the fucking Tito and Ken fight, and get ready to fight the winner."

I told Dana, "No way."

Then the argument got really high-minded. Dana said to me, "Screw you, no way, screw you."

"Screw you," I countered. This is how we talk to each other. I was still as close to Dana as I'd ever been. But I wanted a fucking fight against Babalu. I called my attorney, who pointed out to Dana that I had the right in my contract to fight on that card and he had to set it up. Dana's response was, "All right, fuck face, you are stupid and dumb. You got me. You got the fight." That, naturally, made me happy.

With more than 13,000 people in the stands at the MGM Grand Garden Arena and 150,000 buying at home, this was the biggest event in UFC history. With an audience like that, I wanted to make an im-pression. Even if I wasn't saying anything out loud, every time I won, it was a statement that I was the best fighter in the world, no matter who held the title. To do it on this stage, on the same night that Tito was fighting, would only create more of a stir.

At the start of the fight, Babalu and I danced. He went for a low leg kick; I probed with some left-handed jabs. He didn't make a move to shoot for my legs, the way a lot of the jujitsu guys do. He was willing to stay on his feet and move in close with some kicks to my legs. I hurt him after the first minute with a big right, then around twenty seconds later followed that up with another looping right. This one felt heavy; you could hear the air compress out of my glove. I was determined to push this fight. Babalu was a tough guy and I wanted to rattle him. My eyes were so wide-open during the fight that even the announcers could see I wanted to get the knockout fast. The longer we were in there, the more of a risk I was taking. I just needed one opening. And I got it.

Babalu went in for a low leg kick, leaving himself wide-open. I leaned in for a big right, and when he ducked, I gave him a left hand to the face and then a left leg kick into the forehead. He went down fast and hard. As soon as I pounced to finish him, the ref was jumping on top of me, knocking me off. This fight was over. TKO. Afterward I jumped up, pointed to the crowd, went to help Babalu up, and felt as relieved as I have in a long time. I was still fighting my way, setting myself up for the title my way. Now I could sit back and join the rest of the crowd to watch Tito and Ken.

From the beginning, it was worth the buildup. Ken came out first, introduced by a video of him saying, "Tito Ortiz is a punk," which repeated over and over. Then the stadium went dark, and when the lights came back on, Ken was standing on a platform near an entrance to the arena, with his arms raised. The crowd went nuts. This guy had fought in UFC 1. He had done professional wrestling. Now he was back to try to swipe the title from the guy he thought was disrespecting the sport Shamrock had built.

Tito came out to even more mayhem. He had pillars of fire shoot-

I was whaling on Babalu in UFC 40, until I knocked him out with a kick to the head.

ing up around his entrance platform. When the lights came up to show his face, he was dancing on his platform, waving an American and an Irish flag and wearing his UFC light heavyweight belt. He was amped, bouncing down his ramp into the cage, where his feet barely touched the ground. You could tell the whole thing was making Ken sick. When Tito bounced his way, Ken almost charged him, before the fight even started. When they stared down at center ring, Tito couldn't stop moving, while Ken just stood there looking pissed.

So many of these big fights start off slow, with the opponents feeling each other out. But in this one, the guys seemed to have so much built-up aggression, they couldn't wait to unleash it on each other. They sprinted to the middle of the cage and started swinging. Tito locked Ken up right away, then hit him with a punch, then a knee to the face. Ken swung back, but then Tito got his hands wrapped around the back of Ken's head, pulled his face down, and started kneeing him just above his eyes. Tito had spent seven weeks at Big Bear getting ready for this fight, and he looked as good as he ever had. The crowd was chanting his name, and he took Ken down to the mat, where he beat up on him for the rest of the round. A big cut was bleeding over Ken's eye as the first round ended.

The second round was much of the same. Tito got Ken on the mat again and kept up the ground-and-pound. Ken had a good defensive guard, with Tito locked between his legs, but then Tito pulled himself out of it and got a side position. He kneed Ken to the body again and again. Ken's a warrior, one of the originals, and he wasn't about to tap out. He made a beautiful spin move from the ground and got back on his feet as the round ended. But he looked beat-up and tired. When he threw punches, they were tentative and from too far away, as if he didn't want to get too close.

By the third round, Tito was trying to set Ken up for the knockout. He took one of my moves, a big looping left hand. Then he unleashed a vicious combo of knees and punches before taking Ken down to the mat again. Ken could do nothing. He was too winded and his face was a mess, while Tito looked as if he had barely started fighting. Ken pulled himself off the mat with about a minute left in the round, but Tito came at him again with more combos of kicks and punches. This was a five-round fight, and the third round ended with Ken just trying to keep Tito at bay. Ken could win only if he knocked Tito out. If it went the distance, the fight was Tito's.

It didn't get that far. Between rounds, after looking at Ken's face, the ref called it. Then Tito acted like the punk that he is. When Ken tried to walk over and give Tito a hug, Tito walked away. He put on his postfight T-shirt, which read, I JUST KILLED KENNY, YOU BASTARD. Only after people had seen it did he take it off, go back to Ken, and embrace him. Then Ken walked around the cage with Tito's arm held high. The guy was all class. Tito, the champ, not so much.

But he had put on a devastating display of mixed martial arts and dominated one of the legends of the sport on its biggest stage. Between Tito's win and the way I'd dispatched Babalu earlier that night, Joe Rogan, the actor and UFC commentator, could only say before he signed off, "I can't even begin to fathom a match between Tito Ortiz and Chuck Liddell."

I could. And I couldn't wait.

CHAPTER 27

LOSING AS A MAN IS BETTER THAN WINNING AS A COWARD

THAT NIGHT, AT THE POSTFIGHT PRESS CONFERence, I heard Lorenzo Fertitta talk about how unstoppable Tito was. How he was the best 205-pound fighter in the world and that nobody could beat him. I was right there and found it insulting. Lorenzo was acting as if I weren't a contender, as if I weren't even a threat to Tito.

Then Tito began waffling about taking me on. There was no avoiding a fight with me now. He was the champ. I was the number one contender. But when the subject came up, he wasn't acting like the most dangerous man in the world. He was acting like a guy who had something to lose. He never said, "I want Chuck, I want Chuck." Instead he started talking about renegotiating his UFC deal. He talked about how we were friends and should get paid if we were going to put that friendship on the line. Five months earlier he had been saying how he was going to kick my ass as soon as he was done with Ken. Now, he wouldn't commit.

But we weren't that close. We hadn't trained together for a while. And even if we were, that wouldn't have been a problem, at least not for me. I am not an emotional fighter; I don't have to not like you to fight you. If you step in the ring, I am going to try to take your head off. That was the first lesson Pops taught me about confrontation: Don't fight angry; it only makes you vulnerable. I still fight that way today. Before the bout I'll have a drink with you. Afterward we can hang at the after party. It's nothing personal, just the fight business.

But Tito was using it as an excuse. I wasn't asking for more money. I would have taken whatever they offered. Tito had the belt and I wanted it. But he was making the personal into business by saying he needed more money if he was going to fight a friend. I knew he was trying to avoid fighting me for the light heavyweight title. It got to the point where I had no choice but to call him out. Sometimes you can't walk away. I wanted to fight in UFC 41 in February of 2003, but Tito claimed he had some injuries that were healing. I wanted to fight in UFC 42 two months later in April, but Tito said he was shooting a movie. I wanted to fight at UFC 43 in June, but Tito claimed he had already committed to hosting a grappling tournament in Huntington Beach that weekend.

The truth was, Tito wanted only fights he knew he could win. And Dana practically went to war with him over the way he was dodging me. He wasn't just keeping a fight from happening; he was practically shutting down the sport, not to mention what he was doing to its credibility. How can a champion not defend his title? The Patriots can't win the Super Bowl one year and then decide not to play again, not to give another team the chance to win the championship. No one in the UFC had respect for Tito now. He had always acted like a punk, but at least he was willing to fight. Now he wouldn't even do that. He refused to step into the cage, at least against me. He was worse than a punk. He was a coward.

So what do you do when someone is holding your title hostage? "Well," Dana said, "screw it." Instead of going into a protracted legal battle with Tito, he decided to put on a championship fight for the "interim" light heavyweight belt. That's the beauty of a sport as new as the UFC. There are no long-established, stuffy traditions to violate. We're just making it up as we go along. To us, nothing matters more than a good fight, and anything that gets in the way of that is likely to get pushed aside.

Tito wasn't getting stripped, but the message was pretty clear: If you don't want to fight, then you can't be the only one they call champ. Instead, Dana set up a matchup between me and Randy Couture for UFC 43. From his perspective, it was a clean solution. Randy was a legitimate world champion, a UFC legend. If I beat him, then no one could question my "interim" title. Tito would just be some punk who was afraid to fight. As far as Dana—and, he hoped, everyone else—was concerned, I would be seen as the UFC's light heavyweight champ.

I've always had the feeling that Randy knew this was coming. We had been working out together for a few days before the fight was announced. His coach asked me how I set up certain moves, especially for getting out of trouble when I am in the bottom position. I have a lot of fakes that get people to bite, which is why I am so hard to hold down. But Randy was a heavyweight; I didn't see us fighting anytime soon. Besides, I wasn't giving away all my secrets. Then I learned a valuable lesson: Everyone is a potential opponent.

Soon after we finished training together, I got a call from Dana. He was setting up a fight for me—against Randy Couture, who may go down as the greatest champ in UFC history. He's won the heavyweight title three times and the light heavyweight title twice. He's one of only four fighters in the UFC Hall of Fame. The guy's got two nicknames, Captain America and the Natural, and he's perfectly suited for both. He's an army vet, so there's no form of fighting that doesn't come easy to him, or at least look as if it does. He was an all-American wrestler in college and an alternate on the U.S. Olympic team.

The good news was, heading into our fight, he was struggling. In his two fights in 2002, he had been beaten down by strikes from heavier opponents. Looking to create a marquee fight, Dana suggested he drop down to light heavyweight. It was a golden opportunity: a great payday and a chance to beat the hottest fighter in the sport, me.

I loved the idea. But I would have loved the idea of fighting anyone. I had been begging Dana to find me a match and get me back into the cage. The more I had to talk about taking on Tito and the more he ducked me, the more anxious I was to perform. Rhythm is so important when you're a fighter, and I had been fighting every five months for a few years. But by the time I was scheduled to step into the ring with Randy, in June of 2003, it would have been seven months since my last fight. Nothing you do in training can compare to the reality of a fight. I needed to get my timing down and get my wind back and prepare my body for the punishment of close combat.

I was trying a lot of new things in my workouts. I did some stand-up wrestling and sparring and added a lot of interval training. We'd set up six markers around a field and I'd have to sprint to one, backpedal to another, do a bear crawl to a third. I'd have to do each one in less than around twenty seconds; then I'd get to rest a minute before having to do it again.

But about six weeks before UFC 43, I had a setback. While sparring one morning I tore the MCL in my knee. It wouldn't keep me from fighting, but it would drastically alter how I trained. Severe lateral movement, the kind that comes from the violent twists and turns of wrestling, was out of the question. Instead I could work on only my stamina and my stand-up. There would be no going to the mat.

By the night of the fight, though, I thought the injury to the MCL was a nonissue. Even after the long layoff, my timing had come back in my last few weeks of sparring and I felt strong. Most of all, I was just pumped to be back in the cage, and still a little annoyed that Tito was such a punk. I told one reporter who asked how I felt about going against Randy, "He has balls, unlike some people I know."

Randy has a rep for being at his best in fights that he is expected to lose. And he strolled up to the cage that night as if he didn't have a care in the world. He was dressed in sandals, red shorts, a white fleece-lined jacket, and a blue cap. He could have been going to the beach. He also looked about thirty pounds lighter than he had been. That he was dropping down in weight and had lost two fights made people think I had the advantage. The money in Vegas was coming in heavy on my side.

Randy is such a skilled fighter that you never know if you're going to have to stand and strike with him or spend your night trying to keep from going to the mat. I'm always looking for the knockout, the earlier the better. It feels good, but my punching power is my strength as a fighter. No matter how prepared you think you are for it as my opponent, it doesn't compare to actually taking a hit, which is why I came out punching against Randy. But he had his hands held high, and when I got in too close, he gave me a couple of knee kicks. I countered with a left shin kick; then *boom*, he got his hands around me and slammed me to the mat. It was that fast. I can't lie: It hurt a little bit. I was able to get in a couple of knees to his thigh, but his jabs were coming in quick and were landing. I was eventually able to get up, but I did change my strategy a bit. I wasn't thinking I was slow when I was in the ring, but that was how it looked afterward. Randy was cutting off the Octagon, and I was dancing around trying to find my way in for a punch. But Randy moved in on me again and put me on the ground, keeping me there for the rest of the first round.

I was frustrated walking back to my corner. My knee wasn't hurting, but I had no reaction time when it came to grappling. I could barely move out of the way the first time he took me down, and it wasn't because I didn't see him coming. I had trained to protect my knee, but it had cost me more than I thought it would. I was not conditioned for wrestling, and my timing was way off.

I could have stayed on my feet and punched all day. And for the first two minutes of the second round I felt great—despite a small cut that had opened above my left

WHAT HURTS MORE THAN UFC:

1. Dentist
2. Listening to Antonio sing karaoke
3. Pushing 220 pounds in a wheelbarrow up a hill
4. A paper cut
5. Sitting through an afternoon of *Dora the Explorer*

eye—as we boxed back and forth. After the fight a lot of people said that they were surprised Randy could go toe-to-toe with me. I wasn't. He had never lost to someone considered a striker. And he had as many fights end because of knockouts and submissions from punches as he did from any moves he made on the mat. I had no reason to think he wasn't dangerous, no matter how we fought. He had a steady jab that kept finding its way past my defense, and a right that was on the money that night. Eventually, in the second round, he forced me up against the cage, and while I escaped, he caught me and brought me down again. This was where the lack of wrestling endurance caught up to me. For about thirty seconds I had the top position and was landing punches. But they didn't really hurt Randy because I had so little behind them.

Randy was beating me at my own game, something he had done to other fighters. When he'd fought for the heavyweight title against Vitor, he'd adapted his style and mimicked what Vitor did.

The third round was more of the same. We traded punches for about two minutes before Randy was able to get me on the mat. For most of the fight I had been pretty good at warding off his worst blows, which kept the ref at bay. But this time, he had the perfect position, mounted right on top of me, and he went after my head. He must have gotten off fifteen punches, all of them landing. It was a classic ground-and-pound. The ref knew there was no way of tapping out, no matter how many blows to the head I took, which forced him to jump in and stop it. With 2:40 left in the third, Randy Couture was declared the winner, and interim light heavyweight champion of the UFC. And what did he say during his postfight interview? "Tito, if you want this belt, you will have to come and take it."

Meanwhile I was headed to the hospital. I got stitched up, went back to the hotel, took a nap, then headed home.

Honestly, I can live with losing if I deserve it. And I deserved to lose that fight. I could also live with the fact that I was no longer the number-one-ranked contender, that I had just lost for the first time in four years, and that I had missed out on achieving what I had been working toward my entire UFC career. I could live with the idea of having to prove myself all over again before I got another shot at the title. I could even live with that it would take me two more years to get the payday I would have gotten for my next fight if I had beaten Randy.

But here's what really killed me about losing that night: I let Tito off the hook.

The guy had been dodging me for seven months and had been talking a lot of shit. So were his fans. He was making it sound as if I were stabbing him in the back by even wanting to fight him, as if he had taken me off the street and taught me how to fight. I was the one asked to help him train in the beginning, not the other way around.

While I was training to fight, he was talking about injuries and money. While I was willing to get in the cage with anyone, he was trying to pick and choose his opponents. Ultimately, he was rewarded for being afraid. But, to me, losing as a man is better than winning as a coward.

The problem was, now I had to claw my way back into contention.

CHAPTER 28

YOU CAN WORRY ABOUT LOSING, OR YOU CAN DO SOMETHING ABOUT IT

HAVE A HARD TIME SITTING ON THE COUCH FOR LONG periods between the fights that I win. But when I lose, it's as if I were caffeinated 24/7. All I want to do is get back in the cage and fight. I need to purge myself of the loss and remember what it's like to kick someone's ass. I don't dwell on my losses; it's not like that for me. I'm just damn anxious. My feeling is this: You can worry about losing, or you can do something about it.

I prefer to do something about it, which means getting back to fighting. Dana understands this about me, and the beauty of our relationship is, even though he's technically my boss now, he never puts what's best for the UFC in front of what's best for me. He knew after the fight with Randy that I would want to get back in action as soon as possible, much sooner than he'd be able to figure out who my next UFC opponent would be or how things would shake out in my weight class. He had to worry about putting together Tito and Randy first. That was the marquee fight, the one that was going to bring another huge payday for the UFC. After that, it would be my turn again. But I couldn't wait for that.

A Pride tournament began in August, just a couple of months after my fight with Randy. I thought I had a good chance at winning, and

Dana wanted to get me busy. I was one of his assets, yet he was pushing me to do it for my mental stability, knowing I'd go crazy waiting
for my next UFC fight.

Pride, a Japanese mixed martial arts league, has always been the
UFC's biggest rival. It started back in 1997 when a Japanese promoter
wanted to pit a popular pro wrestler against Rickson Gracie, the Brazilian jujitsu champ. The fight was staged at the Tokyo Dome, and
forty-seven thousand people showed up, not to mention what seemed
like a rep from every media outlet in Japan. The event was such a big
hit, the promoters turned it into a regular event, creating Pride tournaments that lured the best fighters in the world to Japan.

There's long been a debate about whether Pride or UFC has better
competition, which in the mixed martial arts world translates to the
tougher fighters (this is dying down these days, since the UFC bought
Pride early in 2007). Before Dana and the Fertittas swooped in, the
rules in Pride had always been different. The first round is ten minutes,
followed by two five-minute rounds. While pile-driving an opponent,
stomping on his head when he's down, or kicking him when he's lying
on his back are illegal in the UFC, they're fair game in Pride. From a
fighter's perspective, they're both full of equally badass guys. And
most UFC guys had always been thrilled to have Pride as an option.
The payday was great, the competition was top-notch, and mixed
martial arts—while just gaining mainstream popularity in the United
States—has always been immensely popular there. While we were getting crowds of ten thousand to fifteen thousand fans for fights in Vegas,
Pride events were drawing ninety thousand. It was the difference between a band with a cult following doing arena tours and the Rolling
Stones doing a stadium tour. Fighters in Japan were rock stars. During
a visit I made to a mall, security had to be called in to control the
mob.

In 2003, Pride announced it was holding a middleweight grand
prix that would span two tournaments. The first round of matches
would be in August; the semifinals and finals would be held in Novem-

ber. As a UFC fighter, if I agreed to compete and won in August, I was taking myself out of the UFC rotation until the end of the year. I couldn't wait to sign up. I needed the action. Besides, I was handcuffed until the Tito-Randy fight for the UFC light heavyweight title, which was scheduled for September 26, 2003.

My first Pride fight was against Alistair Overeem at the Saitama Super Arena in Saitama, Japan. This was the first round of a three-round tournament that spanned four months. Still, thirty-seven thousand people packed the arena to the rafters to see the seven-fight card. Overeem was a good challenge for me. He's a six-five Dutchman who specialized in Muay Thai, a form of kickboxing. While we'd been MMA fighters for the same number of years, he'd had six more fights than me and had lost only three. At times in 2000 and in 2002 he was basically fighting once a month. By the time we met, he had won twelve straight fights, with only two of them lasting into the second round. All of them ended by a submission, TKO, or knockout. There wasn't a judge's decision in the bunch. Regardless of his skill level, I knew I was getting into the ring with a seasoned vet, a guy who could stand with me, kick with me, and give me a good fight.

So imagine my surprise when I knocked him out at 3:09 in the first round. We came out punching and kicking pretty hard. He even connected on a shot with my head that cut me pretty deep. Within the first minute of the fight I could feel blood trickling through my Mohawk and down onto my forehead. But when he went for another knee to my head following a combination by me, I took him down. Then I took full advantage of the Pride rules. I had him facedown and underneath my chest, so I took my knee and went to town on his head.

Overeem has long legs and got himself out of the bottom position and back on his feet. But I still had his upper body locked up. So I kept kneeing his ribs and his abdomen, which were left unprotected. For a minute he escaped and showed some life, connecting on a looping right, then giving me a pretty good shot with his knee to the body. But

I locked him up again to stop his momentum, and when we separated, I hit him with a straight right and he tried to shake it off as if it didn't hurt him. He even smiled at me. But he looked like a different fighter. He looked as if he were done. He tried a spinning kick that missed and almost knocked him off balance. Then he threw a wild punch and could barely get his hands up. I knew it was over. He had spent all his adrenaline. I hit him with a big right that landed smack in the middle of his forehead. His hands fell to his side, his head dropped down, and I went in to finish.

If you're watching on TV or in the stands, this is the moment when mixed martial arts looks the scariest. It's like those *When Animals Attack!* shows on TV. We see someone who is wounded or vulnerable, and defying all human compassion, we go after the guy. But as a fighter, that's exactly what you are looking for. There should be no hesitation when you see an opponent teetering on the edge of consciousness. You have to finish him. And that's what I did to Overeem. I moved in with two more big rights; then I kneed him in the head; then I threw another combination. The flurry of punches lasted less than ten seconds. Then the tall man just folded up, like a building that was collapsing from the bottom to the top.

Afterward Dana, who was in town for the tourney, ran into the ring and gave me a hug. He was happy for me, of course. But, with Ortiz-Couture just a month away, he was also glad to know his number one contender was ready for whoever won.

Being a fighter doesn't make you a thug.

The Iceman death stare. I was born with it.

My early wrestling days.

My wrestling strategy: Take the guy down.

I train to be a winner, and I never aim for anything less.

From my early days at the Pit.

I couldn't get enough sparring at the Pit.

A man can never have too many belts.

Jeremy Horn may have won UFC 19, but I stopped him in UFC 54.

UFC 29 vs. Jeff Monson. It was a kicking match, and Monson wouldn't put his hands down. But I still won by decision.

I never show mercy, even when a guy is down. Just ask Vitor Belfort (who lost that night).

My adrenaline was on fire after winning against Ortiz in UFC 47. (That's him knocked out in the left-hand corner.)

The sweet victory of winning against Couture in UFC 52. I was the best light-heavyweight fighter in the world, and I had the belt to prove it.

Entering the Octagon with the music pumping and the lights going and all the fans screaming and cheering—makes me want to win (and I did that night).

UFC 57. Couture was down, but I was still going strong. I eventually knocked him out.

I took the title from Couture in 2005 and then knocked him out a second time almost a year later. It feels good to be the champ.

UFC 76. Jardine won, but you'd never guess it from looking at his face.

CHAPTER 29

IT NEVER PAYS TO MOUTH OFF

'M NOT SURE WHY TITO WAS AFRAID TO FIGHT ME but wouldn't hesitate to fight Randy. Maybe he felt he had to fight or else he'd become even more of a joke as a champ than he already was. Or maybe it was the money: Tito was getting $125,000 for fighting and another $50K if he won. Randy was getting $105,000 for showing up and a $70,000 win bonus.

The fight was held at the Mandalay Bay Events Center in front of seventy-six hundred people. And as he always did walking into the Octagon, Randy looked calm and collected. In fact, he was grinning from ear to ear, as if he had a secret that no one else knew. Tito came in looking as intense as he ever had, and once he was in the cage, he did that bounce he does, lifting his knees up to his waist while jumping as high as he can. Maybe he does it to get himself pumped or to get the blood flowing. But he ends up looking like a character in *Donkey Kong*. It definitely didn't do much to scare off Randy, who just kept smiling, as happy as could be.

Unlike Tito's title fight with Ken Shamrock, which started out fast and furious, this one felt more calculated. Both fighters came out slow, feeling each other out. Then, around 2:30 into the fight, Tito tried to get in a few knee shots. But he got in too close and left himself vulnerable, because Randy took him down. For a minute Randy had the better position and tried choking Tito out, but it was still too early in the match and Tito had too much energy for Randy to finish him off. Tito slithered away and tried to box with Randy for a minute or so. But, again, Randy used his superior wrestling skills to take Tito down. With two first-round takedowns Randy not only won the round, he had shaken Tito's confidence. You could see in his eyes that he was rethinking his strategy. No one during his title defenses had so easily put him on his back. Now Randy had done it twice. This was an interesting fight.

Clearly rattled, Tito came out in the second round with a high kick, trying to catch Randy off guard. It didn't work. Randy deftly avoided the kick and soon had Tito on the mat again. This time he forced him against the fence and administered the kind of ground-and-pound he had given me in our first fight. Tito was utterly defenseless, both in that instant and, as everyone watching began to realize, against Randy's superior fighting skills. At the end of the second round, unable to get anything going physically, Tito was reduced to yelling at Randy from across the cage, trying to get in his head with some trash talking. It didn't work. Randy was up two rounds to none.

When Tito began the third with a lunging attempt at a takedown, Randy sprawled, which sent both fighters scrambling for position. Somehow, Tito ended up on top, only to have Randy reverse. When they got to their feet, it didn't last long, as Randy again threw Tito to the mat. This fight, like a lot of fights, had a pattern. Randy was happy keeping Tito on the ground and put him there every chance he could. He wasn't all that interested in striking, and once he realized the fight was his, he had no reason to take that kind of chance. Besides, he was scoring points and doing damage. He was neck-cranking Tito against the fence while delivering elbows, forearms, and punches. Randy is a freak of nature. At forty he looked stronger and hungrier and better prepared than Tito, who is twelve years younger. Tito just seemed exhausted and frustrated by Randy's constant ability to foil his game plan. Round three went to Randy.

As long as he avoided a knockout, Randy was going to win this fight. Tito's corner knew that, too, which was why they were screaming for him to strike Randy hard as soon as the round began. But Tito's moves had no impact. Randy took him down again and delivered some more ground-and-pound. It was becoming a familiar sight. Things were so bad for Tito that Randy nearly choked him out. The ref was right on top of the action, ready to call it, looking for a sign Tito was gone. He escaped, but was forced against the fence again, where Randy threw punch after punch that connected.

In the fifth Tito came out swinging again, but it was no use. Randy had him on his back by the middle of the round. As soon as Tito got back up, Randy threw him down again. It was unbelievable how much Tito was dominated in this fight. He spent the entire match either trying to escape Randy's grappling moves or on his back, protecting himself from punches. In one final, drastic move Tito rolled over and attempted a kneebar. But Randy avoided the hold, and with Tito's butt exposed, Randy pretended to spank him. He actually pulled his hand back and acted as if he were punishing a child. It was hysterical, as though the Hall of Famer were giving the young punk a lesson. This is how you act before a fight. Bam. This is how you win a fight. Bam. This is how you completely demoralize an opponent. Bam. So keep your trap shut and, from now on, focus on fighting. Setting yourself up for embarrassment like that is one more reason why it never pays to mouth off.

Tito must have learned something. After the fight was over and Randy was declared the winner by a unanimous decision, Tito grabbed his belt and wrapped it around the waist of the new UFC light heavyweight champion.

The only question for me was, what would my next fight be? A rematch with Randy? Or a grudge match with Tito?

CHAPTER 30

NEVER LET 'EM BREATHE

BUT, BEFORE EITHER OF THOSE FIGHTS, I HAD TO finish my business with Pride. After beating Overeem in August, I was scheduled to fight Quinton "Rampage" Jackson in Japan in early November, just six weeks after the Tito-Randy fight. As a fighter, Rampage had a style pretty similar to mine. We were about the same size. And he began as a wrestler in high school. He even planned on becoming a pro wrestler when he finished school, before moving over to MMA. And while he was good on the ground, he liked to stay on his feet and trade punches. Or, more accurately, throw punches and knock the snot out of whoever was standing in front of him.

Rampage had never fought in the UFC. He claims it was because he was such good friends with Tito and didn't want a potential fight to get in the way of that. At least Tito had been able to convince one potential opponent that being buddies was a good reason not to fight. Instead, Rampage came up through these small MMA tournaments such as King of the Cage, which used to take place almost entirely at casinos on Indian reservations. That's another way we were similar: The way we came up, we clearly just wanted to fight; against whom, for whom, in front of whom didn't matter. If it took place on a street corner with no one watching, that would have been fine with us. Getting paid was a bonus.

Rampage's big break came when he was invited to fight in Pride in Japan. He was matched up against one of the country's most popular wrestlers, who was a Pride veteran. Rampage was raw, but he was tough. For most of the first round, no matter how many times he was taken down or how many joint locks were attempted on him or how exhausting every choke attempt was, he kept wrestling his way free, often lifting his opponent off the ground and slamming him back down. Finally, he submitted to a choke. But by then he had won over the crowd and earned a deal with the Pride execs to fight for them full-time. Over the next two years he fought in six of the eleven Pride tournaments. He had battled and beaten such guys as Kevin Randleman and Murilo Bustamante, just as I had. As far as fighters went, we were as evenly matched as two could be.

Pride Final Conflict, which is what they were calling this round of the tournament, took place in the Tokyo Dome. More than sixty-seven thousand people were in the audience. For some perspective, that's more than most baseball, basketball, or hockey games, and even heavyweight title fights in boxing. It's about how many people pay to see the Super Bowl in person every year. From the last row of the dome we looked like two action figures moving around on a place mat. But people didn't care, as long as they were inside. The enthusiasm for MMA was unparalleled.

While I was the bigger name in the UFC, this was Rampage's home turf. And you could see that just from the introductions. I was lifted on a platform through a hole in a stage, like some pop star elevating above the crowd before a show. But my intro music was generic, the lights stayed on, and I had no entourage with me. I walked pretty casually down the steps of the stage toward the ring. I even smiled for the camera that was tracking me the entire time. You'd think there's no way you can be fighting in front of that many people and, at least at first, not be jacked up with adrenaline. But I felt calm and re-

Walking into the ring with the crowd going wild really gets my adrenaline pumping.

laxed. I just walked around the ring shaking my arms, trying to get loose.

Rampage, however, had an entrance. For him the lights went down, a rap song he had picked out blasted through the dome's loudspeakers, colored beams of light filled the stadium, and the crowd roared. I was wearing flip-flops, shorts, and a jersey when I came into the ring. Rampage had on a black T-shirt and camouflage pants, with his entourage dressed to match. He also wore his signature heavy chain around his neck. This wasn't a silver necklace, but a real chain, the kind used to keep big rigs from separating. It hung to his belly button. But the best effect was on his face: It was a leather mask with plastic flames flaring out from the sides.

When he was finally at the top of the stage and had the crowd's attention, he pointed his lips to the ceiling and let out a yelp, like a wolf that was howling at the moon. He slowly made his way toward the ring, and every few feet he'd stop to howl. I had gotten to know Rampage that week while promoting the fight, and we liked each other. But I wasn't really expecting this. It was interesting. Even if it did take him a while to finally get to the ring.

While I slipped off my shoes and peeled off my shirt, it took him another few minutes to get undressed. Tonight he was wearing camouflage shorts. But, as an American fighting in Japan, he's also been known to wear Uncle Sam shorts, like the ones that Apollo Creed wore in *Rocky*. You could tell he was pumped to fight. Instead of slipping through the ropes, he jumped over the top and into the ring.

I had worked with Dana a lot before this fight. I actually spent a month at a training camp in Vegas rather than working out at The Pit. It was a big fight for us. Plenty of fans thought Pride was a tougher league than the UFC because it had longer rounds and fewer rules. Because of that rivalry, we were anxious to prove we had higher-quality fighters. There's a great story that Dana was so sure that I—and the UFC—would win that he bet Pride's boss $250,000 on me. The real story is that he bet $250,000 I would beat Wanderlei Silva, because that's whom he expected me to fight. No one thought I'd be going against Rampage.

While I was training, Dana and I did a lot of scouting on Rampage. For a lot of guys that means going to their fights in person or watching them on pay-per-view. But when I'm doing that, I like to go as a fan. I get to as many UFC cards as I can, and when I'm watching, it feels as if I'm just a guy lucky enough to be in the crowd. I can feel my body twitching with the moves; then I start to throw punches at the air. It's easy to get pumped up from the music and the action. I can understand why the crowd is so frenzied when I'm on the other side in the cage. It's fun at home, too. And for a lot of fights I'll have some buddies over to watch. But I rarely sit still long enough to see the whole card.

My scouting is done by watching film. For Rampage that meant watching film of his previous fights. We put together a pretty detailed game plan. In his fight against Bustamante that August, he got caught in a lot of submission moves. He escaped, but it showed that he was getting better as a fighter. Also, because of the trouble I had had against Couture, we felt Rampage would rather take this fight to the mat than stand and strike. So I wanted to get in a lot of low kicks and do some damage to his legs, making him more fatigued and making it harder to lunge the way it's necessary when you want to grapple.

When the fight began, we exchanged a lot of jabs in the center of the ring. Surprisingly, he didn't shoot for my legs at all. He was standing around, happy to make this a boxing match, which wasn't what we had expected while training. We both tagged each other early. I got in a strong high left kick, and he got me on the head with two lefts. Then he came with another left hook that knocked me on my heels. It definitely stunned me. It's when I get hurt or surprised that I'm at my most dangerous. I've got a strong chin—which comes from years of fighting on the street—and I don't get my bell rung easily. Most fighters hesitate, just for a moment, when they think they've tagged someone pretty hard, as if they are waiting to see if the guy falls. That's when I take the chance to attack. So when I fell back on my heels a bit, I immediately came back with a combination that got the crowd into it.

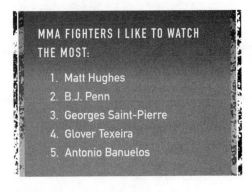

MMA FIGHTERS I LIKE TO WATCH THE MOST:

1. Matt Hughes
2. B.J. Penn
3. Georges Saint-Pierre
4. Glover Texeira
5. Antonio Banuelos

I wasn't throwing any leg kicks and had basically abandoned our game plan. He caught me with another combo and I almost fell walking into the ropes. Then he followed up with a right that landed smack on my face, and it stopped me in my tracks. We were both just throwing wild punches. Since the fight began there hadn't been many jabs, but rather a lot of knockout blows that didn't knock anyone out. Already, I felt exhausted, which was one reason I couldn't kick. I was too tired. I couldn't get my leg up with any force. It felt as if for every combo he delivered, I'd follow up with just one good punch.

Rampage may have won, but not without getting a little roughed up.

The first five minutes of the fight came at a slower pace than anyone had anticipated. And neither of us had tried going to the mat yet.
At the midway point of the first round he had me in the corner and
was delivering a lot of knees and punches to my body. That's what you
want to do when you've got the upper hand in the corner, especially as
a fight nears the end of a round and an opponent is fatigued. Never let
'em breathe.

Then he tried to pick me up and slam me down, but I escaped. To
that point, no one had gotten the upper hand physically after a lot of
trading punches. But after I wiggled out of his grasp, he caught me
with three big hooks to my face and body that had me backpedaling all
the way across the ring. Then he got me leaning the way he needed
and lifted me up into the air for a body slam. You could already hear
the crowd before I hit the ground. It had been waiting for a move like
this. While the impact was huge, the damage was minimal. I slipped
away and was standing again within moments. And the crowd, appre-

ciative of all the MMA skills, cheered just as loudly when I got back on my feet as it did when I landed on my back. But now he was on the offensive. At the end of the round he knocked me down with a left. Rampage moved in for the kill and had me in a vulnerable position on the mat. If the round hadn't ended, there's no telling whether I would have escaped again.

I was breathing heavily, bleeding, and looked exhausted as I made my way back to my corner. Meanwhile, Rampage, who had been winning at the end of the first round, was so tired he knelt for a few seconds with his hands on the ropes before getting up and trudging back to his corner. It was truly a back-and-forth with two evenly matched fighters. Pride couldn't have asked for a better battle. Former UFC heavyweight Bas Rutten, who was announcing the fight on television, said it already ranked as one of his top three favorite fights.

I hadn't done any damage to his legs at all in the first round and needed to find a way to tire him out. Early in the second round, I had him in position in the corner. My arms were locked around his head and I tried to work a guillotine, but I couldn't get the right grip. Instead I leaned my weight on him, trying to make him use his energy to hold us both up. I heard my corner yelling, "Stick to the head, stick to the head," but I wasn't following their instructions. I didn't do enough knees to his body to take his wind away, either. He escaped and we ended up in the middle of the ring trading punches. But mine were lacking any snap. It's hard to respect a guy's punches when there's no power at the end of them.

From the middle of the ring he threw a nasty uppercut. It didn't connect, but came close enough that I fell back. He mounted me and had me facedown with my arms spread. I moved into position to get back on my feet—which drew another round of applause—but he immediately lifted me and threw me down again. That drew even more applause. Now it was a crazy pace, with him coming after me and me just trying to ward him off. When I went down again, he pounced. He was throwing body punches and punches to my head. He had one hand on my neck and chin, pushing my head back while I lay flat on my back, and with the other he was going to town. With more than two minutes left in the round, I had no defense. My guard was down, my arms were providing no resistance. He threw close to thirty punches, all of them connecting with my head or my body. Then the ref ended it.

I wasn't sure why. I hadn't tapped out and wasn't unconscious. Then I realized Hack had thrown in the towel. From his point of view, I was getting pummeled, wasn't improving my position, and had nothing left. Even if I had gotten out of the trouble I was in, the result may have been the same.

Looking back to before the fight began, I had already made a fatal mistake. I should never have worked out at the camp in Vegas instead of The Pit. It might have felt as if I were getting a good workout, but it couldn't compare to what I'd have been doing if John were kicking my ass every day. Of course, I didn't know this until it was too late. I wasn't in the right shape and I pretty much ran out of gas.

But something good did come out of the loss. I think seeing me lose gave Tito some confidence that I wasn't so tough after all. Maybe he thought he could beat me, because, by the end of the year, he had finally agreed to fight me.

CHAPTER 31

IT'S NOT ABOUT STRENGTH; IT'S ABOUT STRENGTH OVER A LONG TIME

T LAST, IT WAS ON. THAT WAS EVEN WHAT THEY w e r e calling the card that Tito and I were set to headline in April of 2004, UFC 47: It's On. At this point, I didn't care that he no longer held the light heavyweight title. I've always fought for more than titles, anyway. And I didn't care that he was slated to make more just for fighting—$125,000 (plus a $50,000 win bonus)—than I would make for fighting and winning ($50,000 for each). And I didn't care if it was because my stature was diminished in his eyes after I'd lost to Rampage. I didn't need him to respect me or fear me. In fact, both of those things might have gotten in the way of setting this thing up. If he thought I was a chump and that got him into the cage, fine by me. After nearly two years of his bullshit; after nearly two years of his ducking me; after nearly two years of his claiming we were too good friends to fight and that I was stabbing him in the back just because I was willing to get in the cage with him, we were finally going to settle it. The time for talking was over. At least, I thought it was.

One of the great things about the UFC bosses is how well they create drama around a fight. The postfight interviews are usually as full of fury and emotion as the fights themselves. It's not just the fighters doing the talking either. It may looked staged, but at times UFC

I love pointing at the crowd after winning a fight and hearing them get all fired up. The UFC is all about the fans.

fighters with bouts coming up will jump into the cage, grab the microphone, and start talking smack about their opponents, firing up the crowd, themselves, and those watching at home. That's part of the culture Dana has created, for the better. We're fucking fighters, and if we're moved by the passion of a fight to get into the cage in street clothes and start talking about beating the crap out of someone, we can do it. It's good for us, it's good for the card, and it's good for the UFC.

Of course, plenty of other times postfight confrontations are staged, or at least planned, as with me and Tito after UFC 46 on January 31, 2004. We were both in Vegas to watch Randy put his light heavyweight title on the line against Vitor. (To give you an idea of how much the Randy fight had cost me—and how much I lost by fighting for the interim title instead of the real title against Tito—I was making $80,000 less in guaranteed money than Vitor was to be paid for fighting Randy. I've never been about the money as a fighter, but if I were looking for one more excuse to want to bash Tito's head in, there it was.)

The fight didn't last long, with Vitor winning by a TKO after he caught Randy above his eye and Randy couldn't stop bleeding. The doctor called it. Afterward, Joe Rogan called me and Tito into the Octagon. As soon as Tito walked out, people started booing. The guy had not only lost his title but, by avoiding a fight with me, had lost the respect of a lot of MMA fans. Meanwhile, I was still an underdog, the workingman's fighter. I hadn't been given my title shot yet. And now that Vitor had won, Randy would be in line for a rematch before I'd get my next chance. I honestly think people were rooting for me as much because of the way Tito acted and because he had shafted me as they were because they liked my fighting style. So while they booed him, I got some cheers.

When we got to the center of the cage, Joe said to Tito, "There's been a lot of talk, a lot of emotion. Tito, tell us what is going to happen on April second."

Tito answered, "Iceman, what's up? With your belly it looks more like Snowman. I can't wait for April second. This fight is finally going to happen. I am going to give you a beating. Let the beating begin."

Then Joe looked at me and said, "Chuck, what do you have to say?"

"This guy has been talking crap for a long time," I said. "He's the one who has been talking crap. He stepped in the ring after I beat Vitor and started saying he was going to kick my butt. Well, he'd better have been practicing his wrestling, because I know he is not man enough to stand in the middle of this ring and strike with me. And if he is, I'll announce to everyone here, if he is man enough to stand in the middle of this ring and strike with me, I'll knock his ass out. And he knows it." Then I pointed right at him. The crowd went nuts. Tito tried to respond but was drowned out by the cheering and the booing. Finally he just walked away and flashed the crowd the finger as he left the cage. The whole confrontation lasted nearly as long as the Couture-Vitor fight. And it may have been more exciting. Even though no title would be on the line, there wasn't a more anticipated fight in the UFC at that moment than Tito and me.

For most fights I'm lucky if I can get eight weeks of training in. But this one was scheduled so far in advance, I had ten to twelve weeks to get ready. My training had more of a slow build, which I liked on two levels: I knew I'd be in peak physical condition, but I also knew I'd have so much pent-up energy and readiness to fight that it wouldn't take long to finish Tito off.

I wasn't in great shape for Rampage and I wasn't in great shape for Randy. So, more than ever, I was committed to my cardio for Tito. I felt we were equal wrestlers, and he might be better with submission moves, but I had the advantage standing up and in punching power. That meant I needed my wind. If I can bench four hundred pounds and squat six hundred, but I can't perform aerobic exercise at peak physical levels for half an hour, I won't last two minutes in the ring. Plenty of cut, muscle-on-muscle guys have stepped into the cage, and if they don't land a knockout punch early in the fight, it's over for them. They were so committed to power they didn't see past the initial rush of adrenaline, when a fight settles down and your body feels as if it's carrying double your weight. Your arms feel heavy, your legs feel heavy, and it's hard to breathe. And that's just when you're dancing. Trying to evade a punch or even taking a punch can bring on the fatigue even faster. Just breathing can be a challenge in this scenario. It sucks to get to that point in a fight, and it's immediately a

I always push myself to the limit when training.

reminder that you've got to train harder next time, because you never want to feel that way again. I've read about players in the NFL who practice a yoga technique called body armor. It's when they take deep and slow breaths, all while their instructor is hitting them in the stomach and the side with a bamboo pole. The idea is to teach yourself how to regulate your breathing even while being attacked. Not easy.

Without good cardio, every fighter will lose most of his strength— as much as 80 percent of it—early in a fight. It's not about strength; it's about strength over a long time. So I did all the things that push my body to its limit. I ran on the beach endlessly, building up my leg strength while struggling to dig out of the sand. They had me running sprints, playing catch with a football, running patterns, then hauling ass back to the guy who was passing me the ball. I need help keeping conditioning drills fun. I really hate straight running—not because of the pain, but because it is so boring. I did the wall ball, where I take a

125-pound medicine ball, throw it against a wooden beam, and make it bounce back at least three feet. It's hard enough picking up the medicine ball. But to make it bounce back is brutal. Then do it five times. For three sets. With just a minute of rest in between. This built up my shoulders and helped my punching power. I would push a wheelbarrow uphill with two hundred pounds, which helped with my stamina, but going downhill it strengthened my grip and my forearms and my shoulders. I knew Tito would try to take me down, and these muscles were what would help me keep him off me. I did the sledgehammer drill, swinging a sixteen-pound sledgehammer into a tire one hundred times, again to improve or maintain my punching power.

Notice how so many of these drills don't use machines or high-tech weights. This is The Pit way, man. It's hard-core. Nothing in a gym can beat pushing two hundred pounds in a wheelbarrow up a hill. I did push-ups, with my hands in different positions and at different speeds. I shadowboxed, jumped rope, hit the bag. Every day, twice a day, for two hours each session, I pushed myself to the limit.

I didn't ignore lifting weights, either. On the days I wasn't with John, here's what I told *Muscle & Fitness* magazine my workout schedule in the gym looked like:

MONDAY: DELTS, CHEST, BACK

	SETS	REPS
Explosive standing military press	3	6
Lateral raise	2	15–20
Tri-set	2	

	SETS	REPS
Flat-bench dumbbell press		12–15 to failure
Incline dumbbell fly		12–15 to failure
Push-up		To failure
Tri-set	2	
Bent-over barbell row		12–15 to failure
Front pull-down		11
Dumbbell pull-over		15–20

Finish with crunches, lying leg raises, decline twisting crunches, and 10–20 minutes of full-body stretching.

WEDNESDAY: LEGS

	SETS	REPS
Squat	3	15–20
Barbell lunge	2	15–20
Barbell side lunge	1	15–20
Compound set	2	
Lying or seated leg curl		12–15 to failure
Romanian dead lift		12–15

Finish with crunches, lying leg raises, decline twisting crunches, and 10–20 minutes of full-body stretching.

FRIDAY: ARMS

	SETS	REPS
Barbell clean	3	6
Tri-set	2	15–20
Barball curl		15–20
Reverse barbell curl		15–20
Hammer curl		15–20
Tri-set	2	15–20
Lying French press		15–20
Seated dumbbell extension		15–20
Cable press-down		15–20

I'd rest sixty seconds between all compound sets and tri-sets. On some days I did a circuit, where I'd do three lifts; then I'd run out on a mat and do sprints, sprawls, and a bunch of other cardio exercises. Then I'd come back and lift again and repeat the circuit.

I took one day off a week, Sunday. Saturday, however, wasn't exactly a light day. That was core-body day. I would do sit-ups throughout the week, but that was just to keep me warm and working so I didn't stiffen up. On Saturdays I had to do core work with a medicine ball, as hard as I could for five minutes at a time; then I'd get a minute of rest. I would do sit-ups where someone throws the ball at my stomach when I go down and I have to throw it back on the way up. I'd do sit-ups from the mat and I'd have to twist at my waist with the ball as well. I also did a lot of plank exercises. Looking at them, they don't look all that tough, because you're basically completely still. But that's what makes them so hard. You get into the push-up position, but you put your elbows on the ground instead of your hands. Then you keep your body as straight as possible and pull your abs in toward your spine, as if you were about to get hit in the gut. Then hold it. For as long as you possibly can. You'll feel it in your sides, up the middle of your stomach, and in your back.

This was a brutal day, but conceivably my most important, for two reasons: (1) I'm a knockout puncher, and all the power in a punch comes from your hips and the torque you can generate. That power is developed when you work on your core muscles. (2) The five-minute intervals were key as well. That's how long a round in a UFC fight lasts. I needed to be trained to go as hard as I could for those five minutes so I knew I could last a round.

Everything I do while training is designed to simulate ring conditions. I aim for high-repetition, explosive lifting, with the goal being to have the capacity to explode powerfully over an extended time. Doing a one-rep max is not going to do much for me. I need to have explosive power for fifteen or twenty minutes. I told *Muscle & Fitness* magazine, "In the ring, I might exert a tremendous amount of energy or strength performing a throw, tackle, knockout combo, or escape, but I'm not going to get a 90-to-120-second rest period to recover and regain strength. I still have to perform. So that's the way I train."

One drill Hack came up with after my first fight with Randy, probably because he could not believe what kind of shape I was in, was a rowing and wrestling circuit. On a basic rowing machine, he'd have me go full tilt, making me row eight hundred meters in less than two and a half minutes. Then I'd have to roll off the machine and onto a mat, where I'd wrestle someone for two and a half minutes more. It would be five minutes of breathless agony. Seriously, it sucked. Then I'd get a minute's rest. Then Hack would have me do it four more times. The rowing would get my shoulders and lats into shape, while the wrestling would help my stamina and strength and keep me in wrestling condition for a fight.

It was hard enough rolling off the machine and onto the mat to grapple with someone in a standard position. But half the time Hack had me starting out on the bottom and made me try to wrestle my way back to my feet. If you haven't been doing that drill for a while, it's a week or so before you don't feel like puking. I hate the wheelbarrow drill more than any of the rest, but this is a pretty close second.

I get so geared toward peaking for a fight that I even change my schedule. I'm a night owl by nature. But fights happen late, as late as 9:00 P.M. Vegas time. I want that to feel like the middle of my day, which means I wake up later than usual—around 11:00 A.M.—and go to bed later than usual—around 4:00 A.M. My diet is reduced to cottage cheese, fruit, nuts, grilled chicken and salmon, steamed vegetables, protein shakes, and occasionally some sashimi or sushi. Someone makes my meals and sends them to me in boxes, so all I have to do is pull one out and heat it up. I follow a 40-30-30 plan: 40 percent carbs, 30 percent protein, and 30 percent fat. I also take supplements such as glucosamine, which helps rebuild my cartilage and wards off arthritis, and MSM, a sulfur-based pill that gives me more energy and rebuilds everything from cells to bone. And, of course, I load up on water.

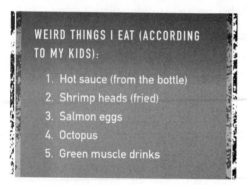

WEIRD THINGS I EAT (ACCORDING TO MY KIDS):

1. Hot sauce (from the bottle)
2. Shrimp heads (fried)
3. Salmon eggs
4. Octopus
5. Green muscle drinks

The deeper I get into training, the less I go out partying, until I've completely removed alcohol from the menu. That doesn't mean I don't go out. In the days leading up to most of my fights, I'm out until midnight or one in the morning. But I'm just drinking water. What's the difference if I sit around my hotel room playing poker on my PSP or if I go out to a club for a few hours after dinner? I wouldn't be sleeping either way. I'll work out from eight thirty to ten at night, then have dinner and go out for a couple of hours. Football players always talk about how the toughest games they play are in prime time, whether it's *Monday Night Football* or the Super Bowl. They're so used to playing in the middle of the day they don't know what to do with themselves or how to recalibrate their schedule. It's the same thing with fighters. By the time I step into the cage for the main event, I need to know my body is going to be comfortable fighting at that time of night.

And before the fight with Tito, I was feeling very comfortable.

CHAPTER 32

WHEN YOU GET AN OPPORTUNITY TO HAVE A GOOD TIME, YOU'VE GOT TO TAKE IT

WHEN THE FIGHTERS GET TOGETHER TO SHOOT those promo posters for Pride and UFC cards, it's usually pretty friendly. Look on YouTube and you'll find video of Quinton Jackson and me joking around and laughing while doing the publicity shots for our first matchup. Often we won't even be in the same place. They'll take my picture in one place and my opponent's in another, then put the poster together.

But Dana, who's a master at building tension and drama leading up to a fight, wanted Tito and me together. He flew us both into Vegas, then had us in a studio, posing nose-to-nose for two hours. We did not speak once. Not a hello, not a how're-you-doing, not even an I'm-going-to-kick-your-butt. I didn't care; it didn't bother me one bit. I had nothing to say to the guy. We'd just stare, less than two inches from each other's face, and look as nasty as we possibly could. I don't think either of us had to try very hard. And I know neither of us was faking it.

I had been waiting so long for this fight, and training so hard, that by the time it finally rolled around, I was as relaxed as I could possibly be. I didn't see any way I could lose or not knock him out. Dana kept telling me he couldn't wait for me to "smash Tito's fucking head in."

The tension between Tito and me wasn't just posing for the camera. I wanted to fight, and soon I'd get the chance.

He even made me promise that, once I won, I would give him my shorts and my gloves so he could put them up in his house.

It had been a while since Tito and I had sparred together. One of the last times was up in Big Bear, where I had hit him so hard he refused to get up and Dana just berated him. That was when he was the champ, the face of the UFC. Times were different now. He knew he had never gotten the best of me. I couldn't see any reason that would change now that we were doing it for real. I could tell he was afraid of me. If he were the champ, he would probably still be ducking me. Now, he understood the only way to regain his status as the ultimate ultimate fighter was to destroy me in front of a huge crowd. He had no other options.

Here's how chill I was in the hours before the fight. A buddy of mine and Tito's stopped by Tito's hotel room to say hello that afternoon and see how he was doing. I remember him telling me that Tito was pretty amped up, as if he were anxious, nervous, and worried about the fight. My buddy couldn't help but laugh as he gave me the details back in my room. That's because he walked in to give me the news while I was wrestling with two girls on my bed.

Now might be a good time to explain a couple things regarding me and the ladies. Since you bought this book, I'm guessing you want to know about the world of an ultimate fighter—the whole world—and not just the fighting and the training and the brutality. And attention from women is a nice benefit of the job I've chosen. I hesitated to put any of these stories in here because I don't want to come off like some kind of Wilt Chamberlain bragging about his conquests. But this is a part of the extreme, ultimate fighter lifestyle that is pretty awesome. And I figured you'd want to read some of those stories, too.

It would be hard to find anyone who loves and appreciates women more than I do. That's how a lot of the people I've dated—including the moms of my kids—become good friends of mine after we break up. I'm a nice guy, I like to think, and once you're my friend, I'll do anything I can for you, within reason. And when breakups happen, I'm pretty honest about why. I'll stay friends with my exes because, usually, there are reasons that I liked them; there are reasons I decided I wanted to spend so much time with them when we were dating. Just because things don't work out doesn't mean a lot of what I liked about someone has disappeared. A lot of times, they see it the same way, and we can move on with our lives without too much drama.

I'm not into drama. If I wanted headaches and hassles and stress, I'd be an accountant. I chose this life because it's fun. And I want to take advantage of all of this carefree, have-fun, do-what-you-want-to-do life I've set up. No matter how hard I train or how seriously I take a fight and my career, when you get an opportunity to have a good time, you've got to take it. And I don't buy into the old cliché that you've got to abstain before a big fight. So if I relaxed with a couple of girls before the Tito fight, no harm. One time, a couple of hours before a title fight, Dana made one of his incessant calls to check on me. I answered, "Can't talk now, I've got two girls in the shower, gotta go." Sure, it freaked him out. But I had a good time.

Before the Tito fight, after the girls left, it was just me, Antonio, and my brother Dan hanging out in my room. I was in the bathroom shaving my body—a lot of fighters do that before a fight because it makes it more difficult for opponents to grab us. Besides, it hurts like a bitch when someone is trying to get a grip on your leg and he's pulling out clumps of hair because his hands are too sweaty to hold on. Antonio and Dan were listening to some music, and we were all yelling back and forth about what we were going to do that night after the fight. There was no tension, no fear, no worry about the fight. I wasn't thinking about strategy or how to stop his submission holds or how to keep him on his feet so I could knock his ass out. If you took a snapshot at that moment, we would have looked like three buddies getting ready to go out for a night of partying in Vegas. And that's what we were. I just happened to have the biggest fight of my life to finish before all that happened.

I wanted someone to talk to while I was in the bathroom, so I asked Antonio to come in. He helped me shave my legs and my back. Then Dan was trying to tell us something but we couldn't hear him, so we told him to come into the bathroom. He walked in, saw Antonio working on my body with the razor, and said, "What the hell are you guys doing?"

I don't know what it looked like, but I knew what I was doing: getting ready for a fight.

CHAPTER 33

WHEN YOU'VE GOT A GUY DAZED, KNOCK HIM OUT

I FELT GREAT HEADING INTO THE TITO FIGHT. I COULDN'T have been calmer or more sure of myself. I may have felt that way if I hadn't had the company of a couple of ladies before the fight, but why take the chance? Plus, it was a good crowd. George Clooney was there. By rule, anywhere Clooney is must be the coolest place to be on that night. Michael Clarke Duncan was there, Joey Pants—the guy who lost his head in *The Sopranos*—was there, too. So were Randy Couture and Ken Shamrock and just about every other big name in the UFC.

When I entered the Octagon, I smiled. I was thrilled—after two years of Tito's using every excuse he could think of to avoid me—that we were finally going to fight. So much had happened in those two years regarding our popularity. I had become a crowd favorite. Tito was now getting booed. Dana has said that he'd made a lot of mistakes when he'd first started running the UFC, but the biggest one was backing Tito Ortiz. When he entered the cage and did his warm-up lap and pulled off another punk move by giving me a little bump, anyone could see why Dana felt that way.

Before most of his fights Tito rips the TEAM PUNISHMENT beanie he wears during his introduction off his head and throws it into the crowd.

Two years earlier someone might have grabbed that and either framed it to be hung in their house or put it on eBay. But tonight, when he tossed it over the side of the cage, someone caught it, then threw it right back at him. That was fucking classic.

While I might have been feeling good, I think Hack was pretty anxious. He offered me a water bottle while we were waiting for the prefight hoopla to settle down. When I said I didn't need it, he drank most of it without taking a breath.

In the final moments before the fight, Tito was doing that stupid Donkey Kong bounce, where he jumps as high as he can and lifts his knees to his chest so it looks as if he's about five feet off the ground. He just kept staring at me the whole time. And I kept staring back, looking as cold and vacant as I could. My natural disposition is to look nasty when I'm not smiling, so I can intimidate without really trying.

Finally, Big John McCarthy, the fight ref, called us to the center of the Octagon. Big John epitomizes how popular the UFC has become. He's a Los Angeles cop and Brazilian jujitsu black belt who studied with Rorion Gracie. He has officiated at more than five hundred MMA fights and helped rewrite the rules for the sport when it was getting resanctioned by all the state athletic commissions early in this century. He refereed his first fight in UFC 2 and has been a central figure in all our fights since. He's got a phrase synonymous with the start of every match—"Let's get it on." He's got his own Web site, his own mixed martial arts school, and his own Big John merchandise. Only in the UFC, where the fans are as rabid as they are, could a ref become the kind of brand name that he's become.

At the center of the cage Big John told us, "Fight clean; fight fair; fight hard." Then he said those magic words that get every UFC fan pumped: "Let's get it on."

And then, after all that buildup, we did nothing. We were both tentative, standing toe-to-toe, exchanging jabs, and just feeling each other out. It was more cat and mouse than badass on badass. I was cau-

Tito Ortiz dodged a fight with me for months. I finally had a chance to knock him out. And I did.

tious, since I didn't want to give him any confidence, but hoped to remind him how hard I could hit.

Then he went for a shoot to take me down. I avoided it and threw a left hook that just missed. Tito just smiled. Seconds later he caught me with a quick jab on my jaw, and I thought, Hmm, he's been working on his skills. Then it was back and forth. He hit me with a few inside kicks, and I fired off a left-right combination. He hit me with a left; I hit him with a right. I don't think either of us was hurting the other. He tried for another takedown and I moved out of the way.

I was giving him too much respect. He was keeping his hands up, blocking a lot of my punches. I went for a kick, which missed, and he slapped his head, basically saying, Come on, is that all you got? I was doing what I always do in a fight: looking for the knockout. I'm not the most patient fighter. My strategy is to find an opening, land a big hit, and end the fight as soon as possible. I don't mind going the distance, but I'm a striker, and I like these things to end because I knocked my opponent out cold.

Tito and I were playing a little back-and-forth, but eventually I would knock him off his feet.

As the first round ended, I saw my opportunity. He hit me with a right and then a leg kick to the body. I countered with a big looping right, probably my favorite punch, but he ducked under it. But I quickly followed with a left-right-left combo that caught him. Then I nailed him with a left-right-left-right-left-left-right and a right high kick, which caught the back of his head. With only five seconds left when I began my flurry, I had him trapped along the side of the cage. And that kick to the head really stung him.

The crowd was going absolutely nuts. It was so loud I don't think anyone around the cage could hear the bell ringing. Big John actually jumped in, and Tito seemed shocked. He pushed Big John out of the way and started yelling, at Big John and at me. I thought he was challenging me, asking me if that was all I had. I'm not sure he knew the round had ended. Even Joe Rogan, sitting ringside, wondered aloud, "What's he doing?" when Big John stepped in. That's how hard it was to hear. Even Rogan didn't realize the round had ended.

But it had ended in my favor. Tito was looking loopy. I knew what was going to happen next. When you've got a guy dazed, knock him the fuck out. We started the second round and he hit my thigh with a solid shin kick. But he had yet to get close enough to get me down. And that was the only chance he had to win this fight. There was no way he could stand with me and throw punches. He's not strong enough or tough enough. I'd known that since I'd

FAVORITE UFC CHAMPIONSHIPS (IN ORDER):

1. Tito Ortiz KO (Punches) UFC 47 4/2/2004 Las Vegas
2. Randy Couture KO (Punches) UFC 52 4/16/2005 Las Vegas
3. Randy Couture KO (Punches) UFC 57 2/04/2006 Las Vegas
4. Tito Ortiz TKO (Strikes) UFC 66 12/30/2006 Las Vegas
5. Vitor Belfort Decision (Unanimous) UFC 37.5 6/22/2002 Las Vegas
6. Renato Sobral KO (Head Kick) UFC 40 11/22/2002 Las Vegas

put him on his knees at Big Bear and he wouldn't get up. The guy was a grappler. Not a striker. He moved in to throw a combo and I caught him in the eye with my glove. Three seconds later I seized the moment. I threw every punch in my arsenal: jabs, rights, hooks, and uppercuts. I was throwing as fast as I could, working in a rhythm fighters only hope for, as if I were working a speed bag. Only the bag was Tito's face. But really, it could have been whomever I was fighting. It's not Tito I'm throwing punches at; it's just a guy, and I am trying to connect and keep on going. I know if I land, I will knock him out.

As much as Tito tried, he couldn't stop me. All of my punches found the holes in his guard. His face was bloody as he fell to the ground. Then Big John leaped in and called it.

Thirty-eight seconds into the second round, I had knocked Tito out.

Here's what happens when you win a big fight: Girls flock to you. I was once at a club in Vegas with my girlfriend after I had beaten some guy up, and right in front of my girl, another woman came up to us

Tito talked a lot of smack before the fight, but I'd shown him the floor. And it took less than two rounds.

and handed me her key. When I fought Tito, I wasn't dating anyone seriously. So after a night of celebrating at the clubs, I brought some company back up to my room. A lot of company. I can't remember how many women, but I know it was more than two. I had promised Dana the gloves and trunks from the fight, and he had forgotten to get them in the celebration after. He came by my room in the morning, knocked on the door, and someone let him in. He saw two girls asleep in the living room, two more girls in the bathroom, and a girl in bed with me. None of us had any clothes on. And Dana remembers seeing condoms hanging from the lamps, on the floor, pretty much everywhere. He looked at me, asked me for the gloves and the trunks, then said, "Get me the hell out of here." I ended the morning by having sex while doing an interview on the phone with a radio station. Again, I'm not trying to brag. This is just the way it was.

What else can I say? It's good to be the winner.

CHAPTER 34

PATIENCE DOES PAY OFF

BY BEATING TITO WHEN I DID, MY TIMING COULDN'T have been better, both for me and the UFC. While Tito had been the first face of the rejuvenated sport, I was becoming the new face. It proved to me that patience does pay off. Meanwhile, mixed martial arts were only becoming more popular, more accepted, and more mainstream. My fight with Tito had been one of the biggest pay-per-view draws in the sport's history, making the UFC gobs of money and drawing in legions of new fans. And Dana had an idea that would help push it over the top.

He wanted to do a reality show. He'd put sixteen of the best un-signed mixed martial arts fighters in the country in one massive house in Vegas. There'd be eight middleweights (185 pounds) and eight light heavyweights (205 pounds), split into two teams with four fighters from each class on each team. The show winner in each weight class would get a contract to fight in the UFC. He wanted me and Randy Couture to be the team coaches. When the show was over—after our two teams had spent weeks battling each other—we'd have our re-match. It was a brilliant scheme—with only one major obstacle: Dana had no idea who would put it on the air.

CHAPTER 35

HAVING A GOOD CHIN COMES NATURALLY

F DANA'S PLAN WORKED, THE SHOW WOULD BEGIN airing for three months in January of 2005, with Randy and me having our rematch that April, at the end of the series. That meant I'd go a year without a fight. That wasn't going to happen. I'm not doing this to be a TV star; I'm a fighter.

A fight was set up for me for UFC 49 in August 2004 with a journeyman mixed martial artist named Vernon White. A small-time player in the game, he was always talking but not always backing it up. For years he'd been saying he deserved a fight with me, going so far as to claim that I was ducking him. Not likely. We had once tried to fight back when Dana was my manager, but the money wasn't good enough and Dana turned it down. Now, it was a good grudge match. Vernon had been around long enough that people knew who he was. He'd be a legitimate fight, a challenge, but not a huge risk.

Vernon began fighting in 1993, and by the time we finally hooked up he'd had nearly fifty MMA fights. While he couldn't talk a very good game—or fight one, for that matter—he was experienced. He knew how to cover up, how to take a punch, and how to get himself out of trouble. Plus, if you've had close to fifty mixed martial arts fights and haven't become anything more than a guy people fight to stay sharp, you're only in it because you like to get beaten up or have nothing else to do. It's not because you think your next fight will be the one that puts you over the top.

By the sounds of the crowd during the introduction, it was clear that Vernon was a long way from winning any fans. When the cage announcer said his name, he was met with a few boos, but mostly indifference, which is actually worse than being hated. If you're going to do something as visceral and emotional as fighting, you at least want to get the crowd to pump you up. Whether they love you or hate you, it can motivate you. But for Vernon there was just disinterest. Joe Rogan said cageside, "I don't think I heard one clap for the guy."

The reaction for me was a little different. As the crowd gave me a standing O, one of the announcers said, "Wanna be a crowd favorite? Knock out Tito Ortiz."

We both came out aggressively. He threw a looping right that barely connected, then came back with a kick that missed. I connected with a good shot to his chin that dropped him; then we grappled for a few seconds. There was good action in the fight. He wasn't backing down, which I liked. But when I had him on the ground, he didn't give me many openings. He'd just cover, not fight. There were no vulnerable spots to hit. And I wasn't in the mood to just sit there. I hate to lose more than anything, but I don't just want to win because my opponent refuses to fight. From the ground I pushed up and gave him some room to stand. He looked confused, surprised that I was letting him get back on his feet. I actually had to motion to him to stand back up.

We went right back at each other. A big left from me, a low kick and big right that connected on the top of my head from him. I always love that look in an opponent's eyes when he knows he's hit me with a solid shot and then realizes that I'm not all that fazed. Having a good chin comes naturally. Nothing I know of can train you for that. That moment when an opponent is stunned that I wasn't rocked back is also crucial. It gives me an opening. Against Vernon, I threw a big right that knocked him down. I pounced and just pummeled him. I was throwing left after left against his head, with enough force that you could hear me grunting across the cage, even though the crowd was cheering. But none of the punches were doing any damage, which was frustrating. Vernon just spread his fingers against his head, and all I got was the back of his hand.

So I backed off again, he got up again, and I went at him again. This was becoming the rhythm of the fight. This time I got him with a looping right that nearly twisted his head right off his neck. Down he went. Again. And I let him back up, again, because I wanted to fight. I had spent a couple months training. I knew I might not get to fight again until Randy in April of 2005, which was eight months away. We danced around for a minute; then I just stood there, waiting for him to make a move. He went for a low leg kick, then took a wild swing that missed. So I knocked him down again. I was bored with just punching him while he wasn't even trying to move. He looked like a kid cowering in the corner, turning his head and begging the bully not to hit him. Finally, he got up again and this time showed some life. He tried a reverse kick and had me backing up a bit. I looked over to Hack and John Lewis in my corner, and they both gave me a look that said, Knock him out already. So I did. I caught him with a good right to his chin and he just dropped. He didn't make a move to cover himself up. The ref jumped in and called it with less than a minute left in the first round. It was a good punch. Good enough that it would become a staple on *UFC Unleashed* shows over the next several years.

CHAPTER 36

YOU NEED TO BEAT SOMEONE OVER THE HEAD TO GET WHAT YOU WANT

T WAS A BRILLIANTLY CONCEIVED IDEA. *THE ULTIMATE Fighter* pulled together all the elements that were making reality TV so popular. It had people desperate for a chance, from different backgrounds, forced to live together. It had a large cash prize at stake. It had competition. And the beauty was that none of it was contrived. Things were settled in the ring, not with votes and immunity and backstabbing. You don't like someone; get him in the ring and knock him the fuck out.

But nobody wanted it. Dana and the Fertittas pitched it to every network, and they all turned them down. This was a problem. Because, while the fights were drawing big pay-per-view buys and the sport was only getting more popular, it still wasn't a huge money-maker. It lost close to $50 million the first three years Dana and the Fertittas owned the company. While it had made progress—from getting sanctioned by more than twenty states, to generating huge pay-per-view numbers, to getting on live-broadcast television—it needed one more hit to cross over. One that would show the broadest audience possible that this was not a sport of savages but of elite athletes who could punch, grapple, and force submission with skill. Looking back, it happened exactly as it should have. No one had ever accepted the UFC from the moment Dana and the Fertittas bought it. Every bit of success had come from Dana basically forcing people to appreciate the UFC by proving there was an audience. The suits who made the decisions wanted no part of the sport, until they saw the numbers. But even then, it was like cutting through layers and layers of bureaucracy. As the stakes got bigger, the skepticism grew, despite the proof Dana provided. Sometimes proof just isn't enough. You need to beat someone over the head to get what you want. This was just one more example, which is why Dana and the Fertittas decided to produce the shows themselves. They'd finance it, edit it, package it, then offer it up for free to whoever wanted it. It was a risk-free deal for some network that didn't know how lucky it was about to get.

Dana and the Fertittas spared nothing. They bought a huge house for the sixteen contestants to live in. In less than three months they converted an old warehouse into a UFC training center. It had mats, speed bags, an Octagon, dressing rooms, offices, and bigger-than-life-size posters of me, Randy Couture, and other high-profile UFC fighters for inspiration. Between crews, cars, props, production costs, food, and everything else, the show would cost $10 million to produce. There was no guarantee they'd make a penny back. It was just as likely they'd make the show and no one would ever see it as it was that a network would pick it up.

Still, when Dana described it to me—I'd coach one team and Randy Couture the other—I wanted in, even though I hate reality shows. That people could see what we do, that a network was going to show fights for free on television, seemed to be exactly what the sport needed to break through. It was going to be important, and I didn't think I could miss out on it. My manager, who was one of Dana's close friends and had actually taken me on when Dana bought the UFC, strongly disagreed. The pay was crap, just $800 a week, and my manager wanted me to hold out for more. But I was also in the middle of negotiating a new deal, and my manager thought I should use this show as leverage. I wouldn't listen; this show was going to be too big—at least I thought.

We became so contentious that he quit working for me when I decided to do the show. For a long time, he wouldn't talk to Dana either.

I moved out to Vegas in September, just after I had bought a new house. And I wasn't thrilled about taking off for two full months of being locked down in corporate housing. I was going to miss my kids, my house, my life in San Luis Obispo. I also finally understood why my friends who live in Vegas are always telling me living there sucks. Friends come to visit constantly, and for them, visiting Vegas is usually several days of strip clubs, bars, and not sleeping. But living there is different. I would tell my friends that I'd take them out, get them in where they wanted to go, but then they were on their own. I had to go home and get up in the morning.

Like everything else in the UFC, we were working without a script. Literally. The first day that we showed up at the training center to start shooting, we had no clue what we were going to do. Same was true for the next day and the next. We were still trying to figure out who these contestants were and whether they really were great fighters. Dana found one guy, Kenny Florian, after he lost an MMA fight in Revere, Massachusetts. This was reality in every sense of the word. Nothing about this show started off looking slick or packaged.

The rules for the guys in the house were pretty simple: You couldn't do anything. You want to create some tension in a house real fast? Put sixteen amped-up amateur fighters in there and tell them they can't watch TV, read books, listen to music, or go out. The only thing they can do is stare at each other, eat, and think about fighting. Otherwise, as Dana once told *Playboy*, "It's not good television. You don't want to tune in and see these idiots sitting around watching TV for eight hours or reading books. It's not easy. It starts to drive them crazy. Imagine me and you in a house together every day, training against each other and knowing that eventually we have to fight each other. These guys start to get on one another's nerves. They've got fifteen roommates, and the house is a mess because no one does the dishes. All these things build up."

Me, Randy, and Dana from season one of *The Ultimate Fighter*. Team Liddell was strong, but we had some tension in the house. We're fighters, for God's sake.

It didn't take long either. On the first night in the house—which was stocked with beer and liquor—several of the guys got drunk. One of them, Chris Leben, whose story line of instability dominated the first half of the season, actually pissed on another guy's bed while the guy was in the bathroom showering. Randy and I woke the guys at five the next morning; they had all slept around three hours, and some of them were still drunk, and we put them through a hellish workout.

Guys were puking in buckets on the mat. They were hitting themselves in the side of their stomachs to work out cramps rather than stop running. It was pure anguish, but also great television. These guys, like a lot of fighters, lived to the extreme. They pushed themselves to the brink when they were having a good time and past it when they were training. Eventually we had them working out more than four hours a day. In fact, that was all they were doing, which helped ratchet up the tension in the house.

Later in the show a light heavyweight named Stephen Bonnar, who was hysterically funny, got mad at a middleweight, Diego Sanchez, who was just plain weird, for cutting off asparagus tips and leaving the stalks behind. Diego's response: "I don't know what asparagus is." (Before one fight Diego practiced yoga in a rainstorm because he thought he could harness the electricity from the clouds.) Another guy walked around in tight shorts that barely covered his ass and slathered himself in baby oil. These guys got bored fast. So bored that Forrest Griffin had some of his roommates actually punching him in the face . . . for fun.

We had them doing some crazy stuff, too. Once they were broken down into two teams—Team Couture and Team Liddell—we'd take them into the Mojave Desert for some challenges. The first pitted my light heavyweights versus Randy's. They had to carry us through an obstacle course while we were sitting in heavy recliners. They had to paddle a kayak across a dry lake bed, filling their boat with weights as they went along. They had to work as a team to carry a telephone pole from one spot to another, then saw it into four pieces, clamp the pieces back together, and carry it back. For those first few challenges, a person was eliminated from whichever team lost.

But, as I wrote, we were working without a script. And this was a show about fighting, not about stupid stunts in the middle of the fucking desert. We decided after one of the early challenges that each show should end with a fight between someone from the team that won the challenge and someone from the team that lost. Loser goes home. You'd think these guys would be dying to get into the cage and go at each other. But no one expected they'd actually be fighting until the finals of the show. The truth was, we didn't even know if they'd be fighting.

On the day the producers told the contestants they were going to step into the cage, Dana was in meetings with potential sponsors for the show. But Lorenzo Fertitta had stopped by to see what was going on. He listened as a producer explained there would be a fight after the next challenge. Before she could finish, the guys were asking how much they were going to get paid. She said, "You're not getting paid. You're fighting for a contract in the UFC. That's it." That didn't sit well. I believe the response from one of the guys was, "Screw that. We ain't fighting. We get paid to fight." Here was the problem: *The Contender*, the show starring Sylvester Stallone and Sugar Ray Leonard, had just started airing on NBC right before we put everyone together. The season was three episodes old when our guys moved into the house in Vegas, and by then they knew that the boxers on *The Contender* were getting paid $25,000 per fight on the show. When they learned they'd be fighting for free on our show, well, they grumbled.

That made Lorenzo nervous. He called Dana and said, "What's going on down here?"

"What's going on where?" Dana answered.

"I'm on the set. And all these guys are saying they are not going to fight unless they get paid."

"Dude, I am on my way down there. And I guarantee you they are fighting."

All the guys had gone back home and were griping about fighting for free. Then, at ten p.m., Dana called me, Randy, and the fighters back to the training center. Dana's a stocky guy with a shaved head who, even though he's not a fighter, would challenge any of these guys in a second. He's perfectly suited for his role as carnival barker of the UFC. That night, he gave a speech that is still written about in the dozens of UFC blogs. It's called the "Do You Want to Be a Bleeping Fighter?" speech. Here's how it goes:

"Gather around, guys, get close over here," Dana said after walking into the gym. "I'm not happy right now. I haven't been happy all day. I have the feeling that some guys here don't want to fight. I don't know if that's true or not true or whatever, but I don't know what the bleep everyone thought they were coming here for. Does anybody here not want to fight? Did anybody come here thinking they were not going to fight? No? Speak up. Anyone who came here thinking they were not going to fight, let me hear it. Let me explain something to everybody. This is a very, and when I say *very*, I can't explain to you what a unique opportunity this is. You have nothing to bleeping worry about every day except coming and getting better at what supposedly you want to do for a living. Big deal, the guy sleeping next to you bleeping stinks or is drunk all night making noise and you can't sleep. You got bleeping roommates. We picked who we believe are the best guys in this country right now. We did. And you guys are it. Bleeping act like it, man. Do you want to be a fighter? That's the question. It's not about cutting weight. It's not about living in a bleeping house. It's about do you want to be a fighter. It's not all bleeping signing autographs and banging broads when you get out of here. It's no bleeping fun. It's not. It's a job, just like any other job. So the question is, not did you think you had to make weight. Did you think you had to do this. Do you want to be a bleeping fighter? That is my question. And only you know that. Anybody who says they don't, I don't bleeping want you here. I'll throw you the bleep out of this gym so bleeping fast your bleeping head will spin. It's up to you. I don't care. Cool? I love you all, that's why you're here. Have a good night, gentlemen."

Then he walked out the door. The next day he promised that any fighter who knocked a guy out or forced him to submit would get a $5,000 prize. And the question of these guys getting paid for fighting wasn't an issue anymore.

CHAPTER 37

WE'RE FIGHTERS. A LOT
OF US HAVE ISSUES.

THIS SHOW WAS JUST LIKE ANY JOB. DANA CALLED us back to the training center for speeches at 10:00 P.M. and meetings at noon. We were training these guys twice a day, and we went for fifty-eight days straight. No one trains that many days in a row. I was responsible for someone else's schedule, seven days a week, and was on call whenever I wasn't at the training center. One night during taping, Antonio was fighting in Reno. I had arranged for a plane to take a bunch of us from Vegas to see him fight. But Dana and the producers told me I couldn't go. I wasn't allowed to leave lockdown, even to see one of my guys fighting. All for a show no one was sure would air anywhere.

The only time we saw footage of the show was when Chris, the kid who pissed on a roommate's bed the first night, was nearly kicked off.

After the guys had been in the house a few weeks and were going stir-crazy, Dana decided to take everyone out for dinner and to get drunk. Some guys drank more than others. Chris, Josh Koscheck, and Bobby Southworth certainly did. Chris and Koscheck, both middle-weights, had been ripping each other the entire show. They clearly hated each other. Southworth, a light heavyweight, and Koscheck were best friends in the house. Late that night Southworth started go-

Every fighter needs to warm up before a fight—even a champion.

ing at Leben, eventually telling him he was a "fatherless bastard." Up until that point Chris had never backed down and usually instigated every confrontation in the house. But Bobby crushed him. Chris just put his head down and started crying. He was so upset he couldn't even sleep in the house. Instead he took his blanket and went to sleep on the front lawn. That was when Koscheck and Southworth decided to fuck with him some more. While he was sleeping, they turned on the hose and sprayed him.

This sent Leben over the edge. He punched a hole through the glass in the front door, slicing off the skin on his knuckles, then tore down one of the bedroom doors. Blood was all over the wall and splattered on the floor. It was nasty.

Of course, Dana got a call about the incident around seven in the morning. Then he called Randy and me into the training center. This is what overnight-summer-camp counselors must feel like. We talked about kicking Koscheck off the show, and about kicking Southworth off, too. When we got to Leben, though, I didn't think he deserved it.

He needed a thicker skin for sure. UFC opponents will do worse things than call you a "fatherless bastard" and pour water on you. But, as I told Dana, "Chris has issues. But who doesn't? We're fucking fighters. A lot of us have issues."

Then we decided to settle it the way we settle everything else: in the cage. Koscheck versus Leben. Too bad for Chris. Koscheck, a former NCAA wrestling champ, got him on the mat and never let him up.

Despite the workload, which I wasn't used to at all, working the show had its benefits. It reminded me of one of the things I love about mixed martial arts, which was teaching younger guys. I was their coach, and I started to feel protective of them, which led to some intense screaming matches with producers. Before one fight, the tape guy—the one who wraps up a fighter's hands before he puts on his gloves— showed up late. By the time he was done, my fighter barely had a chance to warm up before a producer was in the dressing room telling him he had to go out and fight. Now, these fights weren't live. They could have waited a few more minutes for him to finish preparing. He was the one who was competing for his life, not the producer. So I told her he wasn't ready, and she lost it on me, as if I were one of the production assistants. I'm a grown man; you can't talk to me like that. Besides, I told her, I was hired to teach these guys how to fight and to take care of them. I'm going to defend them as if they were fighting for me and Hack at The Pit. When she still wouldn't back down, I finally said to her, "Okay. Go talk to the guys who pay for the show and ask who they want, you or me." That ended the fight. And my guy got to finish his warm-up.

Most of us in the UFC stick up for each other because, except for jackasses such as Tito and Vernon White, we are a collegial group. We help each other when we train, teach each other new moves, explain how to improve various aspects of each other's game. We respect everyone who is giving it a go, no matter how talented he is. That's because so many guys who study martial arts do it for reasons other than wanting to kill people with their hands. They're interested in pushing themselves, taking on a challenge to learn as much as they can in sports that are thousands of years old and constantly evolving. The jujitsu specialists or karate experts in the UFC still have a passion for those disciplines that moves them to teach, even if they're helping someone who may one day be an opponent.

It was the same way with these guys. The strikers gave tips to the grapplers. The wrestlers taught kickboxers how to sprawl and avoid takedowns. Submission guys explained how to break out of choke holds. When those guys faced each other in the cage, they wanted to kill each other. But when they were on the mat at the training center, they were as concerned with helping each other as they were with helping themselves. I don't know that every sport is like that.

There were two other positive side effects: First, all the downtime allowed me to have my knees examined. I had torn the MCL in one knee before the first Randy fight, and the other one had been nagging me for a long time. The doctor told me that a decade earlier he would probably have put me under the knife to fix them both. Now, he said, I could just ice it aggressively and be fine. By my doing ice baths after every workout, my knees were pain-free for the first time in years.

Second, halfway through shooting, I started dating the show's host, Willa Ford. It happened by accident. Willa wanted to go out, but she wasn't allowed to hang out with any of the fighters. So Dana told me to take her out and show her a good time. Pretty soon we were together all the time. The show wasn't even picked up yet, but I was already reaping the benefits of being on television. My girlfriend was a pop star whose biggest hit was called "I Wanna Be Bad." She was one of *Maxim*'s one hundred hottest chicks and a future *Playboy* model. When we finally got to go out with the fighters on the show the last night of taping, we all ended up in a strip club. Willa was pretty loaded, and somehow the guys coaxed her onto the stage to do a dance. While she was letting loose to "Pour Some Sugar on Me," her shirt was ripped off by one of the dancers. A stripper said to her, "Nice tits." Willa answered, "Thanks, you, too."

Really, I didn't have much to complain about.

CHAPTER 38

SOMEONE UP THERE HAS A GREAT SENSE OF HUMOR

AS SOON AS THEY STARTED EDITING THE SHOW, Dana says he knew it was gold. Now he just had to sell it. Luckily, as much as the UFC lived by an oh-screw-it mentality, so did a TV network geared toward the UFC's audience: Spike TV.

Spike was like one of those lad magazines come to life. It branded itself as the "first network for men," and it launched with a party at the Playboy mansion. In the beginning it aired adult-oriented cartoons and reruns of *The A-Team* as well as Pamela Anderson classics such as *Baywatch* and *V.I.P.* Spike even copied the *Maxim* and *FHM* model of the Hot 100 issues and aired an original special called *The 100 Most Irresistible Women*.

The network—which began as the Nashville Network in 1983 and then became the forgettable TNN before being renamed Spike in 2003—could afford to take chances. So few people were watching and its programming was so targeted, if one of its shows drew 1.5 million viewers—hit shows such as *Grey's Anatomy* pull in between 20 and 30 million—it was considered a huge hit, especially with advertisers. There's not a more coveted group for the guys selling stuff than men between the ages of eighteen and thirty-four. Luckily for the UFC, those are our fans.

Spike had had success airing pro wrestling. And in yet another stroke of good luck, Spike's contract with the WWE was coming to an end in the middle of 2005. Rumors were that it wasn't going well. If the network was looking for something to get on the cheap and hope it could pick up where wrestling left off, *The Ultimate Fighter* was a nice alternative. So when Dana came by with a show that featured roommates peeing in each other's bed, guys punching out windows and doors, and real fights in which guys were bloodied and then sent home, how could they resist? Especially since Dana and the Fertittas had paid for it all, which meant it would cost Spike nothing. They agreed to put it on the air in January 2005. It was a barter deal, which meant they provided the airtime, but Dana had to find the advertising. For the first two shows, almost no one wanted to buy a piece of it.

The network had pretty low expectations. It didn't do any promos for the show. And most of the reviews that came in were filed under the "other new shows" category. Only the papers from towns that had fighters on the show—such as the *Boston Globe* (Alex Karalexis, Kenny Florian, Chris Sanford) or the *Augusta Chronicle* (Forrest Griffin)—gave full writeups. Even then, it was about the fighters defending the sport, explaining that the days of bare-knuckle brawling were over. From the inside it always seemed as if we were making headway into the mainstream; then the media would write stories like that and we'd be reminded that most people still thought of us as nothing more than thugs.

The show debuted on January 17, 2005, at 11:00 P.M. Immediately the headlines changed. *"Ultimate Fighter* Surprise Hit for Spike." *"Ultimate Fighter* Knocks Out Competition." Somehow, people found the show. Nearly 2 million people watched the premiere, almost half of them men between eighteen and forty-nine. In the eighteen-to-thirty-four age group, a little less than four hundred thousand guys watched the show. I don't think anyone realized how starved the fans were for something like this. So many gyms—dojos, kickboxing schools, jujitsu academies—were buying UFC fights on pay-per-view, then inviting

Some people think UFC fighters are a bunch of street thugs, but many of us are highly skilled martial artists.

forty students to come and watch. Imagine if all those kids were now watching the fights for free. The numbers improved nearly every week. Mixed martial arts was breaking through on basic cable TV, just a few years after it had been declared dead and less palatable to broadcasters than porn. It wasn't just the fights that drew people in. It was the fighters. They weren't at all what people expected. Sure, they were aggressive and eager to fight. But they were college-educated. They spoke in complete sentences. They trained as hard as any other professional athletes. As Dana once told *Playboy*, "Suddenly people were watching mixed martial arts without realizing they were watching it, because they got caught up in the story lines. You also get to learn about the characters and see that these guys aren't a bunch of fucking gorillas who just rolled in off a barstool. You can see how hard they train and that they have real lives and families."

Too bad we couldn't sit back and enjoy it. Despite pulling such big numbers for the network the first couple weeks, Spike had yet to pick up *Ultimate Fighter* for a second season. Paying $10 million again to produce it themselves was out of the question for Dana and the Fertittas. They wanted a deal with a network that was going to pay them. This was the biggest hit Spike had had in its most recent incarnation, so it seemed like a no-brainer. Then, at the end of January, it became obvious why nothing had been done. The head of the network resigned because of "creative differences." A new guy was coming in, and no one knew what he wanted to do. In fact, people were too worried about their own jobs to be negotiating rights deals. They were practically hiding under their cubicles, hoping to stay out of the way and not get canned. Meanwhile, Dana was flying to New York twice a week trying to make sure Doug Herzog, Spike's new boss, had *Ultimate Fighter* on his radar.

He did, of course. How could he not? The ratings were improving every week. In mid-March Herzog announced Spike wasn't going to renew its deal with WWE, but was working toward a second season of *Ultimate Fighter*. Negotiations dragged on for weeks. The night of the finale, while Stephen Bonnar and Forrest Griffin fought, Dana was putting the finishing touches on a deal in the alley. He and Herzog's rep from Spike actually agreed to air a second season from the fucking alley during the last fight of season one. We'd spent all this time trying to prove we weren't just back-alley brawlers, and then that's where the deal that finally proves it gets hammered out. Someone up there has a great fucking sense of humor.

If Dana had held out a little bit longer, who knows how much more money he could have made. Because the ratings for the finale weren't just better than they had been for the season premiere. They were the highest ratings Spike had ever had. In every category that was important—overall viewers, eighteen-to-forty-nine-year-old males, eighteen-to-thirty-four-year-old males—the numbers went up, peaking in the last show of the year. We wound up averaging 1.7 million viewers per night. The size of the audience grew nearly 20 percent during those first twelve weeks. In April, when the finale aired, Spike was ranked the number one network overall among men eighteen to forty-nine and eighteen to thirty-four. That finale, which aired on a Saturday night in prime time and drew more than 3 million viewers, was not only Spike's biggest show, but the most watched show among men that night. More people were watching UFC fighters on Spike than watched NBA games on ESPN.

Not only had we gotten the exposure we wanted, we were a television phenomenon. And the timing couldn't have been better. A week after the finale aired, with a bout that more people watched than any other in UFC history, Randy and I were going to have our rematch.

This time I'd be ready.

CHAPTER 39

IF A GUY SAYS HE'S READY, HE'S READY. WHO AM I TO SHOW MERCY?

I DIDN'T WATCH THE SHOW WHEN IT PREMIERED. IN FACT, I haven't seen more than a handful of episodes. I hate seeing myself on television. I don't like the way I sound or the way that I talk. I won't even watch my fights when they are replayed, and I have a problem watching the highlights that flash on the screen.

But obviously, plenty of people were tuning in. And not all of them were the type of people I expected. I knew my life was changing when I was walking through a mall in Florida after the first couple of episodes and a man in his sixties stopped me to tell me how much he liked the show. A few steps later a woman about the same age stopped and asked me if I was the guy from that fighter show. When I said yes, she told me how much she liked the show, too. I might have laughed at the notion of doing reality TV, but it was no joke. Whether I liked it or not, whether I thought it was good or bad, television gave me instant credibility. Before TV I was a fighter in a thug sport. Now I was a recognizable face on this cool new show. On that same trip to the mall I stopped at a nail salon to get a pedicure. I'd never put polish on my toes, but a bunch of the guys at The Pit were doing it for fun, painting their toes black. So when the lady asked if I wanted mine painted, I said sure. She was going to do all black; then I told her to make the big toe pink, just to mess with people and see what kind of reaction I got. It's the same reason I like to dance when I'm ringside at one of my guys' fights. At first people were staring at my feet—but I was used to that, given my haircut—and then I just sort of forgot about it. Then a week later I went to a Chargers game in flip-flops and one guy looked at my toes, looked up at me, and said, "Hey, if anyone can pull it off, you can." Now I step into the cage with nicely painted toes and no one even thinks twice about it. But all of this—the elderly man and woman who stopped me, people staring at me and my toes and not making fun of me—just proved to me how powerful the show was, and that, when you need to sell, there's no better pitchman than television.

I like to paint my toenails. So what? Here are my favorite toenail polish colors:

1. Blue
2. White
3. Pink
4. Black

I had to be careful now, too. I don't like to say no to anybody. If you want to hang out with me, buy me a drink, take a picture, I'm all for it. For most of my life, nobody wanted anything from me. That was starting to change. I had more people hanging around me that people in my inner circle didn't know. Dana called them the Klingons, and I was going to have to learn how to recognize those who wanted something from those who didn't.

One way to deal with my newfound celebrity was to seclude myself and just focus on training for the Couture fight. The reality was, as much fun as being famous was, if I lost the rematch with Randy, I was going to be just another guy who had once been on TV. With the show taking off and the sport going mainstream, I wanted to be on the ride for as long as possible. Which meant I had to leave the cage a champ, not a chump.

I lost the first fight because I was out of shape. Part of the problem was my knee, which wasn't an issue anymore, and part was that I just didn't have any wind. Hack was going to make sure that didn't happen again. I did almost all of my training at The Pit, which I hadn't done for several years. The strength training was back-to-basics stuff such as pushing the wheelbarrow, not the circuit weight training I had done in the past. And I did the wrestling and rowing drills—in which I rowed eight hundred meters on a machine in two and a half minutes and then wrestled someone for two and a half minutes. I also did extra wrestling cardio with some buddies, including Eric Schwartz. For one minute we sprinted around the cage as fast as possible; for the next minute we did takedowns, as many as we could in sixty seconds; for the next I'd have to work my way up from being on the bottom. We'd do five one-minute drills; then I'd get a one-minute rest; as always, we were trying to simulate the conditions in a typical UFC round.

Also, for the first time, I watched the tape of my first fight with Randy. This was a revelation. I saw how I was just hanging in there, how low I was in my stance, how flat-footed I was, and how dead tired I was. I thought, If I am in shape, I got this. It's over.

The fight took place in the MGM Grand Garden Arena in front of more than 14,500 fans. It was the largest crowd ever to watch a mixed martial arts fight in the United States. The entire atmosphere felt more like a UFC bazaar than the usual card. The bottom of the MGM was so packed with vendors selling shit and fans buying it up that it would have been hard to slip a piece of paper through the crowd. By the early afternoon of the fight, there wasn't even any parking left at the hotel. The impact of *The Ultimate Fighter* on UFC 52 was obvious, not just from the crowd, but from the media attention. Not only was every UFC credential accounted for, but nearly a hundred requests couldn't be fulfilled. I couldn't even answer my phone anymore. I finally left a message on my outgoing voice mail that said, "You've reached Chuck Liddell. I don't have any more tickets, so quit bothering me."

I was in better shape for this bout, no doubt. But I also felt I had a better game plan. Even Randy had said that I needed only minor adjustments to beat him. I was pretty sure I knew what those were and couldn't wait to prove it.

As soon as Big John McCarthy yelled, "Let's get it on," Randy and I tapped gloves. We both came out looking to strike but danced around each other warily. After a lot of quick punches, we'd back out. Hack had me move, always moving. I thought that anytime I got flat-footed, I was risking getting taken down. So I was moving side to side and forward constantly. I ceded the center of the ring to Randy and probably did more moving. I might tire myself out just from the extra distance I was covering, but the risk was worth taking if it kept him from getting me on the mat.

One of us would throw a low leg kick, then jump back out. I didn't want to get so close that he could grab me and take me down, turning this into a grappling match. And he didn't want to get so close that I could finish the fight with a single punch. My stance was more defensive in this fight and my hands were higher. Twenty seconds into the fight he came in fast with some punches. In previous fights I would have stayed still for an extra second or two, accepted a little bit of punishment, then looked for an opening to make a big knockout punch. But this time I countered quickly, just to make him aware that coming in close would cost him; then I jumped out of the way so he couldn't take me down.

Before the fight, Randy's trainer had talked about his theory on "controlled aggression," which meant being aggressive enough to lure an opponent into your strategy, but not so aggressive that you're pulled out of yours. Early on, I didn't think either of us was doing that. Randy, if anything, was a step slower than he had been in our last fight. He didn't have the speed to close the distance on me that had led to all those takedowns. Even his punches seemed to be coming at half speed. Instead of the quick jabs he used to counter my looping punches in our first match, he tried looping hits himself. They were easy to see coming and relatively easy to avoid.

He did connect with a nice left about ninety seconds into the fight, which helped him catch up with me against the side of the cage, where we clinched. He had his hand on the back of my head, which was leaning in toward his. Then we both threw several punches at each other's

I got in some sweet punches before I caught Randy's eye and he went down.

face. One of the dangers of the type of gloves we use is that our fingers are exposed, unlike in boxing. As I was swinging, one of my thumbs caught Randy in the eye. Everyone in the crowd gasped. No one, least of all me, wanted the fight stopped and me declared the winner because of a doctor's call. That's just a cheap, unsatisfying way to win a fight. Besides, after all I'd gone through for a chance to win the light heavyweight title, I wanted a legit win.

For several seconds Randy stood against the opposite side of the cage from me as the fight doctor and Big John examined him. He blinked and rubbed his eye, trying to get it to stop stinging, willing it to be okay. He wasn't about to lose his title because of a poke in the eye. Finally, he nodded that he was okay. As he got back into his stance, he shrugged his shoulders loose and gave me a nod, too, letting me know all was well.

Randy was down, but I still needed to get on top of him to win the fight.

Good, because now I could go kick his ass. If a guy says he's ready, he's ready. Who am I to show mercy? Randy immediately moved in and I caught him with a left hook that looked as if it hurt him. He tried to counter with a hook of his own, but the force of his throw knocked him off balance. I countered with a compact right cross that got Randy square on the chin. Not many people can stand after that. He was out. Honestly, I didn't even want to jump on him when he was down. Randy is such a class act, and he was completely unconscious. It was the first time in my career I haven't wanted to hit somebody when he went down. Normally I want to kill him. But I pounced anyway. Because that's what you do in the cage. Two more punches connected; then Big John pushed me off him. A little more than two minutes into the fight, I had won the light heavyweight title.

After that I was a blur of emotion. I did my trademark pose—back stiff, head back, arms by my side, full body flexing. Then I ran to the cage, straddled the top, and pointed to my buddies in the crowd. Finally I jumped into Hack's arms. All the frustration of not being the champ the previous few years had been washed away. Tito ducking me, losing to Randy, having to fight my way back into contention. I had been vindicated in every sense. There wasn't a bigger name in the sport at that moment. I made $140,000 ($70,000 for fighting and $70,000 for winning) when I beat Randy. But not for a minute did I think about that money when I was dancing around the cage. All I could think was, no one could question whether I was the best fighter in the world.

I had the belt to prove it.

CHAPTER 40

A MOHAWK ENHANCES YOUR COMMERCIAL APPEAL

NATURALLY. AFTER WINNING THE TITLE I WENT TO Disney World. Because of the show I was stopped a lot more often than I used to be, even when I was with my kids. Sometimes fans would ask Trista if it was okay for them to say hello to me. I'm not sure if they were being polite or wondering if I'd beat the crap out of them. As I walked out of the park at the end of the first day with Trista and Cade, a guy stopped me to tell me he was a big fan, which I always appreciate. Then he told me he was a bigwig at Disney World and would be happy to help us out with anything if we were coming back. Here's where fame is fun: Not only did he hook us up at the park, but he made us grand marshals in the daily Disney World parade that marches down Main Street. Trista, Cade, and I rode in one of the fancy cars, and I even wore mouse

Trista, Cade, and I got the royal treatment at Disney World after I took the title.

ears on my head as we waved to the crowd. Later that night I'd get nods from dads as we were sitting at dinner, as if to say, Nice job. I didn't know if they were talking about the fight or the parade.

Eventually, after the parties ended and my buddies left and I had a minute of peace to think about what had happened, it felt no less extraordinary. When I'd first started fighting as a mixed martial artist, I told Eric Schwartz that I was going to be a light heavyweight champ. Now I was. The funny thing was, considering how many near misses and obstacles I had overcome to finally win the title, my timing couldn't have been better. If I had fought Tito a few years earlier and beaten him, or if I had outlasted Randy the first time we fought, my career might have turned out differently.

THE BEST PERKS OF BEING FAMOUS:

1. Free stuff
2. Restaurants stay open for you
3. Being on *Entourage*

The Ultimate Fighter had helped change people's minds about the sport. They didn't just hear *UFC* and immediately think of unsanctioned, no-holds-barred violence. It had been obvious we trained hard, had backgrounds as athletes, and that most of us had even gone to college. We were guys with families who were struggling to take care of them, or former accountants and teachers and firemen who had chucked it all to chase a dream. The show humanized us. Here's the irony: The sport might have been less bloody before everyone started watching.

It used to be that so many guys who wrestled in college were becoming UFC fighters that a lot of the bouts were fought on the mat. Submission holds dominated. The ex-wrestlers did a lot of lying and praying—getting a guy on the mat and lying on top of him, praying he'd stay there until the end of the fight—to neutralize how much they were going to be hit. But, in an evolution, the wrestlers learned to fight upright and became better strikers. They practiced more than good takedowns and good takedown defense. And it wasn't just guys like Randy Couture, a former all-American wrestler, who can punch with anyone. Around 2005, kids who were fans and trying to become UFC fighters were more than just converted grapplers or kickboxers. They were bona fide mixed martial artists who had been studying all the moves since they were young. This was happening across the entire sport just as *The Ultimate Fighter* was gaining traction. Fights had more action. Now it was becoming a lot less ground-and-pound and a lot more sprawl-and-brawl. Fans were really beginning to understand what we were doing in there. I was at a fight in Sacramento where people went nuts when two guys were throwing punches nonstop for about twenty or thirty seconds. Then they booed when they took a rest. Then, in a later match, they cheered when a guy made a good move to pass a guard. In the early days, no one recognized that kind of thing as difficult. Now it drew applause.

I'm glad people finally recognized mixed martial arts fights for what they are, and what they were always meant to be, going back to their early days in Brazil: contests to gauge which form of fighting was the best in the world.

Sometimes I like to stay out late and sleep in, but the lifestyle never keeps me from winning a fight.

I think people now enjoy watching my style of fighting most. I'm dangerous and explosive and can knock people out. It helps that I look the way I do. A Mohawk enhances your commercial appeal. Especially when you beat people up for a living. But it also helps that, right now, just as the UFC is getting the most attention it ever has, strikers have become popular. As much as critics want to slam us, the fans are tuning in because of what we offer. Besides, no matter how vicious our fights look, we are still nowhere near as damaging a sport as boxing.

After beating Randy in front of the largest in-house crowd ever to witness an MMA fight, as well as the largest pay-per-view audience ever to buy one, I was the face of the UFC. Which meant there was a lot more scrutiny. I've never tried to hide when I go out, nor have I ever wanted to stop going out. I live a fighter's lifestyle, which means I'm pretty low-key when I'm training and I like to stay out late when I'm not. But suddenly a lot more people were interested in what I was doing. Nothing could prepare me for videos of me showing up on YouTube doing something as mundane as teaching a kickboxing class. Forget about clips shot from a phone of me making out with two chicks giving me lap dances at a club. I quickly stopped reading newspapers or going online. It's still that way. The only time I know someone has said something about me or posted something I've done online is when a friend tells me or I get a call from a radio station asking me to comment.

Of course, there were a lot more perks, too. I signed a seven-figure endorsement deal with Xyience, the largest deal ever given to an MMA fighter. I had always been popular in Vegas—for UFC fights our faces are plastered on every billboard and cab in the city—but now I got stopped everywhere I went. I once stopped by a friend's house with a stack of my pictures that I was supposed to autograph. I looked at him and said, "I don't even know how to sign my autograph," and we both started laughing.

Even in San Luis Obispo it was different. People had always recognized me, partly because of my look. But now Antonio and Dan had to put me in the corner of a booth and sit around me; otherwise I'd be signing autographs all night. Even in New York, where most people seem immune to celebrities, people took my picture while I was walking down Fifth Avenue, stopped me at hot-dog carts for autographs, or said hello to me in Saks Fifth Avenue. One night, while I was passing a red carpet party at the Cartier store, the paparazzi saw me coming and turned their backs to the red carpet to take my picture. I've been sitting at dinner and the waiter will tell me that another customer has paid for my meal. Sometimes, the people who buy me dinner don't even stick around to say hello. They do it to say thanks, then leave before I can do the same. Of course I'm flattered and honored. But the whole thing feels absurd at times, to me and to the people who were my friends long before I was famous, the guys who are still my closest friends. But it's cool to get us all free shit and not wait in line whenever we go out.

CHAPTER 41

REVENGE IS PRETTY DARN SWEET

'VE RARELY ASKED DANA TO SET UP A FIGHT FOR ME. He tells me whom I'm going to fight and I say fine. But that doesn't keep me from dropping hints about whom I'd really like to face in the cage if I had my choice. Now that I was the champ, I wanted to avenge all the losses on my record, because, let's face it, revenge is pretty damn sweet. I had taken care of one L when I beat Randy. Now I wanted to fight Jeremy Horn.

Hard-core UFC fans, the ones who had been with us from the beginning, had wanted to see a rematch of this fight for a while. Fighters respected Jeremy because he was a pro, and fans appreciated him because he was so skilled on the ground. Losing to him was nothing to be ashamed of. But I hadn't had a chance to get at him again, because he hadn't fought in the UFC since 2001; instead he was working a bunch of minor-league circuits mixed in with an occasional Pride fight. With my newfound clout and the fans clamoring to see the matchup, Dana anted up to get Jeremy into the cage.

We faced off in UFC 54 on August 20, 2005, at the MGM Grand Garden Arena in front of more than 13,500 people. My confidence was sky-high. I didn't recognize myself in the fighter Jeremy had beaten six years earlier. Back then I was a raw talent who had the urge to knock people out but was still figuring out how to do it. I was undisciplined on my feet and unskilled on the ground. Now I was a professional. No situation in the cage made me feel anxious—I could pass every guard, escape every hold, or take every punch. Going into the fight with Jeremy, I had won six straight by stoppage, and I expected to take people out early in every fight. I even said before the bout that I was going to knock him out in the first round, but if I didn't, he was going to wish I had.

Jeremy didn't back down. He promised he wasn't going to dance around trying to avoid my punches. I knew he wasn't that kind of fighter. He was a pro. No way he was going to be nervous, no matter how much I talked about testing his chin. In ninety-four career fights over nearly ten years of fighting, the guy had never been knocked out. I think a lot of fans started believing he had a shot, too, because the money in Vegas was coming in his way late. Too bad they didn't bet on me.

Midway through the first round I threw a powerful right that split his defense. I've got such a rep for throwing punches from all different angles, I'm not sure he expected one to come straight at him like that. But that is what was open, and he crumbled to the mat like three-day-old cake.

I pounced and pummeled and was being a tough guy, but Jeremy was protecting himself on pure instinct, finding a way to get his hands and his guard up that kept me from doing any serious damage. Finally I stood back up and told him to get up, too. Big John was reffing that night. He always gives a little more leeway to guys who look as if they are in trouble during title fights. But when we had spoken in the locker room before, I told him not to stop this thing. I wanted to fight.

After the match a couple reporters asked why I let Jeremy off the mat. Well, besides the fact that I wanted to keep going, there's no reason for me to ever be down there. I'm not going to win down there. The best way for me to finish fights is standing up. I can hit harder when I am on my feet. So when I know I've hurt a guy, as I did Jeremy that night, I get up and say, "Let's go."

Jeremy is a survivor. He stood up, although he looked unsteady, and I eased back. I knew this fight was over. When the round ended and his corner put out his chair, Jeremy told his guys, "I can't see. Everything's blurred. I can't see."

His vision didn't clear during the minute between rounds, and I took him down again with another straight right. I knew the guy couldn't see, so there was no need to bring my punches from anywhere except straight ahead. But he knew enough about fighting to protect himself when he was down. I was throwing and connecting on a lot of punches. His nose was bleeding badly. For the rest of the fight he'd use one of his gloved hands to helplessly wipe at it. But he was doing just enough fighting back, even if he was swinging blindly, to keep Big John from stopping it, and me from getting him to tap out. When he got up again, his legs were shaking. He went for some takedowns, but it seemed like he did it more for a rest than for any real advantage.

Between the second and third rounds Jeremy told his corner that he was still having a hard time seeing. Not that it stopped him from coming out for a third round. He kept his distance this time and even connected on a few hard kicks. But even if he won that round—one judge scored it that way—he'd need a knockout to win the fight. And that wasn't going to happen.

When we came out for the fourth round, Jeremy's face was in bad shape. He had a cut above his eye, and his nose was still bleeding. I know they were just trying to wait me out, hoping I'd get tired and run out of punching power. I had been sick for a few weeks before the match, and some prefight stories said it might affect my strength in late rounds. But that wasn't going to happen, not tonight. It was time for me to end it. I wouldn't go into a fifth round and wait for the judges to decide it, even if I knew I was dominating the fight.

I threw one more straight right punch—something we had been

working on a lot in the weeks leading up to the fight—and Jeremy went down again.

He reached for his eyes and, as he tried to stand up, told Big John he couldn't see. That was it. Big John called it. I earned $80,000 for fighting and another $80,000 for winning. But I'd done something better than win a big payday. I'd avenged my first mixed martial arts loss. Now, between Jeremy and Randy, that was two down. Which meant only Quentin "Rampage" Jackson was left.

Jeremy Horn took a beating that night. Then I knocked him out.

CHAPTER 42

YOU CAN'T WAIT TO FINISH A GUY

WITH RAMPAGE STILL UNDER CONTRACT TO PRIDE, it would take a while for Dana to set up that fight. No worries, though. Plenty of big-money fights were waiting for me in the UFC, beginning with Randy Couture, who wanted a rubber match.

My feelings about how to fight Randy hadn't changed: If I kept moving, stayed in good position, and made him pay every time he moved in for a takedown, I was confident I could win. Hack also had me working on a new punch, called a fishhook, that people hadn't seen from me, and which we both thought could stymie a grappler who liked to get close, the way Randy did.

The fight with Randy was scheduled for February 4, 2006. I had been an MMA fighter for seven years, and a professional fighter longer than that, yet I could still learn something new. That discovery is still a draw for me, in the same way it made me want to keep going in karate when I was a teenager. Fighting is as much about the internal challenge as it is the external battle.

Hack suggested the fishhook while we were goofing around during a sparring session. This short uppercut hits someone on the side of the chin, rather than coming straight up underneath it with a good, hard, clean punch. It was more of an annoying blow that surprised people than one that could really cause a lot of damage or knock someone out. But if he rushed in and tried to tie me up, it would knock an opponent off balance and make him think twice about coming in again.

I was hoping to use the move against Randy. It's always nice to debut something in front of a big crowd. And every Ultimate Fighting Championship card seemed to be setting a new record for attendance. When Randy and I fought in UFC 57 at the Mandalay Bay Events Center, the gate was $3.3 million, the largest ever, with tickets scalping for as much as $3,600. Once, Dana and the Fertittas had a goal of two hundred thousand pay-per-view buys. The total for my rubber match with Randy was estimated to be more than four hundred thousand. The numbers—and hunger—for UFC cage matches seemed boundless.

MY FAVORITE LOCALES FOR FIGHTS:

1. Mandalay Bay
2. MGM
3. The Palms
4. The Hard Rock Hotel

When we walked into the cage and the fight began, the eruption from the crowd was deafening as I circled to my left and threw a few jabs. He had his hands up and I wanted to wear him down a bit, even if my punches didn't make it through his guard. Meanwhile my hands were down a bit. Randy is a good striker, but I wasn't worried about his power as much as I was his takedowns. That's why I was just feeling him out at first, never standing in front of him for too long, never giving him a clean target to aim for. That first minute of the fight was actually some great hand-to-hand combat: I jabbed; he defended. I threw a left hook to knock his hands down; he got them back up. He came back at me with a right-left combo. I faked; he countered with a right and then a cross that I blocked. I tried to land a big right, but he deftly took a step back to avoid the blow. Neither of us had an advantage; we were just looking for an opening.

We battled back and forth like this for most of the first round. But I could tell that my jabs, while not bringing any knockout power, were definitely starting to have an effect. A little more than two minutes into the round Randy was getting red around his right eye. Thirty seconds later I landed a pretty big left. About forty seconds after that Randy came at me with a right, then tried to move in for the takedown. But I caught him with a left, a big right, and an uppercut. He was stung. I could tell that the right I threw was especially painful. He was bleeding pretty heavily from his nose, and smaller cuts were opening up above his eyes.

I got too excited after the right and went after him. That impulse cost me a bit, because when I got close, it gave him an opportunity to take me down. And he did. But I kept working to get up. I got against the cage and got back to my feet. But he was still locked onto me. I thought Big John would separate us, but he didn't make a move. Instead I kept working to release myself. That's all you can do when you are locked up like that, work and work, so the other guy has to worry about tying you down instead of hitting you. It's one of the hardest, least glamorous, least rewarding acts you can do in a fight. But if you don't, you'll leave yourself vulnerable.

We were moving across the cage, as if we were dancing partners, as Randy tried to take me down again and I worked to keep myself up. I remember a lot of blood as the round ended. And I was glad it was his, not mine.

Before the second round began, Randy's nose was still bleeding pretty badly, so much that he had to keep wiping it. But it wasn't stopping him from taking the fight to me. He had to; I had won the first round and he was hurt. Plus, when blood is pouring from your nose, it impacts the judges. You've got to work that much harder to win points. So while I was able to keep jabbing away at his face and making it sting and bleed a little more, he had to take some shots. He threw a big left, and I responded with a combination. Then he tried to throw another big left and slipped a little. I countered with a big punch, and already off balance, Randy just dropped to the floor.

For a moment, I hesitated. In this instant, I didn't try to finish Randy. I wanted to calculate, Is he out or should I finish him? I didn't want to hurt him if he was done, because sometimes, even in the cage, you try to be human. Then I remembered something. In the split sec-

I'd taken the title from Randy in our last fight, but it felt just as good to knock him out a second time.

ond between Randy's falling and my jumping to finish him, a scene from *The Ultimate Fighter* played in my head. I remembered telling one of the kids that you can't wait to finish a guy. You have to go get him; otherwise you're giving him a chance to recover. With that flashing through my memory, I pounced. After a few punches Big John jumped in and ended it.

For the second time, I had knocked out the most decorated champion in UFC history. And I earned $250,000 for the pleasure.

CHAPTER 43

SCREW IT. RETAKE IT.

THE SHOCKER OF UFC 57 WASN'T THAT I HAD PUT Randy on the ground. He had bigger news than that. With tears in his eyes, he retired from the UFC. Not only had I punished him twice, but I had actually knocked him out of the sport. "This is the last time you'll see these gloves and these trunks in the Octagon," Randy said. "I'm going to retire them tonight."

Of course, every jock has a hard time avoiding a comeback, especially when the public is clamoring to see you again and big money is on the table. So why should the guys in the UFC be any different? Within a year Randy had announced he was coming back, then went out and reclaimed the UFC heavyweight title. I'm glad. The guy was forty-three years old and became champion of the world again. If he can fight at that age, it makes me think maybe I can, too.

At the time, however, I wasn't thinking about retirement or comebacks. I was just enjoying being the champ. The sport's popularity grew every day. I was on the road making appearances to promote the UFC. There were TV shows and radio shows and interviews with fan Web sites that covered us and mainstream media who were finally catching on to what so many others knew: We weren't going away anytime soon.

One day soon after the fight with Randy, I was on the phone with Dana. We were just bullshitting and I mentioned to him how much I liked the show *Entourage*. I knew he was friendly with Mark Wahlberg, so I started giving Dana a hard time, telling him to call his buddy and get me a cameo on the show. I had done some acting when I was younger. As a ten-year-old I played a bit part as a Cub Scout in the Jack Nicholson movie *The Postman Always Rings Twice*. That's what I was thinking for *Entourage*. I just thought it would be fun to do something small, like the guys would pass me at a party and say, "Hey, Chuck, good luck in the fight," or, "Nice fight last night." By the way, this was another sign of how far the UFC had come. A couple years earlier the notion that some of us were becoming so recognizable that we could joke with Dana about cameos on a hot show was laughable. Now I had reason to think it could happen.

Like everything else in the UFC, it turned into something bigger than we expected. I have a manager in Hollywood named Brad Marks (yeah, I know, also inconceivable just a few years earlier). He's buddies with a guy who writes for the show, who is a big UFC fan. Once Brad heard I wanted to be on, he hounded his guy to write me into an episode. He did, and the writers came up with a great idea. I played myself, and I wanted to kick Drama's ass for cutting me off for a parking space and swearing in front of my daughter. On the show, this was all a setup. Drama, played by Kevin Dillon, was acting tough because he thought he was being filmed on a new candid-camera show with Pauly Shore. But I didn't let on. In fact, I got so angry I threatened to knock his teeth out right there. Suddenly Drama thought I wasn't part of the show and that he had just pissed me off. Later that day I left him a message telling him I was coming after him. He showed up at one of my fights that night trying to apologize, but I made him come down into the cage and get on his knees to beg me not to kill him. That's when I told him he was basically being punked.

Doing the show was a lot of fun, although taping was hurry-up-and-wait. So Dillon, Jerry Ferrara, the guy who plays Drama's buddy

Turtle, and I spent a lot of time hanging out and talking. They asked me about the fights, and I asked them how to act. They made it so easy. Whenever I messed up, which was plenty, whoever was running the show would say, "Screw it. Let's retake it." It's a good policy for most things: Screw it. Retake it.

It takes a long time to put those scenes together. I'd say my dialogue a dozen different times so they could set up cameras and shoot it from several different angles. Then I'd say my lines with no camera so they could film an actor's reaction. It was a lot of standing around for a show that's less than thirty minutes, even if it probably is the best show on TV.

I taped the show in August of 2006, and this was a big month for me. Soon after shooting, I had a rematch with Renato Sobral, the Brazilian jujitsu master they called Babalu. When we had fought nearly four years earlier in UFC 40, Dana begged me not to take the fight. I was the number one contender. On that same card, Tito was fighting Ken Shamrock, then was supposed to take me on, as long as I beat Babalu. Dana thought I was an idiot for demanding the fight because Babalu is so tough. Then I knocked Babalu out with a kick to the head.

Now I was the champ, and I still expected to get my hands on him and knock him out in the first round. Some people saw this as a bridge fight, something to keep me in shape between Randy and a bigger match with Tito or Rampage or the Pride champ, Wanderlei Silva. But that wasn't the case. I wanted to fight, and Babalu was the toughest opponent out there for me. Definitely tougher than Tito, as far as I was concerned. I knew to take this match seriously. Babalu had only gotten better during the four years since our first fight. He had filled in a lot of the holes in his game. And I had been battling a foot injury, too. My workouts were good and I had a lot of energy, but just before training I weighed 233 pounds. At the weigh-in I was still six pounds over the 205-pound limit and had to cut weight. Sure, I planned on winning; I just didn't expect it to be easy.

I was totally relaxed before the fight. The guys from Sherdog, one of the leading MMA fan sites, came up to my room before the fight and did an interview with me. Of course, Dana was calling me every couple of hours to make sure I was ready for the fight. He finally stopped at around six o'clock that night, a few hours before the fight. That's because I told him on the phone, "Dana, can't talk right now. Got two girls waiting for me in the shower. Gotta go. Bye." Either he thought I was so confident he didn't need to build me up or so far gone that not even his incessant calls were going to save me.

For the first few seconds of the fight we danced around. Babalu seemed hyper; I couldn't tell if he was anxious or amped. There is a

I connected with some good punches before the final blow that knocked Babalu off his feet.

difference. The guy who's anxious moves quickly but he's jittery, as if he's ready to defend against an opponent's slightest move. A guy who is amped isn't worried about defending himself. He's looking for an opening to take you down. During the first thirty seconds of the fight, I wasn't sure which one Babalu was. He came at me with a straight kick and then a side kick, neither of which hurt. I didn't even throw a punch for the first forty seconds of the fight.

A minute in, he took a leap and threw a big overhand right, the kind that looks a lot scarier than it actually feels. It scores points, but doesn't inflict any damage. Then he threw a left and a right and his arms started flailing. One of his strengths is how fast he is, and his fists were moving like pistons—so fast and furious, in fact, that he left himself completely defenseless.

That was when I nailed him with an uppercut. It was the fishhook move that I'd practiced before the Randy fight and never got to use, and it worked exactly as planned. He was moving forward almost blindly, so I threw the punch at a bit of an angle and got him on his chin. It stunned him—no doubt it hurt, too—and stopped his progress. Now I was throwing everything in my arsenal. As his back was against the cage, I squared up and threw a straight right that caught him smack in the face. Perfect punch, like hitting that baseball through the middle of the infield. His head snapped back and soon he was on the mat, where I was just pummeling him. Big John was circling, looking to see if Babalu could protect himself or make any aggressive moves. He could, but barely. I got up, moved to his side and past his guard, then leaned over to give him another big sweeping right to the side of the head.

Now it was over. Big John jumped in. The fight was barely ninety seconds old, and I had just made another $250,000. Not a bad payday.

Poor Babalu was in such bad shape he had no idea where he was or who was around him. He actually started trying to fight Big John, unaware the match had been called and I wasn't on top of him anymore. Renato made $21,000 for that fight, but this is how much the

Fertittas look out for their fighters: Before he was driven away in an ambulance, they handed him a bonus check. That helped him feel a little bit better.

Meanwhile, back in the cage, I saw Tito sitting in the crowd and invited him to come inside. Nothing like a postfight show. He started out classy, congratulating me on the win, then had to come after me, too. I've never had rock-hard abs, so Tito pointed out that if we were going to fight, we should wait until December, so I could drop some weight first. Then Joe Rogan asked if I'd be more interested in a rematch with Tito or a first go-around with Silva. "I don't care," I said. "No matter who my opponent is, they're going to last less than one round."

I had just proven I was a man of my word.

IT'S A PRETTY GREAT LIFE
WHEN YOU MAKE IT DOING
WHAT YOU LOVE

SOON AFTER THE BABALU FIGHT, ANTONIO AND I moved into my new house in San Luis Obispo. This place is sweet. Outside it has a pool with rocks the size of boulders at one end, which lead to a deck fifteen feet high. It has great views of the mountains, a hot tub, a gourmet-caliber grill. Inside, a spiral staircase connects the living room downstairs to another living room upstairs. It even has a stripper pole, which always comes in handy. The house isn't a mansion, but it's got more bedrooms and bathrooms than I had growing up and is definitely *Cribs*-worthy. It's even made an appearance on the show. I put in a massive TV with a sound system that makes the walls shake in the living room. The guy who set up my remote put a picture of me knocking someone out on the controller's screen, which I tap whenever I want to turn everything off. I even have the video trivia games that people play when they're in bars on top of the bar that surrounds my kitchen. The list of high scorers is a combination of me, Trista, and Cade.

This life is a long way from the $500 I was getting for kickboxing. I had the new house, plus I had kept the other house as an investment. I was managing fighters with Hack and still had a piece of SLO Kickboxing. Somehow I had morphed from a guy who liked to fight into a freaking Iceman brand. This was proof I had made it as a fighter, what I had wanted to do from the day I realized I had to get a job. And now I was even setting my family up for the future. It's a pretty great life when you make it doing what you love. My garage has enough room for the Hummer II I won after one of my UFC fights and the $330,000 Ferrari that Dana gave me just for being a guy the UFC counts on. It was a pretty sweet gift and came as a total surprise. Dana had asked me to meet him in LA for lunch one day. I was out all night, barely made it down to eat, was exhausted, and sat through a pretty boring meeting. We could have done it on the phone, and I wasn't quite sure why we had to meet face-to-face. Then, we were waiting for our cars at the valet, and this silver Ferrari pulls up. Dana hands me the keys and says, "Enjoy." I hit 130 miles per hour driving the three hours back to San Luis Obispo that afternoon. And despite how tired I was, I had no problem staying awake.

Dana began working on setting up a rematch between Tito and me as soon as the Babalu fight was over in August. By the end of September 2006, just before UFC 63, we had a deal. It was set for December 30, 2006, at the MGM Grand Garden Arena. Naturally, Tito couldn't just sign the deal, have some class, and quietly get himself ready for the fight. He had to create a spectacle and put himself at the center of it.

At the weigh-ins for UFC 63 he walked out onto the stage, waving the contract for our fight. He said, "Liddell, so you know, I am not afraid of you. I know you are champion, but I am coming back to get my belt around my waist. I did sign it; it's completely signed. So come December thirtieth you are going to come and see Tito Ortiz, the new light heavyweight champion of the world. Then come on down to my after party, because Chuck Liddell is going to have a shitty one."

A few weeks after his little show, Tito beat up on his old buddy Ken Shamrock. I may be the only guy he wanted to beat more. The Shamrock bout was Tito's third that year; I'd be his fourth, which meant by the time we faced off he'd basically been in peak shape for twelve months. He'd also won five straight fights. He was always talking about what good shape he was in, about how working out in Big Bear was making his cardio so good. Clearly he was building toward making the fight with me last as long as possible. That's how most guys fight me: They avoid the big knockout punch early, make it last, wear me down, and hope I'll tire out on the mat.

I might have had to wait twice as long as Tito between fights, but I was working hard, too. There was little difference between how I trained when I first started out and how I did it as a champion. Sure, now Hack had a $15,000 stopwatch and I drove up to his house in a Ferrari—as opposed to the beat-up Ford Ranger I had had and the $2 stopwatch he had had—but the sessions were just as intense, if not more. Now we knew what being the champ was like and didn't want it to go away. I did a lot of running on the beach. I did the wrestling and the rowing and the wheelbarrow and the sledgehammer. I did the heavy bag and sparring and the medicine ball. My guys, such as Eric, came out to work with me. I swear some of them might never hit the gym if they weren't coming out to help me train.

Hack and I knew that Tito was going to shoot for my legs to take me down. So my strategy was to be patient and not get too close. I'm always looking for the big knockout punch, even when Hack and John Lewis are telling me not to. But this time that was the best game plan. I wouldn't throw a combination—allowing him to move in underneath the punches—until he was hurt and vulnerable. Then I'd set up the knockout with a few jabs.

It seemed that new gate and viewer records were set with every big UFC fight, and mine and Tito's was no different. Tickets were going for as much as $1,000. Andre Agassi and Steffi Graf were there. Kid Rock flew in from doing a show in Iraq. They were part of the crowd that paid a total of $5.4 million to see the fight. And on pay-per-view? More than 1 million buys. Here's a little perspective on what that means: In April 2006, WWE held WrestleMania 22, and 925,000 fans bought it on pay-per-view. A month later, boxing's golden boy, Oscar De La Hoya, fought Ricardo Mayorga, and again, 925,000 people bought the fight on pay-per-view. I saw a story in the *New York Times* that reported the UFC made $205 million from pay-per-view buys in 2006, while HBO made only $177 million. I was going to make $250,000 that night no matter what, plus a lot more for getting a piece of the pay-per-view money. But for Tito, I'd have fought for a six-pack in the back of a bar.

I'd knocked Tito out the first time, and I was ready to knock him out again.

I could hear the cheering of the crowd when I was halfway through the bowels of the stadium from my dressing room. I couldn't help but start smiling and dancing a little bit as I neared the tunnel. "Intro" from DMX's *It's Dark and Hell Is Hot* was blasting; the bass sounded like firecrackers popping. It was the perfect song for walking out—because the arena was dark and hot. And I felt that I owned it.

Tito had been so scared in our first fight—I could see it in his stance—that I didn't know what to expect when we threw down this time. To his credit, he looked less intimidated, as if he had more of a plan. Maybe he was confident because he had fought so much that year and had been training so hard. After the fight, Dana would comment that Tito appeared more comfortable than he had the first time we fought. He threw some kicks. He tried to shoot for my legs but was too far away, and I forced him down and then back up. He clearly wanted to take it to the ground if he was shooting from that far out. But he also wanted to prove he was comfortable standing and striking with me. About three minutes into the fight he threw a big right that connected and backed me up a bit. But, for me, those hits usually knock sense into me before they knock me out. I responded with a right hand that just glanced off his head, but it was enough to get him bleeding badly over his left eye.

Tito needed something to go his way early to build his confidence even more. His trainers had been saying as much in the week leading up to the fight. It's one thing to train hard and watch tape and feel that you can win. It's another to get in the cage and prove it. So far, Tito hadn't gotten what he needed. As he stood wiping the blood off his face, I stepped back and even dropped my hands to my waist a bit. I wasn't doing it to show him up; I don't even think I did it consciously. But it clearly showed how little I respected his punching power.

With a little more than a minute left in the round we both squared off and I nailed him with a right-left-right combination. He staggered for a moment, then did a face-plant onto the mat. He was awake, but hurt, and he landed headfirst at my feet before rolling over into a defensive position. It was an eerily similar position to that of the first time we fought. I had him against the side of the cage and just went off on his head. I was pummeling him as hard as I could, so badly that the ref looked as if he were about to stop it. I could hear him yelling, "Change your position. You'd better change your position or I'm going to stop this fight." Finally Tito got himself into a better defensive position. Once he did that, I didn't want to waste my energy. He wasn't going to tap now, and the ref wasn't going to call it. So I backed up. As I've said, I'm not going to win a fight hitting someone on the ground. I've got a lot more power standing up.

The beating I gave Tito near the end gave me the round as far as the judges were concerned. And probably the fans, too, because a minute into the second round they started chanting my name, "Chuck, Chuck." Tito knew he had to make up some ground. He threw a big right that missed, then went for a takedown that I snuck out of. He was shooting from way back, desperate to get me on the ground. But from the distances he tried getting to my legs, there was no way he'd make it. I'd immediately sprawl and deflect his move. When he did finally reach me, it was at the end of the round, too late to find a way to make me submit.

In the third round I lowered my stance a bit and started aiming a lot more for Tito's body. I wanted to draw him in and set him up for a big overhand right. I was less concerned about his takedown moves now because I felt I had done a good job of setting him up for the knockout. It was time to take a chance and throw some combinations in advance of that big punch. At one point, while throwing fists at his body, I got so low my knee actually scraped the mat. He responded with a left and a right, and really, it just pissed me off. I should have knocked this chump out already and he was still coming at me. I responded with a left that knocked him off balance. He was down again, and this time I wanted to end it. I got on his side and buried his head in punches. He had his arms up, but his back was to me, and I had his leg locked. He couldn't fight back, and he couldn't slither away. The ref

Tito took the loss like a man. I'm not the type to hold a grudge, and besides, he was pretty hurt and looked like he could use a hug.

was yelling, "Change your position, change your position." But he didn't even try. I thought he was beaten.

So did the ref. At 3:59 of the third round, it was called. I had taken Tito down. Again.

To his credit, Tito handled the loss like a man. At the press conference after the fight he said, "I have no excuses right now. He fought the best Tito Ortiz there is. He may be the best fighter pound for pound in the world right now."

Maybe he is maturing as a fighter, but plenty of people would still like to see us fight again. At the postfight party that night I could barely walk without people grabbing at me. I'd be taking a picture with someone and someone else would be pulling me away before the photo had been snapped. I can't even count how many of those people told me how much they'd like to see me kick Tito's ass a third time. Hey, I'd like to see that, too. But first, I was finally going to get a chance to avenge my loss to Rampage Jackson.

CHAPTER 45

NEVER CHOKE ANYONE OUT UNLESS YOU'RE GETTING PAID FOR IT

THE NEXT COUPLE OF MONTHS WERE INSANE. I'D met a girl, Erin Wilson, in the fall of 2006. She was from Bakersfield, and things were going well enough between the two of us that she decided to move to San Luis Obispo.

I was also on the road for all but four of the next seventy days. And one of those days I was at home for less than twenty-four hours. And here's something I learned while I was traveling: There are people with bigger balls than me. I went down to San Antonio for a tour of the veterans' hospital that specializes in treating burn victims and amputees. The guys I saw were mangled from IEDs and had burns all over their bodies. I met one guy who had a picture in his room from before he went to Iraq. In it he was doing squats with three of his buddies sitting on his arms. Now he could barely speak and had bars coming out of his legs to help keep them stable. When I leaned in close, I could hear him say that he wanted "to get better and go back."

I couldn't believe it, and honestly, I'd never do it. That's the kind of fight I don't want any part of. It was devastating seeing the effect of all these injuries on these guys' families. For the rest of their lives some of these men will have tubes attached to their waists so they can go to the bathroom. Some will have to be connected to machines to stay alive.

Some people in Hawaii like to relax at the beach. I'd rather take a guy down.

Many will constantly need surgeries. It will, obviously, impact how they play with their kids. The sacrifice is unimaginable, and meeting people like that makes the shit that happens to me seem laughable.

A couple of weeks after my trip to San Antonio, I went to Hawaii, where I hung out with my good buddy Lorenzo Neal and his teammate Shawne Merriman. After Hawaii, I kept on going. New York, Toronto, Boston. That's how it's been for me after fights ever since the UFC took off. I don't like to say no, but I can't accept many appearances when I am training. So I put everything off until after a fight. Then I realize I am committed to something in a different city every night for two straight months. I don't think I'm living that hard, but when you're on planes, making appearances at clubs, going out a lot and having a good time, it catches up with you.

For me, that happened in Texas in early March 2007. If you follow the UFC, you've seen the video of me passing out during a TV interview on a Dallas morning show called *Good Morning Texas*. If you haven't, go to YouTube; you won't be disappointed. I was on the road, doing promo work for the movie *300*. I had pneumonia and a hacking cough. I couldn't have sex without stopping to have a coughing attack. So I was struggling. But when you're on the road and get a chance to see buddies you haven't seen in a while, you want to take advantage. The problem is, a lot of times you're going out late and have to get up early to do stuff while they can kick back and recover.

The night before the *Good Morning Texas* interview I went to the W Hotel and had a few drinks with a friend. I got home around 2:00 A.M. and had this appearance planned for eight that morning, which meant I had to be at the studio around seven thirty. I was having a hard time sleeping and took a sleeping pill. But I woke up coughing and decided to down some NyQuil, too. After that I don't remember a thing. Not getting up, not going to the show, not the interview, and not getting on a plane to go back to California. The first thing I remember is walking into my doctor's office.

Of course, I still know what happened on that show. How could I not? The video has been watched nearly four hundred thousand times on YouTube. The host asked me about fighting, and I slurred together an answer. You can't really understand it all. Then he asked me about the movie and there was nothing. No response. I looked to be sleeping. The host said to me, "Are you okay, Chuck?" That snapped me out of it, and I said, "Yeah, I'm all right." And I rallied to talk about the movie for a few seconds and answered another question about how you

MY FAVORITE PLACES:

1. Hawaii—I went there for the first time to hang with John Lewis, stayed for ten days and loved it. How could you not?
2. Boston—I started going there with Dana and it's a fun place. We stay in the harbor area and people there are great to us, because that's where Dana used to be a bellman.
3. New York—One of the first big vacations I ever took was to New York with my grandpa.
4. Vegas—Great place to train and fight and, "um," it's Vegas.
5. San Luis Obispo—Nice place to come home to.
6. Santa Barbara—Because it's beautiful and my friends would be pissed if it weren't on the list.

have to be a warrior to fight. But then he asked me whom I wanted to fight next, and all I could think to say was, "Tommy Morrison." I was freaking joking, although it didn't look like it when I was stammering and my eyes were closed. But Morrison, who retired from boxing in 1996 because he tested positive for HIV, had just come back the week before and knocked a guy out in West Virginia. I thought it would be funny. The host of the show, who later said he couldn't understand a thing I was saying, pretty much ended the interview. He actually seemed genuinely concerned that I was in trouble. He kept telling me to hang in there.

Dana, however, was just pissed. He was in Columbus getting ready for a UFC card that weekend, and, well, I'll let him explain how he found out about it: "Someone called me and said, 'Did you see the Liddell video?' I hear this stuff all the time, so I called Lorenzo Fertitta and asked him to find it and watch it before I decided to rip my best fighter's head off. Lorenzo called me back and said, 'Did you see this?' I said, 'No, is it bad?' He said, 'Dana, I can't even explain it to you.' I was thinking, Oh, my God."

Dana claims he called me and told me to "Get the fuck back on a plane to San Luis Obispo. No more promotions. No more parties. No coming to the fights this weekend. Get the fuck home and don't leave until me and Lorenzo talk to you." But I don't remember a thing. I did get on the plane, got home, and spent the next eight days in bed.

When Dana and Lorenzo came out to see me, they were pretty worried. The Nevada State Athletic Commission wanted me to take a drug test. I didn't give a crap. I wasn't on drugs and I'd pass the test. But the commission had never asked a fighter with a clean record to take a test between fights. Right before and right after, sure, but never randomly between fights. The two of them put me on lockdown and basically asked me, "What the hell are you doing? Are you trying to blow what you've got?"

I didn't think I was blowing anything, although after seeing the interview I could see where they were coming from, especially with the play it was getting. They both live in Vegas, and a couple of the radio stations there were replaying my rambling answers constantly as part of a running gag. But whether they thought I was partying too hard or I thought I was fine didn't matter. I was glad they pulled me off the road. The Rampage fight was set for the end of May. Now I could rest, get healthy, and start training for that. But I was still pissed about the drug test, and I came back clean. But I'll never live down the *Good Morning Texas* interview. Not only do radio stations in Vegas still run the tape, but every once in a while Dana will look at me and say, "Blah blah blah blah Tommy Morrison blah blah blah blah."

Of course, every time I watch it, I laugh, too.

CHAPTER 46

YOU HAVE TO STAY CHILL WHEN THE LIGHTS ARE BRIGHTEST

ETWEEN BEING SICK AND BEING BANNED FROM THE road, I got to rest and recuperate for two weeks before I started training for Rampage. This was the upside to nearly passing out on morning television. Plus, my being home made Hack happy. He knows I've got to be on the road promoting the sport and making appearances on my behalf, but he doesn't love it. When I'm out there, he can't be training me and keeping me in shape. A lot of the pomp and circumstance of all this bugs him. He wants to be about the fighting, and stuff that gets in the way of that is a nuisance.

The workouts for Rampage were great. Even Hack says they were perfect. I had been in such a rhythm since earning the title, winning seven straight fights over three years and defending my belt four times. And I wasn't fighting poseurs, either. I had taken on the best the UFC had to offer. It didn't matter if they were grapplers, submission experts, or strikers; people who hated me or people who respected me. When Dana said it was time to fight, I fought whoever was on the card. Just as I never ducked a fight on the way up, I wouldn't duck any when I had made it there, either. This was the fun part, what I had been fighting for all these years to begin with.

I really wanted to avenge that loss to Rampage, especially having done the same with Jeremy Horn and Randy Couture. I'm a competitive guy, and just knowing someone out there had one up on me made me irritable.

Rampage was also the biggest fight out there for me, presenting a bigger challenge than anyone else in the UFC. I had fought and beaten all the top contenders. This had been a fight that was a long time coming. Only after Dana and the Fertittas bought Pride, and Rampage's contract, did he finally even fight in the UFC. His first battle in the Octagon was in February 2007, a second-round knockout against Marvin Eastman. Rampage looked nervous that night, suffering from some cage jitters. Even he admitted it. But I expected that to change when we faced off. He'd made his debut and gotten that out of the way. Now he was going to fight for the light heavyweight championship of the world. Big-time fighters love as big a stage as possible to prove how great they are. They seem to get calmer the greater the expectations. At least, that's how I feel. You have to stay chill when the lights are brightest. I had to assume Rampage would feel the same way.

The sellout crowd at the MGM Grand Garden Arena stood as soon as Rampage walked out of his tunnel. This was as star-studded a crowd as there'd been for a UFC fight. Kevin James, Adam Sandler, Mandy Moore, Andre Agassi, Eli Roth, and David Spade were all there. The whole sport seemed to be achieving critical mass. My appearance on *Entourage* had aired at the end of April. A couple weeks later Cade and I were on the cover of *ESPN the Magazine*. Another UFC fighter was on the cover of *Sports Illustrated*. *SportsCenter* was airing highlights, and ESPN.com was running a mixed martial arts page that featured news and stories from Sherdog. This was no cult sport anymore.

Rampage didn't notice any of this as he made his way from his dressing room. He just kept looking straight ahead. He had his signature heavy chain hanging around his neck, and an electronic belt buckle that had his name—RAMPAGE—scrolling through it, like some sports ticker in a bar that delivered the scores. When he walked out of

Rampage tried to stare me down, but I wasn't intimidated. I'm never afraid to get in the ring, and my fight with Rampage was no different.

the tunnel he howled, in time with the wolves howling and dogs barking on his intro music. Halfway to the cage, he howled again. Rampage had a new trainer, who had been sharpening his boxing skills. And he had been working out and sparring with professional fighters in Big Bear during his training camp. He was cut and as strong as he had ever been when he walked into the cage that night. And he didn't smile once; he just looked mad.

I was feeling good, and maybe a little too relaxed. As I wound through the tunnel toward the arena, a guy jumped out and started walking with my group. No one knew who he was—he didn't have a ticket—but I didn't even stress. I just laughed. The closer I got to the mouth of the tunnel and the louder the music for my intro got, the looser I felt. I started to dance while walking in rhythm to the music. I smiled. The arena went dark for a few seconds before some blue lights above the cage lit up and bright white spotlights began crisscrossing around the stands. As I walked toward the cage, I slapped hands with as many people as I could. The boos that filled the stadium moments earlier were now cheers. Even when we were face-to-face while Big John gave us our instructions, I almost smiled while Rampage gave me the most intimidating look he could. Finally, Big John told us, "Let's get it on."

Rampage had been saying during interviews that he was going to knock me out in the third round. Like everyone who'd trained in Big Bear and then fought me, he wanted to make the fight last and try to get me tired so my punches would get weaker. I didn't expect the bout to last that long. When journalists told me Rampage had been saying he'd take me down in the third, I said, "That will be interesting, since I'm going to take him down in the first." My plan was to punch him in the face as much and as frequently as possible. But I still had to be disciplined. The one punch I had a hard time resisting was a blow to the body. That brings my hands down, and when you are close enough to hit the body, you're close enough to get hit in the chin if you miss. John told me over and over, "Don't go to the body unless it follows a combination." Otherwise you are just too vulnerable.

We came out and the pace was fast. We weren't throwing punches, but moving around a lot. Neither of us was going to wait for the other guy. I threw a low leg kick. I tried a jab. He threw a right to my face that made me stumble a bit. But mostly, I was dancing around the perimeter of the cage while he pivoted in the middle of it. He seemed to get frustrated that I wasn't just rushing in and throwing punches, so he dropped his hands as if to say, "Come on, man, let's fight."

Rampage did a good job of cutting off the cage. It was making it hard for me to come in at him in a straight line. Finally, a little less than two minutes into the first round, I thought I saw an opening. I did exactly what Hack is always telling me not to do: I went for my opponent's body, but didn't lead with any kind of combination to protect myself. That was not smart. Rampage coiled to protect himself and, in a textbook move, uncoiled as soon as he felt my blow. My hands were down, my chin exposed. I was defenseless as his hooking right hand landed smack on my cheek. I collapsed to the mat. He pounced, threw one shot that missed, then connected on another right directly on my head. Now I was out cold. My body went limp and Big John had no choice but to jump in and stop it. Just like that, no more than ten seconds after I threw the punch that started it all, I was no longer the UFC's light heavyweight champ.

When I got to my corner, I looked up at Hack and said, "What happened?"

"You went to the fucking body," he said.

I've got no excuse. I made a mistake and the guy caught me. He's a great fighter and deserves to be champ. As Hack told the guys at Sherdog after the fight, "The risk highly outweighed the benefit of that technique and he paid the price."

CHAPTER 47

GET THE F**K BACK UP

I WASN'T THE CHAMP ANYMORE. AT LEAST FOR THE moment. While it killed me, it didn't seem to matter to a lot of people. I still went on *Letterman* a couple weeks after the fight. I was still voted the Most Dangerous Man at the *Spike TV Guys' Choice Awards*. I was getting invites to club openings in Denver and to toss the coin at arena football games and play the heavy in big-time Hollywood movies. Someone still wanted me to write a book, too. That, to me, is all proof that the UFC continues to be one of the world's fastest-growing sports, with kids signing up in towns all over the country to learn how to do mixed martial arts. It's not wrestling, which is just pure entertainment. New fans are connecting with the athletes, and they recognize how competitive ultimate fighting is. I was a part of building that foundation, and it will last long after I'm done fighting.

Not that I'm done. Quitting didn't cross my mind even after I suffered another setback in September, just three months after the Rampage fight, losing a split decision to Keith Jardine in UFC 76. It was the first time I went the distance in a fight in over five years. To Jardine's credit, it was too close a fight for me to complain about the outcome. I connected on a lot of hard punches in the first round of that fight, so many that even Jardine said afterward that he was seeing stars. But he didn't back down. He scored a lot of points by consistently kicking me in the leg and in the side. My ribs looked as if they had been treated with a meat tenderizer, but I don't think it affected me during the fight. The only thing that still bothered me even days later were a couple of my fingers.

When I heard the Jardine decision, I immediately walked over to a side of the cage, squatted, and put my hands over my head. I thought to myself that it should never have been that close. I wanted to go for the knockdown but never found a chance to throw that punch. I just couldn't pull the trigger on anything. That night I went to the after party and drank a lot of apple cider. The fight had been in Anaheim and I had plans to go to Disneyland with my kids the next day. And that's what we did. A guide took us around the park, let us skip all the lines, and got us into all the rides. We had a blast. When I got back to San Luis Obispo, I immediately started thinking about what was next: I was back in the gym less than a week after the fight. I started breaking down my losses, trying to figure out what I have to do to string some wins together again. You always have to get the fuck back up. In fact, this is how I know I'm not done: The only thing I wanted to do as soon as the cobwebs cleared after Rampage was start fighting again. Same with Jardine.

It's not about the money. I made $500,000 for UFC 71. And six months after my fight with Tito I was still getting checks in the mid–six figures from my share of the pay-per-view. In June 2007 I spent $1 million buying my mom some property and a house and fixing it up. And I still had plenty of money left over. Remember, I was an accounting major who used to make $500 for a fight. I know things can always be worse. And I know the fight game can last for only so long, and nothing I do afterward will ever pay as well. I could retire, and as long as Dana is running the UFC, I'll have a job with him that keeps me comfortable. He's told me that. But I'm still smart with my money. It's a long life, I've got two kids, and I'm not going to blow everything I've earned. But I still love to fight. That feeling will never go away. So as long as I can throw a punch, I'm going to get in the cage.

This is what I've been doing since I was three years old and Pops taught me how to punch. It's why I took up karate and played football and wrestled and had more interest in beating the crap out of people during high school than in getting drunk. There was no such thing as the UFC when I was growing up. I couldn't possibly have known what was in store for me. But, it turns out, my entire life was geared toward becoming one of the best mixed martial artists alive. The street fighting, the grappling, the karate, those were all things that I'd become an expert at. Who knew that I could spend my entire life training in obscure disciplines such as those, and suddenly, combined, they would become one of the most popular professional sports in the world?

No one knew. Least of all me. But sometimes you just get lucky.

I don't know what's next, but here's what I do know: I'm a born fighter and I love to fight. As long as I can throw a punch, I'm going to get in the ring.

EPILOGUE

WHEN YOU'RE GRATEFUL YOU CAN'T BE ANGRY

THE HARDEST PART ABOUT LOSING TO JARDINE wasn't that it was my second loss in a row. And I wasn't too worried about the career implications. I knew I'd fight again, at least one more time, before every fan of the UFC moved on to the next big thing. No, the hardest part was that I thought I had missed a chance to fight Wanderlei Silva. The guy known as the Axe Murderer had been the Pride champ for years, and this was the one fight—other than me and Tito—that a lot of UFC followers had been hoping to see. I wanted it, too. Dana had told me going into the Jardine fight that if I won, he'd set up Silva. Then I lost. And it felt like when Randy beat me for the interim title and I subsequently missed out on getting Tito. Silva is a vicious puncher whom I'd wanted to fight for six years. Now, after two straight losses, I had no idea if I'd ever get the chance.

But a week after the Jardine loss I got a call from Dana. He still thought Liddell vs. Silva would be a big fight—in fact, my losing to Keith made my going up against Wanderlei an even bigger potential draw than if I had won. Silva had just lost two Pride fights in a row, both by knockouts, and had to hand over his middleweight title belt. His career, like mine, was at a crossroads. And like me, he was desperate for a big-time win against a brand-name fighter. Dana recognized that. So when he called and asked me, "Would you still be willing to fight Silva if I could set it up?" my answer was, "Hell, yeah."

I went from being really down to being totally pumped. It also kept me from having to do some serious thinking about where I was going to go next with my life. While I had planned on taking some time off because I felt beat-up after training for Jardine, I was now energized. I couldn't wait to get back in the gym and start training.

But Hack had different ideas about my program this time. He is all about training and fighting. He's not interested in the fame that comes from my being a champ. In fact, he's most frustrated when the celebrity aspects of the job interfere with the work that actually put me at the top of the ultimate fighting world. He's got no time for the entourages and media requests and selling of the Liddell brand. He's a lot like Mickey, the trainer in the first few *Rocky* movies, an old-school, hard-core fighter's trainer. Everything else is a distraction.

In fact, Hack had drilled into my head that the months of training before the Silva fight, which Dana scheduled for December 29, 2007, at the Mandalay Bay in Las Vegas, would be like *Rocky III*. That's the one where Rocky, after beating Apollo Creed at the end of *Rocky II* for the title, starts living like a world-class superstar. He buys a mansion and gets a statue at the top of the steps of the Philly art museum. Meanwhile there's Mr. T's Clubber Lang, a mean, young, hungry contender who is beating the crap out of people, hoping for his shot at the champ. When they finally set up the fight, Rocky's training camp is mobbed by press and Mickey gets pissed, thinking his fighter isn't training hard enough. So what happens: Rocky gets beaten silly in the fight with Clubber—and Mickey dies. Luckily, Hack didn't kick it, but he took a lesson from how Rocky finds redemption: The fighter went back to basics. He left his posh life to train with his old rival, Creed, running on the beach, working out in hot-box gyms, doing the stuff that he did when he was a hungry young contender looking to take Creed's title. He was looking for the eye of the tiger. That's what Hack had me do, too. I got back to the kind of training I did before

I was a veteran fighter and a comfortable champ and tried to find my edge.

My biggest frustration in losing to Jardine is that I never took a shot. And that doesn't mean a knockout overhand right. I didn't go to the ground, either. In a fight like that, a couple takedowns help you score points in two ways: the takedown and the beating you give an opponent when he gets back up. Plus it gets into a guy's head. Now he's looking for those moves, which makes him less aggressive. That is the difference between winning and losing. But I didn't surprise Jardine at all. I wanted to be more of a mixed martial artist but instead was a one-dimensional fighter, dancing around the ring trading punches, focusing on striking. That's not a crime. My strength is beating people up with my fists. I had been winning most of my fights the past few years pummeling opponents with cement-knuckled KO punches. But I'm also a former kickboxing champ. I was a good wrestler in college. I had studied Brazilian jujitsu. I became a UFC champ because I was a master of all the mixed martial arts disciplines. And I wasn't using them. Hack would make sure that wasn't the case anymore.

He invited Sammie Henson, who won the silver medal at the 2000 Olympics in the 119-pound weight class, to help me train and incorporate the wrestling back into my game plan. Wrestlers are a different breed, man. They take training to a level of intensity that is completely unlike sports such as football and baseball. Their mind-set is about pain and suffering. They want as much of those two things as they can get, and then they want to overcome them. That's the only way they know for sure how ready they are to step onto the mat. Sammie is no different. The guy went 71-0 as a college wrestler at Clemson, winning two NCAA titles. Five years after he graduated he won the world championship. He still has the same intensity as the eight-year-old who told his dad he was going to be one of the world's greatest wrestlers. Of course, this made him the perfect partner for Hack, who loved torturing me and finally had someone with fresh ideas.

We did a lot of drills that worked on my explosion, especially with my footwork so I could get low fast. And Sammie worked with me to clean up my wrestling technique, too. But mostly having Sammie there raised the level of intensity. I didn't realize it, but in previous camps my training partners may have been letting up, even unconsciously. This time, when the energy got too low or Sammie felt guys were lagging—or someone came in to spar with a hangover—he let them have it. He'd be screaming, "What the f***, Chuck has a fight coming up and you're not ready to spar. Show the f*** up and be ready." No one wants to be embarrassed, and having him as a watchdog helped keep guys in line to make sure I was getting their best.

And I did, too. I worked on moves I hadn't included in my arsenal in years. I was jabbing, knowing I wanted to set that up against Silva because I had such a reach advantage. I practiced a spinning backfist, which I had learned when I was a kid and used a lot as a kickboxer. I had never used it in a UFC fight, but I saw Silva go down once from that punch, so I wanted to have it ready. I was landing it two or three times a day on guys who were about my height, which made me feel good about the chances of it working. Every minute of training was geared toward making me a more complete fighter, the kind of fighter I had been before I was a champ. Winning is about adapting, and I wanted to prove to everyone who thought I was done that I could fight any style and still come out on top.

I was working hard on the mental aspects of my game as well. Early in my career Hack had worked some of Tony Robbins's time-management and goal-oriented programs into my training system. Then, right after I lost to Rampage, Hack called Tony and asked him to come out to The Pit and work with me. When he did I was still feeling pretty confident about my skills. I was—and am still—convinced that Rampage got me with a good punch at the right time. There was nothing I could do about that. But Tony will tell you that it didn't seem as if my level of hunger was there. He likes to joke that my appearance on *Entourage* was well-timed. Because before that a night out leading up to a fight was me with Hack and a couple of guys. As the Rampage fight drew near, we needed a couple of tables to fit everyone in my party.

Tony and I worked on finding trigger points, words or ideas that motivated me to work with some urgency. My strategy for a long time has been to wade into a fight slowly and use those first few moments as a warm-up to feel out my opponent. But that can create hesitancy if I see an opportunity early on. We had a good session over the summer, with Tony getting me to the point where, on a scale of 1–10, I felt like my intensity level for sparring would often be at a 13. In fact, 13 became one of my triggers, something that Hack and Tony used to get me locked into a zone. Heading into Jardine, Hack wanted Tony to come back and work with me one more time. He couldn't, but Hack and I both wish he had. For whatever reason, even Hack says he wasn't able to push me where I needed to be in those seconds between the rounds.

So we made sure Tony was in Vegas before my fight with Silva. Soon after he arrived at the Mandalay I said to him, "Let's get upstairs and do this thing." I was pretty motivated. My training had been tight, and I was invigorated by Sammie. Now I wanted to get as mentally focused as possible. As soon as we got upstairs, Tony looked at me and said, "Chuck, did you notice anything?"

"Like what?" I said.

"Your hotel room is on the thirteenth floor. Remember what happened last time we worked; you focused on raising your intensity level to a thirteen."

"That's unbelievable," I said. "Ninety percent of the hotels I stay at don't even have a thirteenth floor."

That put us right into it. Tony pretended to be Silva and practiced how he'd walk into the ring. Then he asked me to walk in. When he worked with Andre Agassi, after Agassi had fallen in the rankings, Tony showed the tennis great old videos of himself walking onto the court. When he won Wimbledon he walked in like he owned the place. Tony asked Andre what he was thinking, and Andre answered,

"I looked at the guy and wondered, Why did you bother showing up?" Then Tony put on a tape of a French Open match after Andre's confidence had been shot. He had his shoulders slumped and was thinking about the last time his opponent that day had beaten him.

The point is, Tony wanted me walking in tall and relaxed and confident. We started with guided meditation. He asked me to do some breathing exercises; then he asked me what was the most important thing that had ever happened to me. He didn't need me to answer out loud; he just wanted me thinking about things. And none of the answers I thought of were fight related. They were about my kids and my family. If anything, I thought about how I liked fighting for a living. That takes a lot of the pressure off.

Then he visually took me through about a dozen of my fights. Before coming to Vegas, Tony had asked Hack which fights in my career had been most important to my development. Then he studied them all. As he talked about each one, he asked me to pinpoint moments of certainty, when I knew I would win or could win, and when I felt a little less sure. I needed the benefit of hindsight, of talking through the fights with someone, to be objective about the answers. Whenever I won, my level of certainty was at a 13. When I lost it was at a 9, and those were the fights in which I was hesitant, when I wouldn't get on the ground with someone, like with Jardine. We did this for forty minutes, going through fight after fight, trying to make sure I was physically feeling the certainty of winning. All the while our eyes were closed, and Tony would be talking about other aspects of my life. He tried to put in perspective how important—or unimportant— losing three fights in a row would be. Tony had a saying: "When you succeed, you party. When you fail, you ponder. I want you to get back to pounding." He reminded me that I started fighting for the fun of it, not for the money or the fame or the entourage. He'd say things like, "Yeah, real tough life you've got, getting paid all this money to do what you love. I feel so bad for you that you're under so much pressure." It made me feel grateful, and when you're grateful, you can't be angry.

And, as Pops always said, you can't fight angry. "The real Chuck," Tony would tell you, "is a guy with a smile on his face."

I slept better that night and woke up happier. Everything was in perspective. My mind-set was, Screw it; I'm going to have fun. I've got nothing to lose.

I don't know if Silva felt the same way. He'd made some changes to his training camp, too, so I know he felt a little of the career urgency I did. For the previous seven years he'd been fighting in Pride in Japan. His last fight in the UFC Octagon had actually been a loss to Tito in 2000. He was a street brawler then, but he'd only gotten savvier as the Pride middleweight champ. He'd gone seventeen fights without a loss, including knockouts of Guy Mezger in the first round and Rampage in the second, that one after he had connected on seventeen unanswered knees. The man is viscous and built like a block of granite, square and solid. But in eight fights since beating Rampage in 2004, Silva was just 4-4; that included his most recent loss before our bout, a third-round knockout against Dan Henderson. I needed to win a big fight to get my career back on track, but he might have needed it even more.

He knew it, too, and so did his fans, who were constantly ripping me, actually telling me how much their guy was going to kick my ass. The taunting from Silva's side became so bad that he tried intimidating me at the weigh-in. After we both got off the scales and were face-to-face, he faked as if he were going to head butt me. I've got no time for that. I'd rather just go about my business, step into the cage, and start fighting. Prefight taunts don't get me pumped up; they don't make me want to kick an opponent's ass any more than I already do. So I just shot him the finger and turned around. Then he came at me with a purpose. Only after Hack stepped in, acting as though he were going to beat the crap out of everyone, did things settle down. At least I knew we were all ready to brawl.

Silva came out of the tunnel at the Mandalay the night of the fight with a big smile on his face. He kept rotating his fists as if they were windmills, and rolled his head around on top of his neck. Either he was feeling loose, or he was faking it and trying to get there. Either way he got a big ovation. On the broadcast, Joe Rogan couldn't stop talking about how aggressive Silva was, how he might be the most relentless attacking striker he had ever seen.

I wasn't too worried. I had plans and counterplans and a strategy. In the hallway between my dressing room and the entry to the stadium I could hear my intro music starting, and it made me bounce and dance a little bit. Then, just before I walked into the tunnel, I thought of my session the night before with Tony. The memory completely put me at ease. I had my kids, my family, and a chance to go out and have a great time in a UFC fight. (The $500,000 payday didn't hurt, either.) There was nothing to stress about now. So I put my head down and smiled, just for a second. The cameras tracing my steps caught it, but I don't think any of the guys standing next to me did.

Inside the Octagon, though, I was all business. Silva was full of energy, constantly moving, contorting his wrists and neck. But when we came to the center of the cage for the ref's instructions, I was perfectly still. I just stared straight through him. Still, when he finally came out to fight, he had settled down. Both of us were pretty cautious, actually, feeling each other out. For a fan, this was a great match-up: two strikers who had six years of pent-up frustration from waiting to fight each other, plus a little desperation mixed in. For the first thirty seconds we just danced around the center of the cage. At one point Silva just dropped his arms, either out of annoyance that we hadn't thrown any punches yet or because he was trying to goad me. He moved in a bit after that, but after another minute we had still barely laid a hand on each other.

Then I finally connected on a jab and followed that up with a hard right. He fell back, but I'm not sure if he was trying to lure me in, because when I moved forward he hit me hard on my chin with a combination. It startled me, but I followed up with a quick right, then a looping left and multiple combinations. He was throwing punches, too, but I was throwing mine faster. And with that speed came a lot of power. For twenty seconds we traded blows, with me landing more than I missed. When we ran out of gas on that exchange, I felt as though I were in control of the center of the cage. It was like I was stalking him as he danced around the periphery.

With a little more than a minute left in the round, I tapped him pretty hard again, snapping his head back. He smartly countered, catching me on the chin and letting out a little smile, but I finished the round strong with a couple of quick rights. He desperately wanted to get inside, but when he tried, I was ready with a jab and he'd just eat my punches. After that first round I knew that not only wasn't I hurt, but that I was winning this fight.

In between rounds, Hack kept telling me to stick with the jab. I had a big reach advantage, and part of our strategy was to maintain distance and create angles. A good jab did both of those things. But Hack also warned me to disguise my follow-up more. When I'd throw the jab, I'd be cocking my right hand back as well, as if I couldn't wait to wind up and lay Silva out. I wanted to put a lot of combinations together, and it was harder to do that if he could see the second punch coming.

If the first round was about us feeling each other out, the second was all about punching each other. It took three seconds for him to come at me and land a couple of hard blows. He clearly felt like he needed to turn up the tempo because I had won that first round on points. Silva hits hard, but his punches are looping and take a long time to land. By the time his fists were able to get close, I had snuck a jab at his mouth and was moving out of the way, another advantage of my long reach. It didn't take long before those punches I was throwing did some damage, as Silva began to bleed from his ear.

Still, he wasn't exactly conceding. He caught me with a good left toward the middle of the round that threw me off balance, and now he was the fighter controlling the center of the cage as I danced around him. With a little less than three minutes in the second round he hit me in the chest with both hands, knocking me off my feet. I popped up, but around forty seconds later I slipped and went to the mat again. Two knockdowns in a minute, during a fight I was controlling. I wasn't panicked, but I needed to reassert myself.

For about thirty seconds or so we circled each other, trading minor punches. But with ninety seconds to go I felt I could make another move. I locked him up in a clinch, and when we broke out of it I swung with a big left that knocked him into the cage. I kept pushing forward and opened up a big cut on his face. I threw an elbow and a right and then locked him up again, throwing elbows while his arms were tied up. I had his blood smeared all over my back. When we finally unlocked he tried to hurt me with a combination, but I responded with a big right. Then it was just a back-alley brawl. For a minute we swung wildly at each other, both of us looking like we had anvils attached to our fists. His face was just a bloody target, his nose a bulls-eye in the middle of it all. I won the round when, with about fifteen seconds left, I was able to take him down, which was how the round ended.

In my corner I realized I was bleeding now, too, but not nearly as bad as Silva. His trainers could fit the entire head of a Q-tip into the gash over his right eye. Hack and I both thought I could knock him out, and we had a couple of tricks we hadn't tried yet. It had been a long time since I made wrestling a part of my game plan, but that was why Sammie was in my camp. And, by lying back and punching for most of the fight, I had been setting Silva up for a quick takedown. Hack felt the same way. Just before I got off the stool to start the third he told me now was the time to go for it.

I didn't even waste a second. I had Silva on his back immediately. And, even though he was up on his feet right away, it was just one more thing for him to think about. The fans were certainly enjoying it, as they started chanting my name. But I had one more move I hadn't pulled out: the spinning backfist I'd been practicing all during camp. With a little less than three minutes left it set up perfectly. My back was near the side of the cage, and there was good distance between Silva and me. He was being aggressive, knowing he needed a knockout to win, which meant he wasn't thinking defensively. As he approached, I spun and threw a backfisted right hand. Problem was, the guys I had been practicing the move on during camp were all taller than Silva. While I'd been connecting against them, this shot landed a little high, at the top of Silva's head. He clearly wasn't expecting it—his knees buckled—but it didn't end the fight. I pounced after that, hitting him with a right directly on the chin that made his neck snap like a bobble-head's. I had him against the cage and threw as many punches as I could.

He was tired and in trouble and knew he had to explode. But I kept throwing combinations. The guy had a much stronger chin than I expected. I'm not sure how he stayed up for the entire fight, because he was wobbly and couldn't get any power behind his punches. Finally, with nineteen seconds left, I went for the takedown one more time. The match ended with me locking him up.

There was no question when the judges made their call. It was unanimous. Not only had I won—I had proven that I was still a world-class mixed martial artist.

After the fight, I had nothing but praise for Silva. He took a lot of shots—and handed me a lot of shots—and always kept coming. It was exactly the kind of fight fans had been waiting six years to see, and it was worth the wait. I celebrated with an after party at Studio 54. I even invited everyone in the stands and the people watching at home to come by. I was that energized about the win. I still am. It felt good to beat back such a huge challenge, to get back on the track to regaining my title, to prove that I am as skilled a mixed martial artist as anyone who has ever stepped into the cage. But, more than anything, it felt good to throw some punches. "Chuck doesn't care if he fights for a title or just to stay active or for six dollars in gas money," Hack said in an interview later that night. And he's right.

I'd do all this for free.

APPENDIX

CHUCK LIDDELL'S MMA RECORD (20-5 AS OF SEPTEMBER 27, 2007)

LOSS **Keith Jardine Decision UFC 76 9/22/2007 Anaheim**

I wanted to take my shot but couldn't pull the trigger. I can't complain about the decision; it was close all the way through.

LOSS **Quinton Jackson TKO (Strikes) UFC 71 5/26/2007 Las Vegas**

I was frustrated early because we were moving around but not throwing any punches. Then I made a mistake and he caught me.

WIN **Tito Ortiz TKO (Strikes) UFC 66 12/30/2006 Las Vegas**

I hurt him in the first and the ref kept telling him to move or he'd stop it. I let him get back up. He got a takedown and I popped back up and threw an elbow out of a tie-up that took his heart. He didn't tap, but he quit.

WIN **Renato Sobral TKO (Strikes) UFC 62 8/26/2006 Las Vegas**

I think he thought he caught me with something and got excited and ran at me and I just clipped him. Then I just jumped on top and hammered him. I don't think he knew where he was.

WIN **Randy Couture KO (Punches) UFC 57 2/04/2006 Las Vegas**

I caught him with the right in the first and got him pretty good. Then I got overanxious when I had him hurt and got taken down, but I didn't let him do anything with it. Then I came out in the second and hurt him again.

WIN **Jeremy Horn TKO UFC 54 8/20/2005 Las Vegas**

He is a tough guy and took a lot of shots. I wasn't in any hurry to finish him. I was happy to let him take a beating. His corner should have thought about stopping that.

WIN **Randy Couture KO (Punches) UFC 52 4/16/2005 Las Vegas**

We worked a lot more on movement and we made it tough for him to get a good angle and tie me up. I caught him with a left hook that hurt him, and he charged ahead to tie me up, and when he did that, I hit him with a right and knocked him out.

WIN **Vernon White KO (Punch) UFC 49 8/21/2004 Las Vegas**

It was a great fight because he could take a beating. And I gave him one. He annoys me because he still complains I poked him in the eye.

WIN **Tito Ortiz KO (Punches) UFC 47 4/2/2004 Las Vegas**

I think I should have gone after him more. In the beginning I didn't want to give him any confidence with a cheap takedown. But I wish the first round had been ten seconds longer so I could have finished him in the opening round.

LOSS **Quinton Jackson TKO (Strikes) Pride 11/9/2003 Tokyo**

I had a strained quad before the fight and I think I underestimated him a little bit.

WIN **Alistair Overeem KO (Strikes) Pride 8/10/2003 Saitama, Japan**

I wanted to take him down and take him off his game early. I did; then I let him back up and caught him with a straight right and then an overhand right that ended him.

LOSS **Randy Couture TKO (Punches) UFC 43 6/6/2003 Las Vegas**

Looking back, I gassed in the first three minutes; he was just a step ahead of me. I think they stopped it early, but I don't think it would have mattered. The outcome would have been the same.

WIN **Renato Sobral KO (Head Kick) UFC 40 11/22/2002 Las Vegas**

John predicted I would catch him with a kick to the face. And I did.

WIN **Vitor Belfort Decision (Unanimous) UFC 37.5 6/22/2002 Las Vegas**

He shot a takedown right away and surprised me, but he didn't do any damage on top. Then I won a striking war. He had to exchange with me and I caught him with a right hand.

WIN **Amar Suloev Decision (Unanimous) UFC 35 1/11/2002 Uncasville, CT**

Another guy that I gave too much respect on the ground. UFC wouldn't give me footage of him, so I hadn't seen anything. Everyone said he had a great ground game so I just had to beat him up. This is when I started learning not to listen to what other people say.

WIN **Murilo Bustamante Decision (Unanimous) UFC 33 9/28/2001 Las Vegas**

Tough fight, but one of those guys I think I gave too much respect on the ground, which is why it ended up in the judges' hands.

WIN **Guy Mezger KO (Punch) Pride 5/27/2001 Yokohama, Japan**

I got him backed up against the cage and hit him with right hook after right hook and I kept getting his arm. Then I changed the angle and threw a right straight down the middle and he buckled.

WIN **Kevin Randleman KO (Punches) UFC 31 5/4/2001 Atlantic City**

I asked for this fight. He was a former heavyweight champ. I stopped his first shot and caught him with a left hook. It went well for me.

WIN **Jeff Monson Decision (Unanimous) UFC 29 12/16/2000 Tokyo**

Dana was in my corner for this one. I kept throwing kicks and wanted Monson to drop his hands so I could throw a head kick. But he wouldn't do it.

WIN **Steve Heath KO (Head Kick) IFC WC 9 7/18/2000 Friant, CA**

I had to cut weight to make 195. On the day of weigh-ins I was cramping while warming up. I caught him with a right hand, he bounced off the cage, and I caught him with a kick.

WIN **Paul Jones TKO (Strikes) UFC 22 9/24/1999 Lake Charles, LA**

He was a wrestler and I caught him with a good elbow and split his head wide-open.

WIN **Kenneth Williams Submission (Rear-Naked Choke) NG 11 3/31/1999 Hollywood**

I kneed him in the leg and he tried to turn away so I couldn't knee him, and I ended up being able to get him into a rear-naked from the standing position.

LOSS **Jeremy Horn TKO (Arm Triangle Choke) UFC 19 3/5/1999 Bay St. Louis, MS**

I thought I was doing all right and got caught in something I didn't know. I just relaxed and then it was over.

WIN **José Landi-Jons Decision (Unanimous) IVC 6 8/23/1998 São Paulo, Brazil**

The guy could take a beating. He took a lot of shots in a long fight and wouldn't quit.

WIN **Noe Hernandez Decision UFC 17 5/15/1998, Mobile, AL**

I got hit with a right and laughed because I knew he was going to throw it and I still got caught with it.

UFC RULES

Fouls:

1. Butting with the head.
2. Eye gouging of any kind.
3. Biting.
4. Hair pulling.
5. Fishhooking.
6. Groin attacks of any kind.
7. Putting a finger into any orifice or into any cut or laceration on an opponent.
8. Small-joint manipulation.
9. Striking to the spine or the back of the head.
10. Striking downward using the point of the elbow.
11. Throat strikes of any kind, including, without limitation, grabbing the trachea.
12. Clawing, pinching, or twisting the flesh.
13. Grabbing the clavicle.
14. Kicking the head of a grounded opponent.
15. Kneeing the head of a grounded opponent.
16. Stomping a grounded opponent.
17. Kicking to the kidney with the heel.
18. Spiking an opponent to the canvas on his head or neck.
19. Throwing an opponent out of the ring or fenced area.
20. Holding the shorts or gloves of an opponent.
21. Spitting at an opponent.
22. Engaging in an unsportsmanlike conduct that causes an injury to an opponent.
23. Holding the ropes or the fence.
24. Using abusive language in the ring or fenced area.
25. Attacking an opponent on or during the break.
26. Attacking an opponent who is under the care of the referee.

27. Attacking an opponent after the bell has sounded the end of the period of unarmed combat.

28. Flagrantly disregarding the instructions of the referee.

29. Timidity, including, without limitation, avoiding contact with an opponent, intentionally or consistently dropping the mouthpiece, or faking an injury.

30. Interference by the corner.

31. Throwing in the towel during competition.

UFC MANDATORY EQUIPMENT (FROM UFC.COM)

1. Competitors may use only UFC- and commission-approved 4–6 oz. gloves, designed to protect the hand but not large enough to improve the striking surface or weight of the punch.

2. Commission-approved MMA shorts and kickboxing trunks are the only uniforms allowed. Shirts, gis, and shoes, and the problems they present for grabbing, are not allowed.

MMA MAIN SUBMISSION HOLDS

1. *Heel hook*—Grab the heel and twist as hard as possible so the guy feels as if it were going to separate from his leg. In technical terms, you're hyperrotating the heel. Submission that hyperrotates the ankle joint.

2. *Toe hold*—Same as the heel hook, only on the toe, which should feel as if it were being removed from the foot.

3. *Armbars*—From your back, place your legs across the opponent's chest, with one of his arms between your thighs and with his elbow joint against your hips. Then grab his arm with both of yours, so his forearm is on your chest. Got it so far? To lock his arm, lean back and arch your hips at the same time. This creates

intense pressure in the elbow joint. If the guy doesn't tap, his options are torn ligaments, torn tendons, or a broken arm.

4. *Triangles*—Get your opponent's head and one of his arms between your legs and squeeze. This will force his head down and choke off the blood supply to the brain.

5. *Guillotine*—This is almost too easy against grapplers. The move is executed when you are face-to-face with a guy. When he goes for a takedown, wrap his head inside your arm and squeeze hard. If the pressure from your forearm is placed against the windpipe, then you'll get an air choke, meaning the guy can't breathe. If the pressure is on the arteries of the neck, then you will get a blood choke, which means the blood stops flowing to his head. Either way, it's lights-out.

6. *Rear-naked choke*—This works when you're behind your opponent. Wrap one arm around his neck, with the inside of your elbow against his throat. From there you lock the hand of the arm wrapped around the guy's neck on your biceps and use your other hand to push the guy's head down, closing off an airway. Don't forget to hug your arms together and push out with your chest.

ACKNOWLEDGMENTS

I CAN'T REMEMBER EVERYTHING THAT'S HAPPENED TO me during my life. So I've got to thank all the people who helped me piece things together. First, as always, is my mom, Charlene Fisher. But no one would care what I have to say if not for the following people: Trista's mom, Casey Noland; Cade's mom, Lori Geyer; Nick Blomgren, who put me on the road to the UFC; Dana White, who helped guide my UFC career; John Hackleman and John Lewis, who are always in my corner; the guys I've trained with, Scott Adams, Antonio Banuelos, Scott Lighty, Ian Parkinson, Chuck Sandlin, Eric Schwartz, and Glover Texiera. I also need to thank the fans at Sherdog, whose stories provided great details of every fight written about in this book. And, of course, Erin Wilson, for supporting me during this project.

The book wouldn't have come together without my manager at Untitled Entertainment, Brad Marks; my literary agent, Richard Abate at Endeavor; Brian Tart, the president and publisher at Dutton; and his staff, including Erika Imranyi and Jessica Horvath. Thanks to them for pushing me to share my story.

ABOUT THE AUTHORS

CHUCK LIDDELL first stepped into the Octagon in 1998 and became the UFC's light heavyweight champion in 2005, a title he held for two years. An accounting major at Cal Poly San Luis Obispo, he still lives and trains in the SLO. Check out his Web site at www.mmajacked.com.

CHAD MILLMAN, a deputy editor at *ESPN the Magazine*, is the author of *The Detonators* and *The Odds* and coauthor of *Invincible* and *Pickup Artists*. He lives in Montclair, New Jersey, with his wife and two sons. Visit his Web site at www.chadmillman.com.